MW01109990

Principles of
Supervision

Principles of Supervision

Mel E. Schnake
Eastern Illinois University

Wm. C. Brown Publishers
Dubuque, Iowa

Book Team

Editor **Jeffrey L. Hahn**
Developmental Editor **Mary C. Doyle**
Designer **Mark D. Hantelmann**
Production Editor **Carol A. Kozlik**
Photo Research Editor **Michelle Oberhoffer**
Permissions Editor **Carla D. Arnold**
Product Manager **Matt Shaughnessy**

wcb group

Wm. C. Brown Chairman of the Board
Mark C. Falb President and Chief Executive Officer

wcb

Wm. C. Brown Publishers, College Division

Executive Vice-President, General Manager **G. Franklin Lewis**
Vice-President, Cost Analyst **E. F. Jogerst**
Editor in Chief **George Wm. Bergquist**
Executive Editor **John Stout**
Director of Production **Beverly Kolz**
Vice-President, Director of Sales and Marketing **Chris C. Guzzardo**
National Sales Manager **Bob McLaughlin**
Manager, Marketing Research **Craig S. Marty**
Manager of Design **Marilyn A. Phelps**
Production Editorial Manager **Colleen A. Yonda**
Photo Research Manager **Faye M. Schilling**

Cover and part openers © 1986 by Peter Angelo Simon.

Copyright © 1987 by Wm. C. Brown Publishers. All rights reserved

Library of Congress Catalog Card Number: 86–70636

ISBN 0–697–00653–0

No part of this publication may be reproduced, stored in a retrieval system, or transmitted, in any form or by any means, electronic, mechanical, photocopying, recording, or otherwise, without the prior written permission of the publisher.

Printed in the United States of America
10 9 8 7 6 5 4 3 2 1

To Earl Edwin Schnake

Brief Contents

Contents

Chapter 4

Theories of Motivation 75

Chapter 7

Authority, Responsibility, and Delegation 141

Chapter 8

Communicating with Employees 157

Chapter 9

Evaluating Employee Performance 183

Chapter 10

Discipline, Grievances, and Problem Employees 211

Part Two

Supervising Groups

Chapter 11

Group Dynamics 233

Chapter 12
Managing Conflict 255

Chapter 13
Labor Relations 275

Chapter 14

Managing Change and Training Employees 297

Chapter 15
Supervising Special Types of Employees
315

Preface

The job of supervisor is one that grows more challenging every day. Legislation that concerns employment decisions is commonplace; attitudes toward work are constantly changing; the number of women, handicapped, and older persons entering the work force is rising dramatically; and the complexity of organizations continues to grow in the face of the threats of declining productivity, foreign competition, and unstable economic conditions. All are manifestations of today's rapidly changing environment. The job of supervisor will continue to elevate in importance in the face of these changes, largely because supervisors are "closest to the action." Supervisors are expected to ensure that the day-to-day work activities are accomplished efficiently and effectively. As such, they are an extremely important part of any organization's management team.

This book is designed to provide students with information necessary to become supervisors in today's more complex organization. The book will also be of interest to persons currently holding supervisory positions who want to become more effective in their jobs.

This text is not tied strictly to the manufacturing organization. More and more supervisory jobs are in government and the service industries. Although JBS Manufacturing is used as the hypothetical example in all Introductory Incidents and end-of-chapter Cases, this company has large administrative and manufacturing divisions, employing a number of clerical and administrative employees. The Introductory Incidents will involve these types of employees, as well.

Organization of the Text

Supervisors are responsible for achieving organizational objectives by directing the work of employees. This book is organized around the employee in order to emphasize the importance of working with others. An introductory chapter describes the supervisor's role in an organization. The remaining chapters are grouped into two parts: Part 1 deals with supervising individuals, Part 2 with supervising groups.

Chapter 2 provides information on making employment decisions that are in compliance with an increasingly complex set of equal employment opportunity laws. Chapter 3 presents a discussion of some of the problems associated with making selection decisions, and gives some suggestions for orienting new employees.

Once on the job, employees must be directed so that their efforts will contribute to the achievement of organizational goals. This is the emphasis of chapters 4, 5, and 6. Chapters 4 and 5 deal with the complex subject of motivation and chapter 6 provides information about becoming an effective leader.

Chapter 7 stresses the importance of developing a number of different sources of power or authority and explains how delegating authority may be a means for developing employees. Chapter 8 focuses upon methods supervisors may use to increase their effectiveness in communicating with employees. Suggestions for improving both the sending and receiving parts of the communication process are provided. Chapter 9 offers a number of suggestions for improving the accuracy of employee performance evaluations and for providing feedback to employees about their levels of performance. Finally, chapter 10 discusses how to deal with problem employees and grievances, and how to administer discipline or punishment.

The emphasis changes from individuals to groups in Part 2 of the book. Individuals in groups frequently exhibit behavior much different from that which they demonstrate when alone. It is not unusual for supervisors to be faced with a number of different types of groups within the organizations in which they work. Chapter 11 explains the basics of group dynamics: the ways in which groups form, the types of groups that form, and the effects that groups have upon individual behavior.

When people come together in groups, conflict may result. Chapter 12 demonstrates that the outcome of conflict can be positive if it is properly managed. Chapter 13 talks about the problems and opportunities faced by supervisors in dealing with unions. Chapter 14 provides a discussion of environmental change and its relationship to the growing need for employee training. Chapter 15 looks at the changes taking place in the work force and in work, in general. This chapter takes a look at those special types of employees (e.g., women, the handicapped, older employees, and employees in nontraditional occupations) who are entering today's work force in increasing numbers.

Student Learning Aids

Each chapter is supplemented by a set of Learning Objectives highlighting the important points of each chapter. Following each set of objectives is an Introductory Incident illustrating a major concept covered in the chapter. When this idea is reached in the chapter, reference is made back to the Introductory Incident. Every chapter includes a Chapter Summary, Key Terms, Discussion Questions, one or more Exercises, and a Case. Most of the Discussion Questions will not ask simply for repetition of chapter material; rather, most will require some thought and analysis to be given to some basic principles of supervisory management. The Exercises are designed to elaborate further upon a concept discussed in the chapter. The end-of-chapter Cases require the student to apply material from the chapter to a hypothetical, but practical, situation.

Note to the Student

The Introductory Incidents and end-of-chapter Cases all deal with a hypothetical company called JBS Manufacturing. JBS is a large manufacturing company located in the Midwest. The company makes a variety of products including such agricultural and garden equipment as small tractors, wagons, tillers, and tools (e.g., hammers, wrenches, shovels). JBS also purchases some finished products from other manufacturers and suppliers for resale to customers in its own retail stores located throughout the country. These items include small hardware items (e.g., nails, screws, bolts), lumber, paint, and housewares.

Supplementary Materials

This text is accompanied by a comprehensive Instructor's Manual and a computerized test bank. The Instructor's Manual includes:

1. Suggested course outlines for courses of varying lengths.
2. Lecture outlines for each chapter.
3. Detailed answers to the Discussion Questions.
4. Additional readings for each chapter.
5. Suggestions for the exercises. Included are recommendations for possible ways in which the exercises may be used and the typical results of each exercise.
6. Suggestions for the cases. Each case is analyzed and a teaching note provided.
7. A test bank of true/false, multiple-choice, matching, fill-in-the-blank, and essay questions.
8. Transparency masters.

Acknowledgments

A number of people have contributed, either directly or indirectly, to this book. I would like to thank Dr. Mike Dumler of Illinois State University; Dr. Dan Cochran, Dr. Walt Newsom, and Dr. Dennis Ray, all of Mississippi State University; and Ralph Evans, Vice President of Bound-to-Stay-Bound, New Method Book Bindery, Jacksonville, Illinois. I would like to thank Mary Doyle, Lisa Gottschalk, and Carol Kozlik of Wm. C. Brown Publishers for their nonstop support and enthusiasm. I also wish to express my gratitude to two overworked graduate assistants: Doug Waggle and Stephanie Brandt. Thanks, too, to my family— Kathy, Joe, Beth, Susie, and Ben—for their patience and understanding. Finally,

I would like to thank the following individuals for their helpful comments and suggestions in reviewing the manuscript: Tommy Gilbreath, *University of Texas at Tyler;* Donald Pettit, *Suffolk County Community College;* Floyd B. Wente, *St. Louis Community College at Florissant Valley;* Charles H. Wetmore, *California State University at Fresno;* Karen K. Heuer, *Des Moines Area Community College;* Jerry Boles, *Western Kentucky University;* Michael Vijuk, *William R. Harper College;* and Robin E. Butler, *Lakeshore Technical Institute.*

Mel. E. Schnake
Eastern Illinois University

Principles of Supervision

Part 1
Supervising Individuals

Chapter 1
Management and the Supervisor's Role

Learning Objectives

After reading this chapter, you should be able to:
1. explain the basic management process.
2. describe the management functions.
3. differentiate management from supervision.
4. understand the unique role of the supervisor.
5. recognize the important skills required of supervisors.
6. describe trends that could affect the job of the supervisor.
7. understand the importance of career planning.
8. be able to develop a personal career plan.

Beth has been working for JBS Manufacturing Company* for the past twelve years. She started as Accounting Clerk I in the Finance Division and gradually worked her way up to Accounting Clerk V, the company's highest grade of nonsupervisory job. She has held this job classification for the past five years.

This morning Beth's supervisor called her into his office and asked her if she would be interested in promotion to a supervisory position in the accounts receivable department. This position involves supervising the work of eleven accounting clerks of Grades I through V.

This came as quite a shock to Beth since she had never pictured herself in a supervisory position. She felt reasonably confident of her ability to understand the technical nature of the accounts receivable department based upon her twelve years of experience in the Finance Division. She was unsure, however, what other responsibilities she might face in a supervisory position. Beth told her supervisor that she would consider the position and give him her answer by the end of the week. She made a mental note to begin looking immediately for information about what it takes to be a supervisor.

The situation facing Beth is not an uncommon one. Many people who become supervisors for the first time are not well-prepared for the job.[1] Like Beth, many people are promoted to a supervisory position on the basis of their outstanding performance in a technical, nonsupervisory job. Many changes are to be expected in the move from a nonsupervisory job to the job of supervisor. This chapter will define the role of the first-line supervisor in organizations, and will identify the types of information, skills, and abilities that are necessary to be successful in that role.

Becoming a Supervisor

Once you assume a supervisory position, you must be prepared for the changes that you will be confronting. People who are promoted to supervisory positions often continue to behave as if they were still in their old jobs. As a supervisor, you will be assuming responsibility for the performance of others. You must be prepared for less involvement in the day-to-day technical work and for greater involvement in the planning, directing, and controlling of the activities of others. It is sometimes difficult for new supervisors to "keep their hands off" of daily work activities, but it is important that they learn to do so. Even though it may seem easier in the short run to step in and "do it yourself," this is not good strategy in the long run. It may, initially, take some time to develop employees that can perform without close supervision. This initial investment will ultimately save time, however.

New supervisors are sometimes reluctant to supervise. You, as a new supervisor, may feel uncomfortable giving orders or directions, or assigning tasks to employees. These feelings may be even stronger if you happen to be promoted to supervise people with whom you previously worked. It is often difficult to give orders to those who were your peers prior to promotion. It is important to remember that it may be just as difficult for these employees to accept those orders or assignments from you.

*JBS is a hypothetical Midwest manufacturing company. See the "Note to the Student" in the Preface.

The supervisory role demands that the individual possess a greater number and variety of interpersonal skills than would be needed in a nonsupervisory position. Communicating, coaching, counseling, mediating conflict, encouraging, and persuading are all examples of interpersonal skills. If you don't have good interpersonal skills, and your organization does not provide training in these areas, it would be a good idea to seek such training on your own.

When you become a supervisor you must begin to think of yourself as a member of the management team. Your primary responsibility as a member of this team is to work toward accomplishing organizational objectives. While you obviously have responsibilities to the people you supervise, your principal obligation is to the organization.

Managers at various levels within an organization are responsible for directing the work of employees. The term **supervision,** however, generally refers to the job of the first-line manager, a member of that level of management just above nonsupervisory employees. Supervisors generally perform the same basic functions and activities as top-level managers. What distinguishes these management positions and makes the role of the supervisor unique within the organizational structure is the amount of time spent performing each of these functions and activities. A preliminary discussion of the general process of management will provide a background useful in gaining a clearer understanding of the role of supervisor.

The Process of Management

Management Defined

Management is frequently referred to as the act of getting things done through other people.[2] One definition of management is given as the process of reaching organizational goals by working with and through people.[3] Thinking of supervision as part of the **management process** implies that managers must perform a continuous series of interrelated activities. These activities have been given the collective name of management functions. The management process is goal-directed, meaning that its basic purpose is to achieve organizational goals, and that these goals are generally accomplished by giving direction to the activities of others.

The Functions of Management

While different authors may identify slightly different sets of management functions, any set of functions reflects the same basic purpose of the management process. **Management functions** are the activities that all managers must perform in order to effectively and efficiently direct the work of employees toward organizational goal attainment. The five most commonly recognized functions, and the ones used in this book, are planning, organizing, staffing, directing, and controlling. This chapter will briefly describe each of these. Later chapters will provide more detailed discussion of these functions as they relate specifically to the job of the supervisor.

Planning

Planning determines what goals and objectives are appropriate for the organization and develops a list of the specific practices that might lead to the achievement of those goals. Planning involves making an internal analysis of the organization's strengths and weaknesses, as well as an external analysis of the organization's environment. Suppose that certain members of an organization feel that the company's profits would be increased through the introduction of a new type of product. It would be extremely unwise to make this an organizational objective without some prior knowledge of the availability of the raw materials necessary to make the product, without an estimate of the level of demand for the product, and without some awareness of the extent to which competition from other organizations exists. Finding the answers to these questions constitutes **external analysis.** It would also be necessary to determine whether the organization has the capital required to finance, the technology or production facilities equipped to manufacture, and the employers sufficiently skilled to produce this new product line. Finding the answers to these unknowns constitutes **internal analysis.**

This type of planning is called **strategic planning.** Strategic planning is long-term planning (projections may look ahead from one to five years in the future); and, it generally involves the entire organization, or at least large segments (such as the sales division or the marketing division).

The type of planning that you, as a supervisor, will be most involved in is **operational planning.** Operational planning is concerned with the short term—usually less than one year and often just a day or two (see fig. 1.1). Operational planning at the supervisory level is concerned with completing the work assigned to your department. In order to fulfill your responsibilities to the organization you will often have to schedule the work of your employees, assign priorities to tasks or activities, determine how the work is to be done, and set objectives for your employees.

Organizing

Once the organizational objectives have been determined, and the activities required to accomplish these objectives identified, all must be coordinated to ensure that all activities taking place within the organization are in some manner contributing to the accomplishment of organizational objectives. The function of **organizing** is to group similar activities into departments and establish a structure

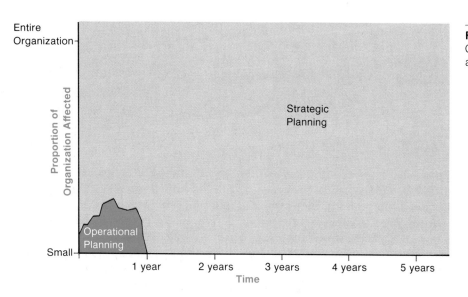

Figure 1.1
Comparison of strategic
and operational planning

of authority relationships within the organization. This internal structure provides employees with a knowledge of their specific areas of responsibility as well
as of the way in which the activities of their group or department are related to
other departments. Organizing is a function performed predominantly at higher
levels of management since it typically involves the entire organization.

Staffing

After the required activities have been determined and grouped together, thus
giving internal structure to the organization, it is necessary to fill these positions
with people who have the skills, abilities, and knowledge necessary to perform
these activities effectively. This procedure is known as **staffing.** While they may
get assistance from others in filling those positions staffing is the ultimate responsibility of the supervisor or manager of each group. Broadly defined, staffing
includes planning for future human resource needs; recruitment; selection; orientation; training and development; performance evaluation; and termination or
retirement.

Directing

In simple terms, **directing** is encouraging employees to behave in ways that contribute to the accomplishment of organizational objectives. Directing may be divided into three areas: motivation, leadership, and communication. Developing
skills in these areas is critical to the process of becoming an effective supervisor.

Figure 1.2
The interrelated functions
of management

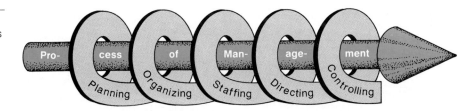

Controlling

Controlling involves measuring current organizational or departmental performance, comparing actual performance with the desired performance level as established in a goal or an objective, and making corrections if performance falls short of the desired level. In other words, controlling is concerned with determining the effectiveness of the organization or department in achieving its stated objectives. If the organization or department has fallen short in accomplishing any of those objectives, then the manager or supervisor must take steps to remedy the performance problem so that the objectives can be achieved in the future.

Planning and controlling are closely related. Plans include objectives or targets for performance; so without planning, there really is nothing to control. At the supervisory level, your emphasis will be on controlling the operational plans that you develop.

Interrelatedness of the Functions

The functions performed in the management process are highly interrelated; that is, the successful performance of one function depends upon the successful performance of the others. For example, the function of organizing cannot be performed effectively until the function of planning has been completed. The outcome of planning is that the goals and objectives of the organization are determined. Managers cannot effectively organize a firm to accomplish objectives unless they first have a clear understanding of those objectives. Similarly, staffing cannot be performed effectively until the types of activities and tasks required to accomplish the objectives have been determined and grouped into an internal organizational structure. Figure 1.2 shows the interrelatedness of the functions of management. While there is some logical sequence to the functions, this does not mean that a manager or supervisor first plans, then stops planning and begins to organize, and then goes on to staffing, and so on. Most of the time these functions are performed on an ongoing basis. Modern organizations are continually changing. Some change rapidly while others alter very slowly, but it is change

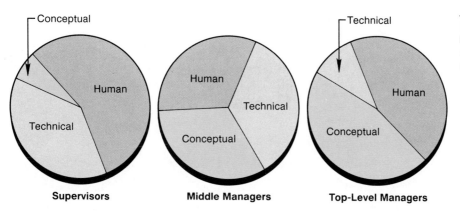

Figure 1.3
Relative importance of
skills for different levels of
management

that creates the need to continuously perform all five functions. Plans may need revision, the organizational structure may need modification, or new positions may need to be filled.

All managers or supervisors should possess three basic skills.[4] **Technical skills** are the ability to perform specialized work activities such as engineering, computer programming, and statistics. **Human skills** incorporate the ability to work with others. These skills include motivation, leadership, communication, and conflict management. **Conceptual skills** include the ability to see the organization, as a whole, and the ability to see how the various departments and activities of the organization relate to and depend upon one another. While all types of managers at all levels need these three basic skills, the relative importance of any skill depends upon the level of the manager within the organization.

 Figure 1.3 indicates that technical and human skills are most important at the supervisory level, and that conceptual and human skills are most important at upper levels of management. All three types of skills are important to middle managers. In general, in moving from lower to higher levels of management, technical skills become less important and conceptual skills, more important. At lower management levels, supervisors are concerned with day-to-day operations. They are responsible for supervising people as they perform a particular task (e.g., production work, clerical work). Supervisors must have sufficient technical skills to ensure that these tasks are performed correctly. The supervisor also needs human skills sufficient to direct employees effectively. Top-level managers are more concerned with long-term planning for the organization as a whole. Specialized technical skills become less important at upper management levels while conceptual skills become more important.

The Basic
Skills of
Management

Figure 1.4
Relationship between
management level and
time spent in
management functions

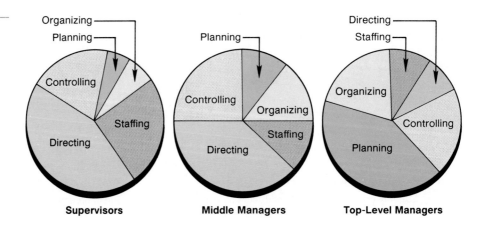

The relative importance of the three basic skills at any managerial level is related to the relative amount of time devoted to the five managerial functions. Figure 1.4 indicates that managers at all three levels perform each function of management. The time spent in each function, however, changes from level to level in the organization. Managers at all three levels spend about the same amount of time staffing and controlling, for example. Time devoted to the function of planning is greater at the top management level, while time devoted to directing is greater at the supervisory level. All supervisors plan, organize, staff, direct, and control, but they spend a greater proportion of their time and energy performing the latter three functions.

The Unique Organizational Role of the Supervisor

While it is true that supervisors are members of the management team, the organizational role of the supervisor is significantly different from the roles played at any of the other levels of management. Supervisors are the only managers who directly oversee a group of nonmanagers. They must work on a daily basis with nonmanagerial employees below them and with managers above them. Supervisors have responsibility to managers above them to ensure that the organization's tasks are performed effectively and efficiently. At the same time, supervisors have responsibility to their employees to try to maintain a suitable work environment, to foster good working relationships, and to provide challenging task assignments so that the employees' needs for personal growth in their jobs can be satisfied. Clearly, the supervisor is a "person in the middle."

Supervisors of the Future

Certain trends in management today are making a substantial impact upon the role of the supervisor. It is likely that some of these trends are directly related. For example, the average age of the work force is increasing. This means that supervisors, increasingly, will be overseeing older workers who may have different values and needs than younger workers. At the same time, educational levels are rising. This means that supervisors will be supervising the older workers as well as the younger workers with higher levels of formal education. Research suggests that people with higher educational levels demand more from their jobs than those with less education—that they seek to participate in the decisions made and want some degree of control over what happens on the job. Finally, antidiscrimination legislation is likely to increase or at least continue to evolve through the courts. This trend will create the necessity that supervisors be knowledgeable about what constitutes fair and unfair employment practices.

Several skills and abilities important to the successful supervisor have been identified.[5] These include the ability to motivate employees, the ability to communicate effectively, and the ability to make sound decisions. This book is designed to provide information necessary for the development of these skills and abilities. It will focus upon ideas and tools that supervisors will find immediately useful in that role. While the following chapters discuss many theories, the emphasis of the book is upon integration (i.e., how the various theories relate to each other) and application (i.e., how the ideas contained in these theories can be implemented and used). This hands-on orientation is reinforced by the cases, experiential activities, and specific issues that are a part of each chapter.

In sum, the book focuses upon what supervisors do and presents useful information that can help them to do it better. Beth, and those who, like her, are contemplating becoming a supervisor, as well as those who are already supervisors, but want to become more effective, will find these chapters helpful.

Once you have accepted a supervisory position, or better, before you accept a position, you should give some thought to career planning. A career is a sequence of jobs that a person holds during his or her working life. **Career planning** is the process of defining career goals and determining the activities that must be performed in order to accomplish these goals. While some organizations may assist their employees with career planning, you are ultimately responsible for managing your own career.

The first step in career planning is to do a self-analysis. A **self-analysis** is a tool used to help you clarify your interests, values, strengths, and weaknesses. It is sometimes difficult to take an objective look at ourselves; however, this must be done in order to conduct a useful self-analysis. A self-analysis can indicate the type of work for which you are best suited and so, is a step most beneficially taken before a position has been accepted. Most schools have counseling or placement offices that will assist you in conducting a self-analysis. The procedure should help you to choose a career that will take advantage of your strengths and minimize your weaknesses. Exercise 1.2, at the end of the chapter, is designed to help you get started in conducting your self-analysis.

Career planning does not become less important after you have accepted a position. You should determine if your organization has developed a career path for employees in your position. A career path is a sequence of jobs within the company through which a person in your current position is likely to progress. If an organization has gone to the trouble to develop career paths, it is a good

Career Planning for Supervisors

sign that it is truly interested in the development of its employees. If your organization does not have a career path for your position, then you should develop one on your own. Pick out a sequence of jobs within the organization that you believe would provide you with the experience necessary to accomplish your career objectives. An individually-developed career path may very well extend outside the current organization.

Any career plan should be flexible enough to allow you to take advantage of new opportunities. Factors beyond your control are bound to affect your career. A career plan helps to establish goals and give direction to your career, but should not be viewed as a strict set of guidelines that must be explicitly followed. As you gain work experience, it is a good idea to consider your career plan on an ongoing basis. A good career plan will be revised to take changing environmental conditions into account as well as to take advantage of unforeseen opportunities.

Summary

While supervisors are members of the management team, their organizational role is unique. They are the only managers who direct the work of nonmanagers. As managers, supervisors perform all of the management functions—planning, organizing, staffing, directing, and controlling. The nature of the job, however, requires the supervisor to spend more time staffing, directing, and controlling than planning and organizing.

All managers need to posses three basic skills: technical skills, human skills, and conceptual skills. Human skills are important at all levels of management. Technical skills are more important at the supervisory level, and conceptual skills become more important at upper levels of management.

Several factors have been identified as having a significant impact upon the role of today's supervisor. These include rising educational levels, an older work force, and increasing antidiscrimination legislation. Each of these will place some demand upon the supervisors of the future, suggesting that the role of the supervisor is becoming more challenging. This book is designed to provide information about, and assistance in developing, the skills that will enable you to give effective supervision.

Key Terms

career planning (p. 13)
conceptual skills (p. 11)
controlling (p. 10)
directing (p. 9)
external analysis (p. 8)
human skills (p. 11)
internal analysis (p. 8)
management (p. 7)
management functions (p. 7)

management process (p. 7)
operational planning (p. 8)
organizing (p. 8)
planning (p. 8)
self-analysis (p. 13)
staffing (p. 9)
strategic planning (p. 8)
supervision (p. 7)
technical skills (p. 11)

1. Why is management referred to as a "process of interrelated activities?"
2. Why do managers at different levels spend varying amounts of time performing the managerial functions?
3. Explain why supervisors generally spend more time directing, staffing, and controlling than planning and organizing.
4. Why are supervisors described as having a unique role within the organization?
5. Will the time supervisors spend in various managerial functions be the same in different kinds of organizations or industries?
6. Why is the process of management referred to as a series of ongoing activities?
7. What trends are likely to affect the job of the supervisor in the future?
8. What are some of the important skills and abilities supervisors need to develop in order to be effective?

References

1. H. K. Baker and S. H. Holmberg, "Stepping Up to Supervision: Making the Transition," *Supervisory Management* 26 (September 1981): 10–19.
2. S. C. Certo, *Principles of Modern Management: Functions and Systems.* 2nd ed. (Dubuque, Iowa: Wm. C. Brown Publishers, 1983).
3. D. Hellriegel, and J. W. Slocum, Jr. *Management.* 3rd ed. (Reading, Mass.: Addison-Wesley Publishing Co., 1982).
4. R. Katz, "Skills of the Effective Administrator," *Harvard Business Review* 52, (1974): 90–101.
5. G. R. Terry, "Speaking from Experience: The Supervisor of the (Near) Future," *Training and Development Journal* 31 (January 1977): 41–43.

Exercise

Ranking Supervisory Activities

Below is a list of behaviors engaged in by most supervisors. Rank these items in terms of their importance to the effective performance of a supervisor (1 = most important, 10 = least important). Add any others you think are important.

planning	motivating
communicating	organizing
scheduling	developing employees
coordinating	training
delegating	performance appraisal
disciplining	interviewing
budgeting	setting objectives
mediating conflict	decision making
conducting meetings	persuading
encouraging	writing letters/reports
public speaking	checking employee's work
safety/accident control	listening

team building	enforcing rules/policies
searching for problems	problem solving
recruiting	collecting information/data
teaching	handling grievances

Questions

1. How did your rankings of these behaviors compare with the rankings given by others in the class?
2. Did you change any of your rankings after class discussion? Why or why not?
3. How would your rankings differ if the exercise asked you to rank the items in terms of the *amount of time* supervisors typically spend performing each behavior?
4. Retain this exercise and look at it again at the end of the course. See if you would change any of your rankings after completing the course.

Exercise

Career Self-Analysis

Listed below are several questions that you should ask yourself when conducting your self-analysis. Complete the questions below and evaluate them in terms of a job or career that you are considering. Do your strengths and weaknesses match this particular job? You may want to take this information to your counselor or placement office for help in developing a career plan.

Questions

1. What are your current career goals or job plans?
2. List any skills you have developed. Evaluate your level of expertise by giving yourself a low, medium, or high ranking for each skill.
3. What do you think are the skills you need to develop in order to achieve your career goals?
4. Describe your plans for developing the skills listed in the previous item.
5. List your favorite activities or pastimes in order of preference.
6. Do your strengths, interests, and weaknesses match your career objectives or job plans? Why or why not?
7. The following are other questions to consider:
   a. How do you feel about traveling? What percentage of the time would you be willing to travel?
   b. What kinds of activities do you dislike doing?
   c. Do you prefer working alone, or with other people?
   d. How hard are you willing to work? Physically? Mentally?
   e. Are you willing to relocate? Do you have any restrictions on geographic area or size of city?

Peggy was extremely happy about her recent promotion. After nine years in the market research department as an administrative assistant, she was promoted to supervise that department. Peggy had replaced Mike Urban, who retired after twenty-three years with JBS Manufacturing. Although he had been well-liked by all of his employees, Mike had done little more than maintain the status quo for quite some time. He had not initiated any changes in the department during the last five years. He had seemed interested only in completing the work that came into the department and had not sought any additional responsibilities or developed any projects on his own initiative.

Peggy had made several suggestions to Mike in recent years, but he had not seemed interested in pursuing them. One of Peggy's suggestions was that research projects be assigned to teams of employees. Currently, no individual was responsible for an entire project. Each person in the department seemed to have his or her own specialty. For example, Peggy's specialty was statistical analysis. Others specialized in questionnaire design or interviewing. Everyone performed his or her own specialty on a given project, but no one was responsible for its completion. Peggy felt that it would be more motivating to everyone to be assigned to a team that would have responsibility for completing an entire research project. She was eager to implement this change as well as several others she had come to feel were needed. Peggy had always gotten along very well with the other employees in the department. Since she had worked alongside most of the people in the department for at least two or three years, she was certain that they would cooperate with her in making these changes.

At the end of the second week in her new supervisory position, Peggy called a meeting of all departmental personnel. She wanted both to outline some of the changes that she planned to make and solicit the support of departmental employees. She especially wanted to implement the work team idea as soon as possible. After outlining her proposals, there was little discussion or comment by the employees. Peggy was a little surprised that they were so reserved. Since there had been very little organizational change in several years she thought the employees would welcome a few new ideas. The employees did not seem opposed to Peggy's ideas, but they didn't seem too excited about them, either.

The following week, Peggy began assigning people to teams to work on research projects. In addition, a team leader, usually a senior employee, was appointed to supervise the project. Almost immediately Peggy began to hear complaints from employees about all of the new changes. One employee with whom Peggy had been friendly prior to her promotion, objected when Peggy assigned him to a second research project. "Who do you think you are, bossing us around like this? You used to be one of us. It seems to me that you really like using your new power to boss around the people you used to work with."

Peggy was shocked to hear this. She had no idea that anyone might feel that way. She wondered if any of the other employees felt that way. It had certainly not been her intention to boss people around. She simply wanted to make some changes that she felt were important to the department. She began to wonder what she could do to improve relations with her employees.

Questions

1. What do you see as the major problem in this case?
2. What mistakes did Peggy make?
3. What should she have done differently?
4. What can Peggy do now to correct the situation?

Appendix

Time Management

Time is the scarcest resource, and unless it is managed, nothing else can be managed.[1] There are only so many hours in the day, so you must learn to manage your time wisely. Too often supervisors get too bogged down in "putting out fires" and handling relatively simple, unimportant activities while more complex and important activities are neglected.[2] In order to begin managing your time more effectively, you must first determine how your time is being wasted. Basically, this involves finding the answers to the following three questions:[3]

1. Where does my time go?
2. Where should my time go?
3. How can I use my time more effectively?

The best way to analyze how your time is currently being spent is to keep a time log. Put simply, a time log is a diary of how you have spent your time, typically recorded in fifteen-minute intervals. It will probably be necessary to do this for at least two weeks before the log will contain a representative sample of your activities. This may seem, on the surface, to be a rather simple exercise, but it is well worth the effort. Many people are surprised when they look back over their time logs at the end of the recording period and discover how much and in what ways their time was wasted.

Figure A.1 is an example of a time log. It is designed to structure the recording of daily activities, the priority of each of those activities, and the person who initiated the activities. This information will be helpful in analyzing the time log. You will be able to see what proportion of time you spend on low-priority activities, see where those activities originated, and take steps to eliminate these interruptions of more important activity.

As you analyze your time log you should try to determine how you could have used your time in better ways. Be particularly alert for the appearance of increasing numbers of low-priority activities or time wasters. Baker identifies twenty major time wasters and categorizes them into internal and external time wasters.[4] Internal time wasters are activities that you initiate, that are largely under your control, and that can be relatively easily eliminated. Examples include procrastinating, failing to assign responsibility, presenting unclear objectives, failing to set priorities, failing to plan, poor scheduling, and attempting to do too much at once. External time wasters are activities initiated by others and are not completely under your control. External time wasters are, or are produced by, such things as telephone interruptions, meetings, visitors, socializing, lack of information, excessive paperwork, lack of policies and procedures, and red tape. Effort should be made to eliminate both types of time wasters.

Time Log

Name: _____

Dates of Log: _____

Time	Activity	Comments
7:00		
7:15		
7:30		
7:45		
8:00		
8:15		
8:30		
8:45		
9:00		
4:00		
4:15		
4:30		
4:45		
5:00		
5:15		
5:30		
5:45		
6:00		
6:15		
6:30		

NOTE: Comments should include an analysis of whether the activity was an effective use of time or time wasted. Ideas on how to prevent time wasters in the future or on ways to make better use of time should be included.

As you are analyzing your time log and identifying time wasters to avoid in the future, begin thinking, also, about specific ways in which you could use your time more effectively. You might do a number of things to make better use of your time:

1. **Set goals.** Determine what it is that you really want to accomplish. Goals provide direction and keep you on the right track. If you keep your goals clearly in mind, you are less likely to be sidetracked to less important activities.
2. **Set priorities.** You should set priorities as well as goals. Many authors recommend starting each day by making a "To Do List."[5] This list should itemize the daily activities that have to be done in order to accomplish your goals.

These tasks should be assigned priorities in terms of their importance in achieving those goals. These activities can be sorted into three categories based on their relative importance: *A* activities are very high-priority items and should receive immediate attention; *B* activities are average-priority items; and *C* activities are low-priority items. You should focus first upon *A* items. Don't begin working on *B* activities until you have completed all *A* items. Save *C* items for brief periods of idle time, such as when you are waiting for an appointment. Be careful, however, not to let the "To Do List" become an end in itself. Remember, its purpose is to help you manage your time more effectively. Sometimes supervisors spend so much time on their "To Do Lists" that the list, itself, becomes a time waster.

3. **Control paperwork.** Try not to handle each piece of paper more than once. When you pick up a piece of paper, give it your attention. Don't just return it to a different pile on your desk.

4. **Make time to plan.** Time spent planning is time well spent. If you find yourself feeling that you do not have time to plan, you are probably not managing your time very effectively. You could be very busy putting out fires and responding to "crises," but still not be making good use of your time.

References

1. P. F. Drucker, *The Effective Executive* (New York: Harper and Row, 1967), 51.
2. L. D. Alexander, "Effective Time Management Techniques," *Personnel Journal* 60 (1981): 637–640.
3. H. K. Baker, *Techniques of Time Management* (Washington, D.C.: Small Business Administration, January 1979), 2.
4. Ibid., 3.
5. G. H. Labovitz and L. Baird, "Managing Time: Positive Clock Watching," *Advanced Management Journal* (Summer 1981): 44–53.

Appendix Exercise*

It is easy to become complacent about managing your time. Many of us think we're using our time effectively when, in fact, we are not. Develop a summary of where your time is currently being spent. This can be a simple listing of several major categories of your daily activity (e.g., studying, watching TV, attending class). Next to each category make an assessment of the amount of time you believe you are spending at that activity each day. After you have completed this list keep a time log for one or two days. Carry a small notebook with you and, every fifteen minutes, record how your time is being spent. At the end of the day (or whatever time period you choose), summarize and evaluate the time spent in each category. How closely did your projections come to the record of actual time spent in each category?

*Exercise developed by Donald Pettit, Suffolk Community College.

Chapter 2

Legal Issues in Employment

Learning Objectives

After reading this chapter, you should be able to:

1. discuss the important federal equal employment opportunity legislation.
2. describe the responsibilities and activities of the Equal Employment Opportunity Commission (EEOC).
3. identify employment practices that might be considered illegal or unfair.
4. explain what constitutes illegal discrimination.
5. explain adverse impact and how it is determined.
6. describe the rights of employees on the job.
7. discuss supervisor responsibilities.

Introductory
Incident

Susan walked in to the supervisor's meeting preoccupied with thoughts of the heavy work-load that had been unexpectedly placed upon her department. She wondered how her employees would react to a request that they work this Saturday. Just then her manager, Bob Foreman, made a comment that caught her attention. Apparently an insurance company, one of the city's largest employers, was being investigated by the Equal Employment Opportunity Commission. One of its employees had filed a complaint with the EEOC charging that she had been passed over for promotion due to the organization's traditional discriminatory treatment of women. Bob said that the personnel director for this insurance company, and Bob's friend, had told him that the company was likely to lose the case if it reached the courts. Bob added that he was certainly glad that none of his employees had gotten JBS into that kind of trouble.

Susan realized that she didn't know very much about fair employment practices legislation. She wondered if any of her actions as a supervisor had been violations of some law with which she was unfamiliar. She decided that it might be a good idea to ask the personnel department if they could supply her with any material on the subject.

Since the early 1960s, the basic relationship between the employer and the employee has undergone drastic change. With the proliferation over the last twenty years of equal employment opportunity legislation, employers have been constrained in their dealings with employees. Many employment practices that were commonplace only a few years ago have, today, either disappeared or undergone modification to comply with federal or state fair employment legislation.

Federal and state equal employment opportunity legislation now affects all phases of the employment process—from the initial advertisement for and recruitment of applicants, on through selection, training, promotion, performance evaluation, discipline, and retirement or termination. Not only are employers prohibited from treating employees differently, but legislation now requires that employers give equal opportunity to all classes of employees and applicants. Nowhere within organizations has this legislation had more of an impact than at the supervisory level. Fair employment issues are often thought of as the concern of the personnel department; however, it is the supervisor who must accomplish organizational goals while dealing equitably with employees on a daily basis. Supervisors must have a good working knowledge of federal and state equal employment opportunity legislation in order to avoid charges of unlawful employment practices and possible court action.

Federal Legislation

This section of the chapter will consider the most important of the federal equal employment opportunity or fair employment practice laws. Most states and many large cities have their own fair employment practices laws and enforcement agencies; however, many of these laws have been modeled after federal legislation. A supervisor must have a good understanding of federal legislation and should be aware of any existing set of laws within the state or municipal government, as well. Some state law is more stringent and sometimes offers protection to groups

Major Federal Equal Employment Opportunity Laws

Table 2.1

Date	Name	Description
1963	Equal Pay Act	Requires the same pay for women as for men doing similar work under similar working conditions.
1964	Civil Rights Act, Title VII	Prohibits discrimination in employment on the basis of race, color, religion, sex, or national origin.
1972	Equal Employment Opportunity Act	Extends coverage of Title VII provisions and gives the EEOC the power to sue on its own behalf or on behalf of a claimant.
1978	Pregnancy Discrimination Amendment to Title VII	Requires pregnancy, childbirth, and all related medical conditions to be treated like any illness with respect to fringe benefits and other personnel policies.
1967	Age Discrimination in Employment Act	Prohibits discrimination in employment based upon age for persons between 40 and 65 years of age.
1978	Amendment to the Age Discrimination in Employment Act	Extends coverage to persons between the ages of 40 and 70.
1973	Vocational Rehabilitation Act	Requires federal contractors and subcontractors to take affirmative action to employ and promote qualified handicapped workers.

not covered by federal law. As such, a supervisor in some states could be in compliance with federal law, but still be engaging in an unlawful employment practice based upon the law of the state. A brief discussion of state law will follow a review of federal legislation. Table 2.1 summarizes the major federal equal employment opportunity laws discussed in this chapter.

Civil Rights Act of 1964, Title VII

The **Civil Rights Act of 1964** constitutes the major piece of equal employment opportunity legislation. Each section of this act deals with a specific aspect of discrimination (e.g., voting rights, education, employment). **Title VII** of the act deals with fair employment. Section 703(a) of Title VII states:

> It shall be unlawful employment practice for an employer (1) to fail or refuse to hire or to discharge any individual with respect to his compensation, terms, conditions or privileges of employment, because of such individual's race, color, religion, sex, or national origin; or

(2) to limit, segregate, or classify his employees or applicants for employment in any way which would deprive or tend to deprive any individual of employment opportunities or otherwise adversely affect his status as an employee, because of such individual's race, color, religion, sex, or national origin.

Section 704(a) of Title VII prohibits discrimination against an employee or applicant for opposing an unlawful employment practice or for participating in a Title VII investigation or hearing. This means that employees and applicants are protected not only against discrimination on the basis of race, color, religion, sex, and national origin in employment decisions, but they are also protected against retaliation should they choose to make a complaint or testify against the organization.

In 1972, Title VII was amended by the Equal Employment Opportunity Act. This act expanded the coverage of Title VII to include (a) both public and private employers (including state and local governments, and public and private educational institutions) with fifteen or more employees; (b) labor organizations (unions) with fifteen or more employees, and; (c) both public and private employment agencies. Organizations not subject to federal law may still be covered by state or municipal (city) laws.

Race, under Title VII, refers to members of racial minorities; however, protection of members of majority races against reverse discrimination is also covered.[1]

Under Title VII, it is unlawful to discriminate on the basis of any religious activity. If the religious activity interferes with a work schedule, the employer must make a reasonable attempt to accommodate the employee. For example, if an employee is scheduled to work on a religious holiday, the employer would likely be required to reschedule work assignments to accommodate the employee.

Most cases of discrimination in the courts today are based upon sex discrimination. The definition of sex discrimination was amended in 1978 to include pregnancy, childbirth, and related medical conditions. As a result, employers are required to treat pregnancy and all related medical conditions as an illness with respect to fringe benefits (e.g., sick pay) or any other personnel policies.

Sexual Harrassment

Besides treating job applicants or employees differently on the basis of their sex, another serious, but common, problem is that of **sexual harrassment.** The EEOC defines sexual harrassment as "unwelcome sexual advances, requests for sexual favors and other verbal or physical conduct of a sexual nature when submission to such conduct is made either explicitly or implicitly a term or condition of an individual's employment; submission to or rejection of such conduct by an individual is used as the basis for employment decision affecting the individual; or such conduct has the purpose or effect of unreasonably interfering with an individual's work performance or creating an intimidating, hostile or offensive working environment."[2]

Allstate settles sex bias suit for $5 million

The Associated Press

WASHINGTON — In one of the largest such settlements on record, Allstate Insurance Co. agreed to give $5 million to female sales agents alleged to have been discriminated against, the government announced Monday.

The Equal Employment Opportunity Commission said the back pay settlement agreement, approved by a federal district court in Sacramento, Calif., affects some 3,000 women employees and ends nearly 10 years of litigation.

The settlement came in a class action case in which Lola Hogan challenged the company's policy of basing starting salaries on prior pay. She maintained that she had been frustrated by earning less than men doing the same job.

EEOC Chairman Clarence Thomas called the wage discrimination settlement one of "historic proportions" and said it "should have significant impact on salary-setting practices in all industries nationwide."

A spokeswoman for Allstate, saying she could comment only if her name were not used, said that in signing the settlement the company was not admitting that it had discriminated against women.

"There is no such finding against us," the spokeswoman said in a telephone interview from Allstate's home office in Northbrook, Ill. "We in no way admit to unlawful discrimination against female sales agents and sales agent trainees in setting the level of guarantees (on women's salaries)."

The spokeswoman said the agreement was signed by Allstate "in order to avoid the continuing uncertainty and delay of further litigation. If this action were not settled, it could have taken three to five years to resolve the dispute," her statement said. "We feel the settlement is a fair compromise and is reasonable, adequate and in the best interest of Allstate as well as the class" of women plaintiffs.

But the spokeswoman also said that Allstate has "realigned the way we compensate our new agents. It's a plan we've been studying for a number of years, and it's not a result of this lawsuit."

"What it will do is eliminate anything like this ever happening again," she said.

Hogan had testified in a retrial of her suit in May that "there's nothing more discouraging than finding yourself working harder, selling more and making less than the person standing next to you."

Hogan, who no longer works for Allstate, filed the suit in 1977 under her former married name of Lola Kouba. She had gone to work for Allstate in 1974 for $825 a month. That was to last during her training period and to serve as the basis for sales commissions.

She said she was told that all new agents make the same, but soon found that newly hired men, doing the same job, were getting $1,000 a month.

A federal judge had ruled in 1981 that Allstate could not rely on prior salaries to determine new sales agents' pay unless it determined that disparities in prior pay weren't caused by sexual discrimination. That ruling was overturned by by the 9th U.S. Circuit Court of Appeals in 1982.

But during a new, three-week trial in June, the EEOC alleged that Allstate's compensation system violated Title VII of the Civil Rights Act of 1964 "in that it discriminated against females sales agents by providing them unequal pay in the form of lower minimum salary guarantees than it provided male employees performing the same jobs."

Reprinted by permission of The Associated Press.

Typically, a supervisor accompanies a request for sexual favors with a threat to withhold a promotion or a pay raise if those favors are not given. Sexual harrassment may range from suggestive remarks, to touching, to demands for sexual favors. This problem may be more serious than many people are aware since many incidents are likely to go unreported. One study concluded that approximately 80 percent of all female employees have experienced some form of sexual harrassment.[3]

To avoid charges of sexual harrassment, supervisors should treat all employees equitably. Certain behaviors and situations are to be avoided, such as driving an employee home after work, working late with an employee, and engaging in sexually suggestive conversations.[4]

Equal Employment Opportunity Commission

The **Equal Employment Opportunity Commission** (EEOC) is the agency charged with the enforcement of Title VII. Before Title VII was amended in 1972, the authority of the EEOC was limited to investigating charges of discrimination and trying to assist both parties in reaching an agreement. The 1972 amendment gave that agency the authority to bring action against organizations in U.S. district courts, either on its own behalf or on behalf of claimants.

The EEOC is an independent regulatory agency made up of five commissioners appointed by the President and confirmed by the Senate for five-year terms. No more than three of the commissioners may be members of the same political party.

The EEOC processes about 70,000 complaints, annually, in its fifty-nine regional and district offices throughout the United States. Complaints may be filed by an individual, a group, or an EEOC commissioner; however, any complaint must be filed within 180 days of an alleged violation. When a complaint is filed with the EEOC, it is first deferred to a state or local fair employment practices commission, if one exists. This state or local commission may immediately give the complaint back to the EEOC, or it may begin an investigation. After sixty days the EEOC may begin its own investigation, regardless of any action by the state or local commission.

Typically, the EEOC immediately seeks voluntary compliance on the part of the employing organization. If this fails, court action may be taken. Cases aggainst private employers are taken to federal district court, and cases against public employers are taken to the Department of Justice.

The EEOC has two other major functions. First, the EEOC issues guidelines for Title VII compliance. Guidelines have been issued in the areas of (a) discrimination because of pregnancy, sex, religion, or national origin; (b) employee selection procedures; (c) affirmative action programs, and; (d) pre-employment inquiries. While these guidelines are not laws, the Supreme Court has indicated that they are entitled to "great deference."[5] This means that the courts will generally find the employment practices that violate these EEOC guidelines to be at least questionable and, perhaps, unlawful.

The second function of the EEOC is an information-gathering function. Every organization with one hundred employees or more must file form EEO-1 with the EEOC each year. The **EEO-1** form records how many women and members of minority groups are employed in different job categories and how much those individuals are paid. Figure 2.1 shows what the EEO-1 form looks like.

Equal Pay Act of 1963

The **Equal Pay Act of 1963** is an amendment to the Fair Labor Standards Act of 1938. Under this act, workers of both sexes must be paid at the same rate for equal work involving equal effort, skill, responsibility, and working conditions. The court has determined that equal work does not mean identical work; however, the work must be "substantially similar."[6]

If an employer is found in violation of this act, the inequity cannot be corrected by lowering the wages of the higher-paid sex. The law specifically requires that an employer raise the wage rate of the lower-paid sex if current practice is found to be in violation of this act.

The equal pay act applies to any organization employing two or more people, when that organization is "engaged in interstate commerce or in the production of goods for interstate commerce." This phrase has been interpreted rather broadly to cover all but a few organizations. The act also applies to government employees, but not to labor unions because labor unions do not set wage rates. This piece of legislation has been administered by the EEOC since July, 1979.

Figure 2.1
EEO-1 form
Source: Joint Report Committee, Equal Employment Opportunity Commission, Office of Federal Contract Compliance Programs.

Joint Reporting Committee
- Equal Employment Opportunity Commission
- Office of Federal Contract Compliance Programs (Labor)

EQUAL EMPLOYMENT OPPORTUNITY
EMPLOYER INFORMATION REPORT EEO–1

Standard Form 100
(Rev. 5–84)
O.M.B. No. 3046–0007
EXPIRES 3/31/85
100–211

SAMPLE

Section A—TYPE OF REPORT
Refer to instructions for number and types of reports to be filed.

1. Indicate by marking in the appropriate box the type of reporting unit for which this copy of the form is submitted (MARK ONLY ONE BOX).

(1) ☐ Single-establishment Employer Report

Multi-establishment Employer:
(2) ☐ Consolidated Report (Required)
(3) ☐ Headquarters Unit Report (Required)
(4) ☐ Individual Establishment Report (submit one for each establishment with 50 or more employees)
(5) ☐ Special Report

2. Total number of reports being filed by this Company (Answer on Consolidated Report only) ______

Section B—COMPANY IDENTIFICATION *(To be answered by all employers)* — OFFICE USE ONLY

1. Parent Company
   a. Name of parent company (owns or controls establishment in item 2) omit if same as label — a.

Name of receiving office | Address (Number and street) — b.

City or town | County | State | ZIP code | b. Employer Identification No.

2. Establishment for which this report is filed. (Omit if same as label) — OFFICE USE ONLY
   a. Name of establishment — c.

Address (Number and street) | City or Town | County | State | ZIP code — d.

b. Employer Identification No. | (Omit if same as label) — e.

Section C—EMPLOYERS WHO ARE REQUIRED TO FILE *(To be answered by all employers)*

☐ Yes ☐ No 1. Does the entire company have at least 100 employees in the payroll period for which you are reporting?

☐ Yes ☐ No 2. Is your company affiliated through common ownership and/or centralized management with other entities in an enterprise with a total employment of 100 or more?

☐ Yes ☐ No 3. Does the company or any of its establishments (a) have 50 or more employees AND (b) is not exempt as provided by 41 CFR 60–1.5, AND either (1) is a prime government contractor or first-tier subcontractor, and has a contract, subcontract, or purchase order amounting to $50,000 or more, or (2) serves as a depository of Government funds in any amount or is a financial institution which is an issuing and paying agent for U.S. Savings Bonds and Savings Notes?

If the response to question C–3 is yes, please enter your Dun and Bradstreet identification number (if you have one): ☐☐☐☐☐☐☐☐☐

☐ Yes ☐ No 4. Does the company receive financial assistance from the Small Business Administration (SBA)?

NOTE: If the answer is yes to questions 1, 2, or 3, complete the entire form, otherwise skip to Section G.

NSN 7540–00–180–6384

Figure 2.1 (cont.)

SF 100 Page 2

Section D—EMPLOYMENT DATA

Employment at this establishment—Report all permanent full-time or part-time employees including apprentices and on-the-job trainees unless specifically excluded as set forth in the instructions. Enter the appropriate figures on all lines and in all columns. Blank spaces will be considered as zeros.

JOB CATEGORIES		OVERALL TOTALS (SUM OF COL. B THRU K)	MALE					FEMALE				
			WHITE (NOT OF HISPANIC ORIGIN)	BLACK (NOT OF HISPANIC ORIGIN)	HISPANIC	ASIAN OR PACIFIC ISLANDER	AMERICAN INDIAN OR ALASKAN NATIVE	WHITE (NOT OF HISPANIC ORIGIN)	BLACK (NOT OF HISPANIC ORIGIN)	HISPANIC	ASIAN OR PACIFIC ISLANDER	AMERICAN INDIAN OR ALASKAN NATIVE
		A	B	C	D	E	F	G	H	I	J	K
Officials and Managers	1											
Professionals	2											
Technicians	3											
Sales Workers	4											
Office and Clerical	5											
Craft Workers (Skilled)	6											
Operatives (Semi-Skilled)	7											
Laborers (Unskilled)	8											
Service Workers	9											
TOTAL	10											
Total employment reported in previous EEO-1 report	11											
(The trainees below should also be included in the figures for the appropriate occupational categories above)												
Formal On-the-job trainees	White collar	12										
	Production	13										

NOTE: Omit questions 1 and 2 on the Consolidated Report.
1. Date(s) of payroll period used: 2. Does this establishment employ apprentices?
                                               1 ☐ Yes   2 ☐ No

Section E—ESTABLISHMENT INFORMATION (Omit on the Consolidated Report)

1. Is the location of the establishment the same as that reported last year?
   1 ☐ Yes   2 ☐ No   3 ☐ No report last year

2. Is the major business activity at this establishment the same as that reported last year?
   1 ☐ Yes   2 ☐ No   3 ☐ No report last year

OFFICE USE ONLY

3. What is the major activity of this establishment? (Be specific, i.e., manufacturing steel castings, retail grocer, wholesale plumbing supplies, title insurance, etc. Include the specific type of product or type of service provided, as well as the principal business or industrial activity.)

Section F—REMARKS

Use this item to give any identification data appearing on last report which differs from that given above, explain major changes in composition or reporting units and other pertinent information.

Section G—CERTIFICATION (See Instructions G)

Check one
1 ☐ All reports are accurate and were prepared in accordance with the instructions (check on consolidated only)
2 ☐ This report is accurate and was prepared in accordance with the instructions.

Name of Certifying Official	Title	Signature	Date
Name of person to contact regarding this report (Type or print)	Address (Number and street)		
Title	City and State	ZIP code	Telephone Area Code	Number	Extension

All reports and information obtained from individual reports will be kept confidential as required by Section 709(e) of Title VII
WILLFULLY FALSE STATEMENTS ON THIS REPORT ARE PUNISHABLE BY LAW, U.S. CODE, TITLE 18, SECTION 1001

Age Discrimination in Employment Act of 1967

The **Age Discrimination in Employment Act of 1967** is also administered by the EEOC. This act has made it unlawful to discriminate against employees or job applicants if they are between forty and sixty-five years of age. In 1978, an amendment to this act extended coverage to employees and job applicants between the ages of forty and seventy. Any employer with twenty or more workers is covered. The age discrimination act also eliminated mandatory retirement for federal employees.

The law does allow age to be used as a criterion in employment decisions if a particular age is a requirement for the successful performance of the job. For example, discrimination against older job applicants would be considered allowable in the hiring of actors to play the role of children in a movie. These types of specifications introduces the idea of **"bona fide occupational qualifications"** (BFOQ) or **"business necessity."** This means that if it can be shown that a particular characteristic is *essential* to successful job performance, it would be permitted even though it discriminates against a protected group. This concept will be further discussed later on in this chapter, and again in chapter 3.

Vocational Rehabilitation Act of 1973

Under the **Vocational Rehabilitation Act of 1973,** all federal contractors and subcontractors receiving more than $2,500 in federal contracts per year are required to take affirmative action to hire and promote qualified handicapped workers. This act defines a handicapped person as one who: (a) has a physical or mental impairment which substantially limits one or more of life's major activities (e.g., walking, seeing, hearing); (b) has a record of such an impairment (e.g., a person who has a history of disability or illness, such as cancer, but who is not suffering from the disability or illness currently), or; (c) is regarded as having such an impairment (e.g., an individual who seems mentally retarded, but is not).

The rehabilitation act, therefore, covers those traditionally categorized as handicapped (e.g., blind, paraplegic) as well as individuals with conditions not traditionally considered handicapped (e.g., persons with diabetes). In 1976, the court extended the definition of handicapped to include alcoholism and drug addiction.[7]

Executive Orders

Executive orders define the position of the executive branch of the government and are aimed at federal agencies, contractors, and subcontractors. The executive branch will stop doing business with an employer who violates an executive order. For the most part, these orders simply echo Title VII; however, they often extend the coverage to include, specifically, federal agencies, and federal contractors and subcontractors.

Executive Order 11246, signed by President Johnson in 1965, prohibited discrimination on the basis of race, color, religion, or national origin by federal agencies, contractors, and subcontractors. In 1967, **Executive Order 11375** added sex-based discrimination to that list.

In 1969, President Nixon signed **Executive Order 11478** requiring that employment decisions and policies in the federal government be based upon merit and actual performance. The directive also prohibits discrimination on the basis of race, color, religion, sex, or national origin. Executive orders are administered by the Office of Federal Contract Compliance Programs (OFCCP).

State Legislation

Most states have their own equal employment opportunity laws and state enforcement agencies. Some state regulations are more strict than federal law. This raises the question of which law applies. Whenever there are inconsistencies between federal, and state or local laws, federal law takes precedence. For example, Ohio state law prohibits employers from asking job applicants for information regarding their race or sex, yet federal law requires that such information be recorded and annually reported to the EEOC. On the other hand, if state law does not conflict with federal law but is simply more stringent or extensive in its coverage of groups, then both the state as well as federal law must be observed.

It should be emphasized that some state law extends coverage to groups not covered by federal law (e.g., obese individuals). So it is extremely important that you become familiar with the fair employment practice laws of your state. The personnel department of your organization may have this information. Otherwise, contact either the state's Fair Employment Practices Commission or its Equal Employment Opportunity Commission.

What Constitutes Discrimination?

In practice, **discrimination** may be defined as adverse impact in the absence of bona fide occupational qualifications (or business necessity).

Adverse Impact

Adverse impact may be defined as employment practices (e.g., hiring, promoting) that exclude members of a protected group (e.g., race, sex, religion) at a higher rate than members of nonprotected groups. Significantly, the intent of the employing organization is irrelevant in judgments of adverse impact. An employer may be acting in good faith and trying to not discriminate, but if an employment practice is found to have adverse impact, the employer may be subject to court action.

Adverse impact may occur under several different sets of circumstances. First, a ruling of adverse impact can be made if blatant discrimination against members of a protected class is discovered. For example, an employer might refuse to hire women for certain jobs even though sex has nothing to do with ability to perform the job. Second, members of a protected class may be receiving treatment differently from that given members of an unprotected class. For example, female job applicants might be asked about their plans for marriage and having children, while male applicants are not. If the rate of selection for female applicants is substantially lower than the rate for male applicants, adverse impact may be found. Finally, adverse impact may be judged even in the absence of blatant discrimination or differential treatment. An employment practice may appear to be neutral (not designed to discriminate against members of a protected class) and the employer may have good intentions; but if the effect or result of the employment practice is that members of a protected class are excluded at a higher rate, adverse impact may be found. For example, suppose you are an employer in a city where 75 percent of the white population, but only 25 percent of the Hispanic population, has a high school diploma. Requiring a high school diploma for employment in this city would most likely result in a ruling of adverse impact, unless the employer could prove bona fide occupational qualification (i.e., that a high school diploma is necessary for successful job performance).

The 80% or 4/5ths Rule

The EEOC has established a rule of thumb known as the **4/5th or 80% Rule.** This guideline is typically used by the EEOC or the courts in determining whether or not adverse impact exists. This rule states that the selection rate and promotion rates for members of a protected group must be at least 4/5ths or 80% of the rate for members of a nonprotected majority. An example using selection or hiring rates will help to clarify this rule.

Suppose that your organization has received applications from 200 black applicants and 200 white applicants. Your organization hired 120 white applicants and 60 black applicants. The existence of adverse impact would be determined by comparing the selection rates of the two groups in the following manner:

Number of Minority Applicants Hired		Number of Nonminority Applicants Hired
————————————	divided by	————————————
Total Number of Applicants		Total Number of Applicants
60	divided by	120
———		———
200		200
.30	divided by	.60
	$= .50 = 50\%$	

Since 50 percent is not at least 80 percent, the 4/5ths Rule has been violated and there is evidence of adverse impact. The selection rate for blacks was only 50 percent of the selection rate for whites. It should be noted that the rule is generally not applied when dealing with small numbers of employees or applicants.

Two important points about adverse impact need to be made. First, a finding of adverse impact does not necessarily mean that an employee practice is discriminatory or unlawful. It only establishes what is known as **prima facie evidence.** Prima facie means "at first view" and, in practice, denotes a situation in which there is enough evidence indicating the possibility of discrimination to warrant additional investigation. Second, the **burden of proof** now shifts to the employer. After adverse impact is established, the employer has two choices— to discontinue the practice immediately, or show either that the practice is job related or that business necessity exists. When employers require that job applicants possess certain traits or skills such as a high school diploma or a particular height, questions of business necessity, or bona fide occupational qualification (BFOQ), may arise.

Employee Rights

This review of equal employment opportunity or fair employment practices legislation has suggested that employees have certain rights on the job and that supervisors need to be aware of them. Your employees have the right to fair and equitable treatment while at work. Based upon the legislation presented earlier, fair and equitable treatment means that employees are entitled to the following: (a) freedom from discrimination based upon race, color, religion, sex, national origin, or age; (b) job security; (c) the confidentiality of their employment records, and; (d) in some cases, access their employment records.

Much of this chapter has dealt with discrimination. The focus will now switch to some other aspects of fair and equitable treatment.

Job Security

Job security is the right to continued employment with an organization and involves the right to due process in case of termination of employment. Employers have traditionally operated under the **"termination at will" doctrine,** meaning that employers reserve the right to fire an employee at any time for any reason, or even for no reason. Recently, the "termination for just cause" doctrine has been gaining favor, making it more difficult for employers to fire employees.

As a general rule, supervisors *cannot* fire employees for

1. engaging in lawful union activity. *(National Labor Relations Act of 1935)*
2. filing unfair labor practices charges with the National Labor Relations Board (NLRB). *(National Labor Relations Act of 1935)*
3. filing discrimination charges with the EEOC, or state or municipal fair employment agencies. *(Civil Rights Act of 1964, Title VII, Section 703(a))*
4. participating in an EEOC investigation. *(Civil Rights Act of 1964, Title VII, Section 704(a))*
5. refusing to work under unsafe conditions. *(Occupational Safety and Health Act of 1970)*
6. reasons related to age. *(Age Discrimination in Employment Act of 1967,* and amended in 1978)

Most union contracts specify the ways in which an employee may be fired. These contracts usually include a due process clause. Due process includes the right to call witnesses and refuse to testify against oneself. It also includes the right to face charges or reasons for termination. Even employees not specifically covered by a union contract are afforded the protection of due process. Court decisions have protected workers from discharge in cases where due process was denied.[8]

As a general rule, supervisors *can* terminate employees for

1. unsuccessful job performance (provided the employee cannot be trained to perform successfully).
2. too many unexcused absences.
3. repeated lateness.
4. verbal abuse.
5. physical violence.
6. falsification of records.
7. drunkenness or drug abuse on the job.
8. theft.

Progressive Discipline

Terminating employees requires documentation. Say, for example, that an employee does not perform well and is repeatedly late for work. You will need specific, detailed records documenting the employee's behavior before that employee can be terminated and before you can expect that the termination will hold up in court if it is contested. One of the best ways to accomplish this, and a way that the courts seem to favor, is to include **progressive discipline** in the process. Progressive discipline may be defined as a specified sequence of disciplinary activities that become increasingly severe with the occurrence of repeated violations. A typical sequence of actions might include the following steps:

1. Giving a verbal warning. Although it is common to make the first warning an informal, verbal warning, it is best to put all warnings in writing. The employee should be required to sign the warning to show that it was received.
2. Giving a written warning that becomes a part of the employee's permanent employee record.
3. Suspending the individual from work. This action is also documented and made part of the employment record. The suspension may be for a day or several weeks, depending upon the seriousness of the violation.
4. Terminating employment.

At each stage of the progressive discipline process, the employee should be warned what type of action will be forthcoming should another violation occur. It is important that the employee be counseled at each step. Specifically, the individual should be told exactly what is wrong, why it is wrong, and what can be done to correct the behavior. The fact that this counseling has taken place should be included in the documentation.

The progressive discipline process accomplishes two things: (a) it gives employees a chance to correct their behavior before their employment is terminated, and (b) it provides the documentation required in case termination is necessary.

Employment Records

Two separate legal issues are associated with employment records. One, employees have the right to have their personnel records remain confidential; that is, employment records cannot be released to third parties without the employee's consent. And two, federal employees and employees in certain states have the right to examine their employment records.

Confidentiality of Records

Several pieces of federal legislation require that employment records (e.g., letters of reference, pre-employment test results, performance evaluations, salary records) be kept confidential. This legislation prohibits employers from releasing information in employment records without the consent of the employee. While these acts apply primarily to federal agencies, many states are adopting legislation to cover private employers, as well. The Privacy Act of 1974, the Federal Fair Credit Reporting Act, and the Family Education Rights and Privacy Act (or Buckley Amendment) are all pieces of legislation that have been passed to protect the confidentiality of the employee's record.

Employee Access to Records

The **Privacy Act of 1974** allows federal employees to examine all records pertaining to their employment. It also allows individuals to amend records that they feel are inaccurate by attaching a statement explaining what they believe to be incorrect. While the Privacy Act applies only to federal agencies, several states have adopted similar legislation covering private employers. (These states are California, Connecticut, Illinois, Maine, Michigan, New Hampshire, Oregon, Pennsylvania, and Wisconsin.) State law differs on which records may be examined, how many times per year the records may be examined, whether or not copies may be made, and whether or not employees can insert a statement in their records noting that the records contain information with which they disagree and stating the reasons why they disagree.[9]

Advice to Supervisors

Supervisors can do several things to avoid problems linked to employment decisions. The following are the major areas in which effort should be applied in order to circumvent potentially difficult situations.

1. *Use only job-related information in making employment decisions.* This is good advice whether the decision involves hiring, firing, promotion, or a salary

increase. If the personnel department has adequately done its job of conducting a job analysis and preparing valid instruments (i.e. job application forms, performance evaluation rating scales), you need to do your job and use these instruments properly. If adverse impact should ever be established, you must be able to prove business necessity. There is no way to accomplish this if you are using information in your decision making that is not job related (e.g., sex, age). Table 2.2 shows what are considered to be fair and unfair pre-employment inquiries based upon federal legislation.

2. *Communicate your expectations.* It is important for supervisors to communicate their performance expectations to employees. Obviously, the clearer it is to employees what it is they are to accomplish, the more likely they are to accomplish it. It might be argued that if performance expectations are not made clear to employees, a supervisor, who is so inclined, could use this ambiguity to discriminate. Since employees do not know what management considers to be "good performance," employees could easily be told they are not performing well causing them to lose out on a salary increase or promotion. Without an understanding of what is expected, it is difficult to argue with the decision. The courts frown upon ambiguity and are likely to find an employment practice to be unfair if it is so ambiguous or subjective that it would be possible for a supervisor to discriminate if he or she were so inclined.[10]

3. *Communicate problems early.* Just as it is important to communicate expectations, it is also important to communicate problems as early as possible. The saying "Ignorance of the law is no excuse" is a familiar one. It means that if you are driving your car and break a law you are subject to the penalty whether or not you were aware of that law. This is not the case on the job. Employees cannot be held responsible for rules of which they are not aware. Communicating problems early allows employees to correct their behavior soon after the problem arises. This communication can, however, and probably should be, documented in case the employee does not correct the problem and discipline or termination becomes necessary.

4. *Treat employees equally.* This suggestion should be unnecessary if you are using only job-related information in your employment decisions. All other factors such as age, sex, and religion should be irrelevant. Only job-related qualifications and performance levels should be considered.

5. *Maintain a complete set of records.* The importance of documentation cannot be overemphasized. If an employee challenges an employment practice in court, documentation is an absolute requirement. If the progressive discipline process already described has been used, it should provide the necessary documentation for problem employees. It is not always the problem employee, however, who challenges an employment practice or decision. It is good practice to maintain objective employment records on all employees.

Table 2.2   Preemployment Inquiry Guide

Subject	Lawful Inquiries	Unlawful Inquiries
1. Name	"Have you worked for this company under a different name?" Maiden name.	Inquiries about the name which would indicate applicant's lineage, ancestry, national origin, or descent. Inquiry into previous name of applicant where it has been changed by court order or otherwise.
2. Address or duration of residence	Applicant's address. Inquiry into place and length of current and previous addresses. "How long a resident of this state or city?"	Specific inquiry into foreign addresses which would indicate national origin.
3. Birthplace	"Can you after employment submit a birth certificate or other proof of U.S. citizenship?"	Birthplace of applicant. Birthplace of applicant's parents, spouse, or other relatives. Requirement that applicant submit a birth certificate, naturalization, or baptismal record. Any other inquiry into national origin.
4. Age	If a minor, require proof of age in the form of a work permit or a certificate of age. Require proof of age by birth certificate after being hired. Inquiry as to whether or not the applicant meets the minimum age requirement as set by law and requirement that upon hire proof of age must be submitted in the form of a birth certificate or other forms of proof of age. If age is a legal requirement: "If hired, can you furnish proof of age?" or statement that hire is subject to verification of age.	Requirement that applicant state age or date of birth. Requirement that applicant produce proof of age in the form of a birth certificate or baptismal record.

Preemployment Inquiry Guide

Table 2.2 (cont.)

Subject	Lawful Inquiries	Unlawful Inquiries
5. Religion	An applicant may be advised concerning normal hours and days of work required by the job to avoid possible conflict with religious or other personal conviction.	Applicant's religious denomination or affiliation, church, parish, pastor, or religious holidays observed. "Do you attend religious services or a house of worship?" Applicant may not be told: "This is a Catholic/Protestant/Jewish/atheist/etc. organization." Request pastor's recommendation or reference or any other religious references. Applicants may not be told that employees are required to work on religious holidays which are observed as days of complete prayer by members of their specific faith. Any inquiry to indicate or identify religious denomination or customs.
6. Race or color	General distinguishing physical characteristics, such as scars, etc.	Applicant's race. Color of applicant's skin, eyes, hair, etc., or other questions directly or indirectly indicating race or color. Applicant's height where it is not relative to job.
7. Photograph	May be required after hiring for identification.	Request photograph before hiring. Requirement that applicant affix a photograph to application. Request that applicant, at his or her option, submit photograph. Requirement of photograph after interview but before hiring.

**Table 2.2
(cont.)**

Preemployment Inquiry Guide

Subject	Lawful Inquiries	Unlawful Inquiries
8. Citizenship	"Are you a citizen of the United States?" "If you are not a U.S. citizen, have you the legal right to remain permanently in the U.S.?" Statement that if hired, applicant may be required to submit proof of citizenship.	"Of what country are you a citizen?" Whether applicant or applicant's parents or spouse are naturalized or native-born U.S. citizens. Date when applicant or parents or spouse acquired U.S. citizenship. Requirement that applicant produce naturalization papers or first papers. Whether applicant's parents or spouse are citizens of the U.S.
9. Ancestry or national origin	Languages applicant reads, speaks, or writes fluently.	Applicant's nationality, lineage, ancestry, national origin, descent, or parentage. Date of arrival in the U.S. or port of entry; how long a resident. Nationality of applicant's parents or spouse; maiden name of applicant's wife or mother. Language commonly used by applicant. "What is your mother tongue?" How applicant acquired ability to read, write, or speak of foreign language.
10. Education	Applicant's academic, vocation, or professional education; school attended. Inquiry into language skills such as reading, speaking, and writing foreign languages.	Any inquiry asking specifically the nationality, racial, or religious affiliation of a school. Inquiry as to what is mother tongue or how foreign language ability was acquired.
11. Experience	Applicant's work experience. Other countries visited.	

Preemployment Inquiry Guide

Subject	Lawful Inquiries	Unlawful Inquiries
12. Conviction, arrest, and court record		Ask or check into a person's arrest, court, or conviction record if not substantially related to functions and responsibilities of the prospective employment.
13. Relatives	Names of applicant's husband or wife, and dependent children. Names of applicant's relatives already employed by this company. "Do you live with your parents?" Names and addresses of parents or guardian of minor applicant.	Name or address of any relative of adult applicant other than applicant's spouse or children.
14. Organization	Inquiry into the organization of which an applicant is a member providing the name or character of the organization does not reveal the race, religion, color, or ancestry of the membership. "What offices are held, if any?"	"List all organizations, clubs, societies, and lodges to which you belong." The names of organizations to which the applicant belongs if such information would indicate through character or name the race, religion, color, or ancestry of the membership.
15. Notice in case of emergency	Name and address of person to be notified in case of accident or emergency.	Name and address of relatives to be notified in case of accident or emergency.
16. References	"By whom were you referred for a position here?" Names of persons willing to provide professional and/or character references for applicant. "Who suggested that you apply for a position here?"	Require the submission of a religious reference. Request reference from applicant's pastor.

Table 2.2 (cont.)

Preemployment Inquiry Guide

Subject	Lawful Inquiries	Unlawful Inquiries
17. Sex	Only if nature of the work or working conditions provide valid reasons. Where a bona fide occupational qualification is reasonably necessary to the normal operation, motif, culture, or atmosphere of that particular business or enterprise.	Sex of the applicant. Any other inquiry which would indicate sex. "Are you expecting?" or "Are you pregnant?"
18. Work schedule	Inquiry into willingness to work required work schedule.	Any inquiry into willingness to work any particular religious holiday.
19. Miscellaneous	Notice to applicants that any misstatements or omissions of material facts in the application may be cause for dismissal.	

Compiled from *EEOC Compliance Manual* (Washington D.C.: Bureau of National Affairs, October 28, 1975) and from the Department of Labor, State of Hawaii. (p. 158)

Any inquiry is forbidden which, although not specifically listed among the above, is designed to elicit information as to race, color, ancestry, sex, religion, or arrest and court record unless based upon a bona fide occupational qualification.

Summary

The equal employment opportunity legislation discussed in this chapter share a common theme. Employment decisions should be based upon job-related information. Factors such as sex, age, religion, national origin, race, color, and handicap should be irrelevant to any hiring decision related to qualified applicants for a job.

It was noted that several states and some large municipal governments have their own fair employment practices legislation, as well as their own enforcement agencies. State law is sometimes more stringent than federal law, and will often extend coverage to groups not protected by federal law. It is critical that supervisors become familiar with the fair employment practices of their state.

In practice, discrimination is commonly defined as adverse impact in the absence of business necessity. One way that evidence of adverse impact is established is through the application of the 4/5ths or 80% Rule.

It is becoming increasingly difficult to fire an employee according to the "termination at will" doctrine; it is being replaced by the "termination for just cause" doctrine. Typically, termination under this standard requires documentation and progressive discipline.

This chapter concluded with a discussion of employee rights on the job. In addition to rights to freedom from discrimination, and to keeping employment records confidential, many employees have the right to examine their employment records. Job security is another right of the employee.

adverse impact (p. 30)
Age Discrimination in Employment Act of 1967 (p. 29)
bona fide occupational qualifications (p. 29)
burden of proof (p. 32)
business necessity (p. 29)
Civil Rights Act of 1964 (p. 23)
discrimination (p. 30)
EEO-1 (p. 26)
Equal Employment Opportunity Commission (p. 25)
Equal Pay Act of 1963 (p. 26)
Executive Orders 11246, 11375, 11478 (p. 30)
4/5ths or 80% Rule (p. 31)
prima facie evidence (p. 32)
Privacy Act of 1974 (p. 34)
progressive discipline (p. 33)
sexual harrassment (p. 24)
"termination at will" doctrine (p. 32)
Title VII (p. 23)
Vocational Rehabilitation Act of 1973 (p. 29)

1. What are the groups protected by the federal equal employment opportunity legislation as discussed in this chapter?
2. Does a thirty-year-old white male have any protection under federal fair employment legislation?
3. Explain adverse impact.
4. Describe how the 4/5ths or 80% Rule works.
5. What rights do employees have on the job?
6. What are some reasons for which you can usually terminate an employee?
7. Do employees have the right to examine their employment records? Do you think employees should have this right? Why or why not?
8. What explanation can you give for the reluctance of management to give employees the right to examine their employment records?
9. Explain progressive discipline.
10. What actions should supervisors take to comply with federal equal employment opportunity legislation?

1. Bakke v. Regents of the University of California, 17 FEP 1811 (1978).
2. *EEOC Guidelines on Sexual Harrassment,* 29 CFR Section 1604.11, 1980.
3. P. A. Somers and J. Clementson-Mohr, "Sexual Extortion in the Work Place," *Personnel Administrator* (April 1979): 23–28.
4. D. J. Peterson and D. Massengill, "Sexual Harrassment: A Growing Problem in the Workplace," *Personnel Administrator* (October 1982): 79–89.
5. Chmill v. City of Pittsburgh, 15 FEP 447 (1977).
6. Schultz v. Wheaton Glass Company, 9 FEP 506 (1970).
7. Connecticut General Life Insurance v. DIHLR, 13 FEP 1811 (1976).
8. Reeves v. Eaves, 15 FEP 441 (1977).
9. "Employee Access to Records," in *Personnel Management Policies and Practices.* (Englewood Cliffs, N.J.: Prentice-Hall, 1984).
10. Wade v. Mississippi Cooperative Extension Service, 7 FEP 282 (1974).

Exercise

The Application Blank

Examine the application form for XYZ Corporation. Identify and describe (1) any unlawful or unfair pre-employment inquiries contained in this application form and (b) the reason why you think each of these inquiries is unfair.

XYZ CORPORATION

APPLICATION FOR EMPLOYMENT

ANSWER ALL QUESTIONS COMPLETELY
PLEASE PRINT IN INK OR TYPE

YOUR APPLICATION WILL BE CONSIDERED CURRENT FOR ONLY 90 DAYS FROM THE DATE COMPLETED. AFTER 90 DAYS, YOU MUST RENEW IT.

| NAME: LAST | FIRST | MIDDLE OR MAIDEN | DATE OF APPLICATION | FOR WHAT TYPE OF POSITION ARE YOU APPLYING |

ADDRESS: NO. OR RT.   STREET OR BOX — HOME PHONE NUMBER

CITY   STATE   ZIP — BUSINESS PHONE NUMBER — HOW DID YOU HAPPEN TO APPLY TO XYZ?

DO YOU ☐ OWN HOME ☐ RENT ☐ OTHER — SOCIAL SECURITY NUMBER

DATE OF BIRTH   HEIGHT FT. INCHES   ☐ SINGLE ☐ WIDOWED, WHEN ___   NO. OF DEPENDENT CHILDREN / THEIR AGES

WEIGHT LBS.   DATE AVAILABLE FOR WORK   ☐ ENGAGED ☐ SEPARATED, WHEN ___   RELATIONSHIP OF OTHER DEPENDENTS

WILL TRANSPORTATION TO WORK BE A PROBLEM ☐ YES ☐ NO   ☐ MARRIED, WHEN ___ ☐ DIVORCED, WHEN ___   DO ALL DEPENDENTS LIVE WITH YOU ☐ YES ☐ NO

	NAME	ADDRESS	AGE	WHERE EMPLOYED
SPOUSE				
FATHER				
MOTHER				
BROTHER				
BROTHER				
SISTER				
SISTER				

NAMES OR RELATIVES AND FRIENDS WORKING WITH XYZ. (1) (2) (3) (4)

DO YOU HAVE ANY PHYSICAL DEFECTS OR DISABILITIES ☐ YES ☐ NO — NATURE

HAVE YOU EVER SUFFERED ANY INJURIES AT WORK ☐ YES ☐ NO — WHEN / NATURE OF INJURY

HAVE YOU EVER BEEN TREATED FOR MENTAL ILLNESS ☐ YES ☐ NO — WHEN / NATURE OF ILLNESS

HAVE YOU EVER BEEN CONVICTED OF A CRIME ☐ YES ☐ NO — WHEN / TYPE OF OFFENSE / GIVE ALL RELEVANT DETAILS

HAVE YOU EVER SERVED IN THE U.S. ARMED FORCES ☐ YES ☐ NO — DATES OF ACTIVE DUTY / BRANCH OF THE SERVICE

DO YOU HAVE ANY MILITARY RESERVE OBLIGATIONS ☐ YES ☐ NO   IF YES, WHAT ☐ READY ☐ STAND BY ☐ RETIRED — UNIT AND BRANCH

LIST BELOW THE NAMES OF PREVIOUS EM-PLOYERS—START WITH MOST RECENT (a) Name of Company (b) Address (c) Phone Number	DATES EMPLOYED		POSITION OR TITLE DESCRIBE YOUR DUTIES	IMMEDIATE SUPERVISOR	WAGES OR SALARY	REASON FOR LEAVING
	Month	Year				
A)	From			NAME	START	
B)						
	To			TITLE	LAST	
C)						
A)	From			NAME	START	
B)						
	To			TITLE	LAST	
C)						
A)	From			NAME	START	
B)						
	To			TITLE	LAST	
C)						

HAVE YOU EVER BEEN EMPLOYED BY THIS COMPANY	☐ YES	☐ NO IF YES, WHEN	FROM TO	REASON FOR LEAVING

REFERENCES: LIST THREE PERSONS NOT RELATED TO YOU WHO HAVE KNOWLEDGE OF YOUR QUALIFICATIONS AND FITNESS FOR THE POSITION FOR WHICH YOU ARE APPLYING. DO NOT LIST REPEAT NAMES OF SUPERVISORS LISTED UNDER WORK HISTORY.

NAME	ADDRESS

If relevant to the type of work for which you are applying, indicate any special skills you may have:

Typing speed (WPM) _____ Calculator ☐

Dictaphone ☐ Other _____

Can You Drive a Standard Shift Automobile

YES ☐ NO ☐

Education	NAME AND ADDRESS	ATTENDED		Did You Graduate?	TYPE OF DEGREE	COURSE OF STUDY
		From	To			
GRAMMAR						
HIGH SCH.						
COLLEGE						
OTHER						

XYZ, INC. IS AN EQUAL OPPORTUNITY EMPLOYER. FEDERAL LAW PROHIBITS DISCRIMINATION IN EM-PLOYMENT PRACTICES BECAUSE OF AGE, RACE, COLOR, RELIGION, SEX OR NATIONAL ORIGIN. FACTS RELATING TO YOUR AGE, RACE, COLOR, RELIGION, SEX OR NATIONAL ORIGIN ARE NOT CONSIDERED IN DETERMINING YOUR QUALIFICATIONS FOR EMPLOYMENT.
I UNDERSTAND THAT ANY FALSE OR MISLEADING INFORMATION OR OMISSIONS IN THIS APPLICATION SHALL BE SUFFICIENT CAUSE FOR REJECTION OR IMMEDIATE DISMISSAL. I AUTHORIZE YOU TO CON-TACT ALL COMPANIES USED ABOVE ABOUT MY EMPLOYMENT RECORD. THE COMPLETION OF THIS APPLICATION DOES NOT INDICATE THERE ARE ANY POSITIONS OPEN AND DOES NOT IN ANY WAY OB-LIGATE THE COMPANY.

IN CONSIDERATION OF MY EMPLOYMENT, I AGREE TO CONFORM TO THE RULES AND REGULATIONS OF THE COMPANY, AND THAT MY EMPLOYMENT AND COMPENSATION MAY BE TERMINATED, WITH OR WITHOUT CAUSE, AND WITH OR WITHOUT NOTICE, AT ANY TIME, AT THE OPTION OF EITHER THE COM-PANY OR MYSELF. I UNDERSTAND THAT NO REPRESENTATIVE OF THE COMPANY HAS AUTHORITY TO ENTER INTO AN AGREEMENT WITH ME FOR EMPLOYMENT FOR ANY SPECIFIED PERIOD OF TIME, OR TO MAKE, ANY AGREEMENT WITH ME CONTRARY TO THE FOREGOING.

DATE	SIGNATURE

Case

Jane's First Interview

Jane was excited and a little nervous about conducting her first job interview. She had accepted a supervisory position with JBS Manufacturing only a month ago. She had already had to mediate conflict between two of her employees and reprimand another for consistent tardiness. After all that had happened so far, Jane was really looking forward to interviewing applicants for a new position in her department.

The title of the position is Computer Programmer I. The responsibilities of this position are to assist other departments within JBS, determine their computer report needs, and to write programs (largely in COBOL and BASIC) that will satisfy these needs. The position requires good interpersonal skills since most of the jobholder's interaction will be with people who have no computer skills or knowledge of programming languages.

The first job applicant to be interviewed was waiting in one of the conference rooms in the personnel department when Jane arrived. She had spent almost an hour this morning going over the applicant's resume and application blank, so Jane felt confident, as she opened the conference room door, that she was prepared for this interview.

The following conversation took place:

Jane: Good morning. I'm Jane Simmons. You must be Lyle Burns.

Lyle: Yes, I am. Good morning.

Jane: I have reviewed your resume and application blank and would like to ask you some questions about your qualifications for the computer programmer job that we have open. First of all, why don't you just tell me about yourself. Are you married? Do you have any children? What are your hobbies?

Lyle: Yes, I'm married and have two daughters. I enjoy jogging and am president of the local runner's association. I guess I'd have to say that micro-computers are also a big hobby of mine. Even though my job involves computers, I'm always tinkering with some micros that I have at home.

Jane: I didn't know that there was a local runner's club. I guess that means you live here in the city?

Lyle: Yes, we just bought a house on the west side.

Jane: So you haven't lived here very long?

Lyle: No, we moved here about a month ago.

Jane: What church do you go to? I'd like to invite you to mine if you haven't chosen one yet.

Lyle: Actually, my wife's parents live in the city. We have been attending their church.

Jane: Great. Say, does your wife work outside the home?

Lyle: Yes, she teaches part-time at the local community college.

Jane: Really. What type of courses does she teach?

Lyle: She's in the business department. She teaches primarily accounting and finance courses.

Jane: Very good. Well, I guess we had better turn our attention to the position we have open before I run out of time. Tell me, what programming languages are you familiar with?

Lyle: Most of my previous work has been with BASIC, COBOL, and FORTRAN. I have done some work with PL1, APL, PASCAL, too.

Jane: That's good. A great deal of the work in this particular position will be with BASIC and COBOL. Another aspect of this position that you should understand is that you will be working largely on your own. In addition, most of the contact you have with others inside the company will be with people who have little, if any, computer training. In addition to writing programs to satisfy their needs, you will often have to help them to determine exactly what their needs are. This will often require a good deal of diplomacy. You may frequently be asked to do things that simply cannot be done because the person making the request doesn't understand computer programming.

Lyle: I think that would provide a challenge and an aspect to the job that most programmers do not have. Frankly, sitting in a room and writing programs all day is not what I want to be doing. I enjoy solving problems and that seems to be what this job entails.

Jane: Right. Well, I'm satisfied that I have enough information. Do you have any questions?

Lyle: No, I believe that I understand what the position involves, and I think it's exactly what I'm looking for.

Jane: Good. I have two more applicants to see this afternoon. I will call you in the morning and let you know what my decision is. Thanks for coming in this morning.

Lyle: Thank you.

The interview was then terminated and Jane returned to her office to review her notes before seeing the next applicant.

Questions

1. Was there anything in the interview that might be considered an unfair pre-employment inquiry? Explain.
2. What are some questions that are likely to get asked in casual conversation during an interview that might be considered unfair?
3. Did you notice any other mistakes that Jane made during the interview?

Chapter 3
Selecting Employees

Learning Objectives

After reading this chapter, you should:

1. be able to differentiate personnel department and supervisory responsibilities regarding the selection process.
2. be aware of the various sources of information about applicants that may be obtainable.
3. be able to evaluate the relative usefulness of the different sources of applicant information.
4. have an awareness of the interviewer errors that are common to the interviewing process.
5. recognize the strengths and weaknesses of different types of interviews.
6. know how to conduct an employment interview.

Joe has just finished his third month with JBS Manufacturing. After graduating from the university last spring, he accepted a supervisory position in the advertising department at JBS. In this position, he supervises the work of four clerical employees.

Early last week, one of Joe's employees notified him that she was leaving JBS in two weeks and was going back to school. Joe immediately notified his boss, who told Joe to begin interviewing people to fill that job opening. Since this was Joe's first supervisory position, he was not sure how to begin the process. He knew that the personnel department had applications on file that he could review in order to find some people to call for interviews. He remembered reading about the increase in legislation concerning employment practices and wondered if there were some things he should be aware of before proceeding. In addition, Joe had never conducted an interview and was not sure what questions he should or should not ask a job applicant. He wondered if the personnel department had any information that could help him.

While it is true that supervisors are involved in every step of the staffing process, they are more involved during some stages than in others. Supervisors work together with, and receive assistance from, the personnel department in many activities related to staffing. For example, the personnel department is generally responsible for recruiting. Even so, supervisors may provide input such as specifying the skills and abilities that candidates for a particular job should possess. Supervisors, on the other hand, are more involved in selecting and evaluating even though the personnel department often provides input, such as determining the performance evaluation instrument to be used. Both the personnel department and the supervisor should be involved in the orientation of new employees. Personnel provides a general orientation to the organization and personnel policies, while the supervisor orients the new employee to the job. Finally, if the organization has an internal training and development program or department (usually located within Personnel), both the personnel department and the supervisor are responsible for the development of new employees. If no formal training and development program exists within the organization, supervisors are responsible for employee development.

In general, supervisors spend more time evaluating than engaged in any other part of the staffing process. This chapter will provide a broad overview of the staffing process as well as a discussion of recruiting, the first step in the staffing process. Since recruiting is largely the responsibility of the personnel department, that step will be examined in terms of what supervisors can do to assist in the recruiting process, thus setting the stage for those later staffing activities in which supervisors will become more heavily involved.

At the most basic level, the objectives and strategies of the organization determine its staffing needs.[1] In developing objectives, managers learn where the organization is going; in developing strategies they learn how the organization is going to get there. Objectives and strategies tell management what kinds of jobs will need to be performed and, therefore, the numbers of employees with particular skills, education, and training that will be required to perform these jobs most effectively. As organizational plans and objectives change, staffing needs are likely to change, also. This suggests that it would be useful to develop some type of formal human resource planning system.

An organization should not be overstaffed or understaffed, either in terms of employee numbers or in terms of the specific skills, abilities, and knowledge those employees possess. In an effort to ensure this balance, a personnel department must provide **human resource planning** on an ongoing basis.[2] Once objectives and strategies have been set, and the kinds and numbers of employees needed have been determined, Personnel is responsible for acquiring these employees. Resource planning generally begins by establishing a comparison between the current supply of human resources and the projected demand. Once human resource needs have been determined, the current supply of human resources within the organization must be established. If objectives and strategies call for a number of employees with a particular skill, the organization may want to determine whether there are employees somewhere within the system who possess that skill before considering outside candidates. One way of accomplishing an internal analysis of human resources is through a **skills inventory.** A skills inventory may be nothing more than a complete list of names, education levels, skills, and training of the people working for the organization.

Human Resource Planning and Skills Inventory Systems

A skills inventory system can range from a very simple hand-recorded index card to a more sophisticated computerized information system. No matter what its particular form, the purpose of a skills inventory is to make available to the personnel department or other managers, detailed information of the skills, training, and education of the individuals employed by the organization. This can be useful to the personnel department in planning for human resource needs, as well as to the supervisor in looking for replacements with particular skills. In addition, the skills inventory is a way of telling employees that the organization is interested in them and in their careers. If employees feel that the organization is interested in seeing them develop and advance, they are more likely to be motivated and committed to achieving the organization's goals.

An example of a skills inventory card appears in figure 3.1. The particular format and information included can and should be modified to fit the organization's needs. For example, some organizations, instead of using codes as in figure 3.1, use computer printouts describing in detail each employee's experience, training, education, and interests.

Obviously, the skills inventory is only as good as the information it contains. Each employee's inventory must be updated regularly to ensure that recent training or education has been added to the set of information. Supervisors must work with the personnel department in order to keep the skills inventory current. If an employee attends a seminar or takes an evening class, this information should be promptly forwarded to the personnel department for inclusion in that employee's skills inventory.

Figure 3.1
Skills inventory card

NAME		DIV.	CLOCK
IDENTIFICATION #		DEPT.	

JBS MANUFACTURING—SKILLS INVENTORY

I. A. Experience Codes YRS.   **I. B. Uncoded Experience** YRS.

1. _____ _____   _____ _____
2. _____ _____   _____ _____
3. _____ _____   _____ _____
4. _____ _____   _____ _____
5. _____ _____   _____ _____
6. _____ _____   _____ _____

II. Foreign   III. A. Education
Language   Degree   Major   Year of   College
Codes   Codes   Codes   Degree   Codes

1. _____   1. ____   _____ ____   _____
2. _____   2. ____   _____ ____   _____
3. _____   3. ____   _____ ____   _____
4. _____   4. ____   _____ ____   _____
5. _____   5. ____   _____ ____   _____

III. B. Years of College   **IV. Years with JBS**
Circle equivalent to full years of college completed
0, 1, 2, 3, 4, 5, 6, 7, 7+   _____

Recruiting

Once the human resource planning process is complete and it has been determined that the organization must seek additional employees from the outside, the organization must be able to attract qualified applicants. **Recruiting** refers to the variety of methods an organization may use to attract applicants with the skills and abilities necessary to achieve organizational objectives.

Recruiting Methods and the Supervisor's Role

Table 3.1 indicates that many recruiting methods are available to an organization and that different methods are used to recruit to different occupations. The first two columns of the table (Office/Clerical and Plant/Services) are probably more relevant to first-line supervisors, while the last three columns apply more to upper-level managers.

Regardless of the particular recruiting method used, supervisory input is critical to the process. The personnel department is responsible for developing a pool of qualified applicants. Supervisors are responsible for selecting an employee from this pool.

Organizational Recruiting Methods by Occupation | Table 3.1

Source	Occupation				
	Office/ Clerical	Plant/ Service	Sales	Professional/ Technical	Management
Employee Referrals	92	94	74	68	65
Walk-ins	87	92	46	46	40
Newspaper Advertising	68	88	75	89	82
Local High Schools or Trade Schools	66	61	6	27	7
U.S. Employment Service (USES)	63	72	34	41	27
Community Agencies	55	57	22	34	28
Private Employment Agencies (company pays fee)	44 (31)	11 (5)	63 (49)	71 (48)	75 (65)
Career Conferences/ Job Fairs	19	16	19	37	17
Colleges/Universities	17	9	48	74	50
Advertising in Special Publications	12	6	43	75	57
Professional Societies	5	19	17	52	36
Radio-TV Advertising	5	8	2	7	7
Search Firms	1	2	2	31	54
Unions	1	12	0	3	0

Note: Figures are percentages of companies providing data for each employee group.

From *Personnel Policies Forum,* copyright 1979, by The Bureau of National Affairs, Inc., Washington, D.C.

Job Description, Job Specifications and Job Analysis

The personnel department recruiters are not as familiar with the position to be filled as are supervisors; thus, the supervisor needs to supply recruiters with information about the nature of the job, the specific duties that will be performed, and the types of skills, abilities, and education that are necessary to perform well on the job. This information is frequently available in the form of a **job description,** or brief summary of the basic tasks performed on a job. Many job descriptions include **job specifications.** These are the specific education, experience, and skills requirements of the job.

The usefulness of job descriptions and specifications depends upon the effectiveness of a job analysis. A **job analysis** is an evaluative process undertaken to determine the tasks or activities to be performed in the job as well as the specific skills and abilities that an individual would need to perform that job effectively.[3] The job analysis, therefore, is an investigation of a position that yields the job description and job specifications.

A job analysis can be conducted in a number of ways: observing an employee at work in the position, interviewing employees, interviewing supervisors, distributing questionnaires, or having employees keep a diary of their activities on the job. Many times, more than one method will be used. If a thorough job analysis has been performed and job descriptions and specifications have been prepared, the recruiter will be able to use this information to screen out applicants inappropriate for the position. If a job analysis has not been performed, a job description and set of job specifications, alone, may not provide information sufficiently detailed or accurate to be of use in recruiting. In such a case, the supervisor must provide the recruiter with information about the job and the requirements of the person holding that job so that inappropriate candidates can be screened out and the qualified applicants retained. In the absence of this information, the pool of applicants is likely to contain candidates without the necessary qualifications. As a result, unqualified applicants will not be screened out until they are interviewed, thus placing much of the responsibility for recruiting in the hands of the supervisor.

The Selection Process

Selection is the process by which individuals are hired from the pool of applicants developed during the recruitment process. While recruiting is the primary responsibility of the personnel department, selection is the primary responsibility of the supervisor. The personnel department may provide input or make recommendations, however, the final decision generally rests with the supervisor.

The recruiting and selection processes are closely related. Often, information gathered during the recruiting process is used again during the selection process. For example, most organizations require applicants to fill out application forms and most recruiters make some record of information obtained during the preliminary screening interview. This information is passed along to the supervisor for use during the selection process. Figure 3.2 shows the relationship between recruiting and selection. Not every step in this example is used by every organization or for every type of job. As was discussed in chapter 2, any selection device used must be relevant to the job being filled; therefore, it may be inappropriate to use certain pre-employment tests for some jobs. Some organizations may choose not to make background checks or require physical exams. Most organizations, however, use application forms, preliminary screening interviews, and employment interviews. The personnel department usually conducts the first two of these pre-employment tests. Supervisors use that information, together with the information collected in the employment interview, to make selection decisions.

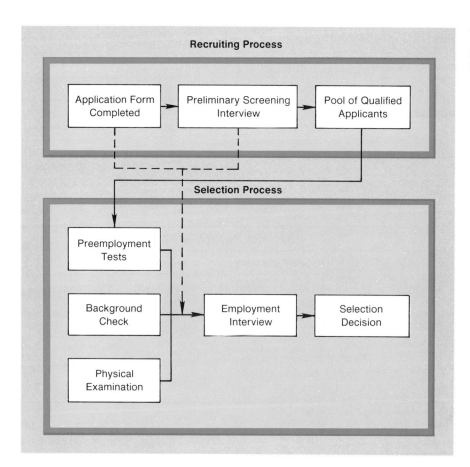

Figure 3.2
Relationship between
recruiting and selection

Each of these selection techniques will be discussed, giving particular emphasis to the interview since it is so widely used and accepted. First, however, the concepts of validity and reliability, both of which are closely associated with most types of personnel or human resource decisions, will be introduced.

Reliability and Validity in Selection

The purpose of the selection process is to choose from the pool of qualified applicants, the one who will be most successful on the job. Selection devices, such as interviews or tests, are used to try to predict how successful the applicant will be if hired. For a selection device to accurately predict future job performance, it must be both reliable and valid.

The first step is to define successful job performance. Suppose that the supervisor has determined that the minimum performance level for an employee in this particular job is thirty units of output per day. Any selection technique employed should tell the supervisor which applicants will be capable of meeting the minimum performance level and which applicants will not. If the selection technique does not differentiate between applicants it will not be very useful.

Table 3.2   Illustration of Reliability

Test-Retest Reliability*

Applicant	Good Reliability		Poor Reliability	
	1st Test Score	2nd Test Score	1st Test Score	2nd Test Score
Joe	96	91	96	47
Beth	42	47	93	39
Susan	89	86	40	88
Ben	39	36	14	71

Interrater Reliability**

Applicant	Good Reliability		Poor Reliability	
	Interviewer 1 Ratings	Interviewer 2 Ratings	Interviewer 1 Ratings	Interviewer 2 Ratings
Joe	9	10	9	3
Beth	4	6	4	10
Susan	7	7	7	2
Ben	3	5	3	8

*Test scores can range from 0–100.
**Interviewer ratings can range from 0–10.

Most personnel departments are responsible for establishing the reliability and validity of selection techniques. An understanding of these concepts, however, will greatly aid the supervisor in making proper use of those selection techniques.

Reliability

If selection techniques are going to be useful in making predictions about future job performance, they must be reliable. The **reliability** of a selection technique is a measure of its dependability or consistency. For example, if a pre-employment test is given to an applicant on three successive Mondays and the applicant's scores were 130, 54, and 92, respectively, these results would indicate that the test is unreliable. The test is not dependable. Which of the three scores is the best predictor of the applicant's ability to perform? There is no way to tell which of the scores is most accurate; this makes the test unreliable. Each score would result in a very different decision about the applicant. Consequently, the test is too unreliable to use. Table 3.2 illustrates the measurement of high and low reliability.

Illustration of Good and Poor Validity				Table 3.3
	Good Validity		**Poor Validity**	
Applicant	**Test Score***	**Performance** **Rating**	**Test Score**	**Performance** **Rating**
Joe	40	5	40	10
Beth	75	7	74	2
Susan	95	10	95	3
Ben	80	8	80	1

*Test scores can range from 0–100.
**Performance ratings can range from 0–10.

Validity

Reliability is a necessary characteristic of an effective selection technique but alone, cannot ensure that effectiveness. A selection device must be valid, as well as reliable. **Validity** refers to the degree to which a test is measuring what it is supposed to measure. A test could be very reliable, but be measuring the wrong thing. On the other hand, an unreliable test cannot be a valid test. Table 3.3 provides an illustration of the measurement of both good and poor validity.

Selection Tests and the Law

The importance that has come to be placed upon demonstrating the validity of selection techniques, or of any technique used in employment decisions (e.g., background checks, interviews, and performance evaluations), has grown out of the fair employment laws discussed in chapter 2. Title VII of the Civil Rights Act of 1964, Section 703(a) prohibits any employment discrimination on the basis of race, color, religion, sex, or national origin. The Tower Amendment (Section 703(h)) to the Civil Rights Act was passed in reaction to the concern that pre-employment testing might be viewed as discriminatory. The Tower Amendment permits the use of tests as long as the contents of the test, the administration of the test, and any action based upon the results of the test are not used to discriminate against any of the protected classes under Title VII. A test case of that legislation took place in *Griggs* v. *Duke Power,* 1974.[4] In the ruling of that case the Supreme Court stated that selection tests should not be used as the basis for employment decisions unless the test can be shown to be a "reasonable measure of job performance."

This decision placed new emphasis upon job qualifications in making employment decisions. It has since prompted the courts to look, first, for evidence of discrimination and then for evidence that the selection technique is job related. To be job related the selection process must be based upon the qualifications necessary to successfully perform the job.

Job Application Forms

One of the first pieces of selection process information that supervisors are likely to see is the job application form. Typically, a supervisor will have reviewed the candidate's application form and already be familiar with the individual's job history. Recently, the accuracy of the information collected on application forms has been questioned. One study found substantial disagreement between information supplied by the job applicant on the application form and information supplied by a previous employer.[5] The biggest discrepancies were found in the reported reason for leaving the previous job, length of time in the previous job, and the salary received. Other studies have suggested that the job application not be considered in the selection decision and that it be used only in obtaining data necessary for company records.[6]

Nevertheless, the application form continues to be a widely used information-gathering technique. Supervisors should be aware of the possibility that the form contains inaccurate information before using it as a basis for making an employment decision.

State fair employment practices legislation must also be considered in the use of application forms. As noted in chapter 2, some state law is more stringent than federal law; thus, an application form, or the questions asked during an interview, may be in compliance with federal law, but at the same time be in violation of state law. This problem becomes particularly serious when an organization operates in several different states and uses a standard application form in all of them.[7] Even if the application form is in compliance with federal, and state or local law, supervisors need to be thoroughly familiar with each of these sets of laws to avoid asking interview questions that could be considered unfair pre-employment inquiries.

Interviewing

Whether or not a pre-employment test, application form, or other device is used in the selection process, it is quite likely that the supervisor will conduct an employment interview. Most supervisors would feel uncomfortable filling a job opening without having first interviewed the person hired, no matter how many other selection techniques were used. Similarly, many employees would feel uncomfortable about being hired without an interview. So it seems that the interview is widely accepted as a selection technique by both employers and employees. Despite the fact that interviewing is a predominant practice, a substantial amount of evidence indicates that this technique is of questionable reliability and validity.

The problems and errors common to the interviewing process will be examined, followed by a discussion of different types of interviews. The last section of this chapter offers suggestions of ways in which supervisors can minimize these problems and increase the reliability and validity, and hence, the accuracy of their interviews.

The purpose of an interview is the same as that of any other selection technique. Supervisors interview job applicants in an attempt to gather information that will help predict how successful that person would be in performing the job.

Qualities Perceived Important for Male and Female Job Applicants

Table 3.4

Qualities Considered Important for Male Applicants	Qualities Considered Important for Female Applicants
Ability to change his mind on an issue	Pleasant voice
Persuasion abilities	Excellent clerical skills
Capability of withstanding a great deal of pressure	High school graduate
	Excellent computational skills
Exceptional motivation	Immaculate in dress and grooming
Being aggressive	Ability to express self well

From Cecil, E. A., Paul, R. J., and R. A. Olins, "Perceived Importance of Selected Variables Used to Evaluate Male and Female Job Applicants," *Personnel Psychology,* 26, 398. Copyright © 1973 Personnel Psychology, Inc. Reprinted by permission.

Common Interviewing Errors

Several problems or errors are common to the interviewing process, each of which reduces the reliability and validity, and thus, the ability of the interview to predict an applicant's potential for job success.

Stereotyping

A common mistake made in interviewing is the tendency of the interviewer to stereotype people.[8] **Stereotyping** in an interview situation occurs when the interviewer has preconceived ideas about a particular group of people that affect the supervisor's judgment of an applicant who is believed to be a member of this group.

Stereotyping can easily contribute to bias and discrimination. Stereotypes about people are commonly created on the basis of their group membership (e.g., sex, age, race). For example, one study examined the qualities perceived to be important for male and female applicants for the same job.[9] Subjects indicated the relative importance of each of fifty variables to interviewers' evaluations of either male or female applicants. Table 3.4 shows that the qualities considered most important for male applicants differed from the qualities considered most important for female applicants. Remember, these were male and female applicants for the same job, yet the lists of important characteristics differed substantially. The qualities considered important for females seem to describe characteristics commonly considered helpful in clerical jobs, while those considered important for males seem to describe abilities most useful in managerial or supervisory positions. Evidently the subjects in this study hold certain stereotypes of males and females. These stereotypes would certainly affect their judgment if they were to interview both male and female applicants for the same job opening.

Primacy and Recency Effects

Studies have shown that interview information presented first and information presented last tends to be remembered longer and given greater weight than information presented in the middle of the interview.[10] These tendencies are referred to as the **primacy effect** and **recency effect,** respectively. From the perspective of a job candidate, it is important to make sure to create a positive first impression, as well as to end the interview with an emphasis on strong points. From the perspective of the interviewer, it is important to recognize that primacy and recency effects are relatively common and to make a conscious effort to give the same degree of consideration to all information collected throughout the interview.

Emphasis on Negative Information

Interviewers seem to place more weight upon negative information than they do upon positive information.[11] This could mean that a good candidate could get bypassed on the basis of a very small amount of negative information. When this occurs the organization misses the opportunity to acquire a good employee.

It is not surprising that interviewers are reluctant to hire an individual about whom any negative information is known considering the way in which interviewers, through feedback, are held accountable for their employment decisions.[12] Interviewers are more likely to get negative feedback about someone they hire who subsequently fails on the job, than positive feedback about someone they hire who performs well on the job. In the attempt to avoid negative feedback, interviewers pay close attention to any negative information uncovered during the interview and weight it heavily. By not hiring candidates with any negative aspect to their credentials, even the most trivial, the interviewers reduce the chance that anyone they hire or recommend will fail on the job. While it is rational for an interviewer to want to avoid negative feedback, supervisors should be aware of this tendency so that they do not overlook a highly-qualified applicant because of a small amount of unfavorable information.

Contrast Effects

Contrast effects are developed when the current applicant is compared with preceding applicants.

A simple comparison of applicants does not constitute a problem. Problems arise when the interviewer substantially overrates or underrates the current applicant as a result of the comparison.[13] For example, assume that a supervisor interviews several applicants with relatively poor qualifications. Then an applicant is interviewed who really doesn't have the qualifications for the job; however, this applicant's qualifications are much higher than those of earlier applicants. The supervisor may rate this applicant too high because of the contrast with the previous applicants. This could result in a poor selection decision. While the current applicant's qualifications are much higher than those of the earlier applicants, they still do not meet the requirements for the job. A decision to hire this applicant based on the overrated interview results could put the applicant into a job for which he or she is not prepared.

Early Decisions

Some research suggests that the selection decision—to hire or not to hire—occurs very early in the interview. One study found that interviewers made their decisions after only four minutes of a fifteen-minute interview.[14] According to these results, a great deal of interview information is not even considered. This tendency, along with that of primacy effects, makes a good first impression of even greater importance to the applicant. Interviewers should avoid making any decision until all information has been gathered. The time for evaluation and decision making is after the interview is over. During the interview, the emphasis should be upon collecting information that will lead to a good selection decision.

Halo Effect

The **halo effect** has been described as follows: "If the interviewer likes the applicant, the tendency might be to rate the applicant too high on many characteristics. On the other hand, if the interviewer dislikes someone, the tendency might be to rate that person too low on all or most characteristics."[15]

In other words, if an applicant possesses a characteristic, positive or negative, that catches the attention of the interviewer causing that interviewer to make a higher or lower evaluation of the applicant than is warranted, based upon the applicant's objective qualifications, the halo effect is at work. This, too, can lead to an erroneous selection decision. The interviewer must make a conscious effort to evaluate an applicant's qualifications as objectively as possible. It should not be assumed that just because the applicant has very high quantitative skills, for example, that he or she also has excellent communication skills. Each characteristic should be evaluated separately and objectively.

Stereotyping, primacy and recency effects, overemphasizing negative information, contrast effects, early decision making, and halo effect have all been shown to be potential sources of interviewer error. Each of these could serve to reduce the reliability and validity, and hence the accuracy, of selection decisions. Before considering ways to minimize the effects of these problems, various types of interviews will be discussed. The type of interview employed also affects the validity and reliability of the interview.

Types of Interviews

Applicants may be interviewed by an individual, by a series of individuals, by a group of interviewers at once, or by any combination of these. Most organizations, however, use individual interviews. Typically, an applicant goes through a preliminary screening interview in the personnel department, followed by an interview with the supervisor who has the job opening. Just as variety may be found in the number of interviewers involved, organizations may use a variety of interviewing techniques. Among these are the structured, semi-structured, and unstructured types of interview.

Structured Interviews

In a **structured interview,** the interviewer asks a series of predetermined questions of all applicants. Often a standard form is used and the interviewer makes note of the applicant's responses on the form. The important characteristic of this form of interview is that the interviewer asks only questions appearing on the form, and asks the same questions of all applicants. This approach can be quite restrictive, however. The interviewer is unable to probe deeply into areas which he or she may feel need more clarification.

Unstructured Interviews

The characteristics of the **unstructured interview** are quite the opposite of those of the structured interview. Often, very few questions are prepared in advance. The interviewer may simply make note of topics to be covered. The basic idea is to get the applicant talking about a topic and, in the process, providing information useful to the interviewer. The role of the interviewer is to keep the applicant talking and to record the information. This interviewing technique is difficult to use effectively unless the interviewer has been trained in its use. While this approach provides the flexibility necessary to probe certain areas, an unskilled interviewer may lose control of the interview and fail to obtain sufficient information on which to base a selection decision.

Semi-structured Interviews

The procedures involved in a **semi-structured interview** have some of the characteristics of both the structured and unstructured techniques. The most important questions are prepared in advance and asked of all applicants. Upon completion of the structured part of the interview, however, the interviewer is free to probe into any areas needing further clarification.

Validity and Reliability of Interviews

The reliability of an interviewing technique is the same, in effect, as the reliability of the interviewer who uses that technique. In other words, if an interviewer, using the same interviewing technique, interviewed the same applicant at two different points in time and reached substantially different decisions, the reliability of that technique (or of the interviewer) would be suspect. Similarly, if two different interviewers, using the same interviewing technique, interviewed the same applicant and reached entirely different decisions, the reliability of that technique (or of the interviewers) would have to be questioned.

The majority of research in this area finds the structured interview to have the highest degree of reliability.[16] This is because the same questions are asked each time an interview is conducted. The less structured the interview, the greater the likelihood that different questions are asked, or that the same questions are asked differently in each interview. How could reliability be anything other than very low if different questions are asked during the second interview?

It is important to recognize that increased structure comes at the cost of decreased flexibility. But without the flexibility to probe deeply into certain areas during an interview, important information may go uncovered. In sum, while some structuring is necessary for reliability, the interview should probably not be entirely structured. Some form of semi-structured interview may be most effective.

The validity of an interview is measured by the extent to which the interview results are able to predict the level of job performance of the applicant. Unfortunately, very little research has been conducted in this area. The few studies that have been done suggest that the structured form has the highest validity, referring to those interviews that were at least partially structured, but not necessarily totally structured.[17] Several other suggestions can be made toward conducting a more effective interview.

Legal Aspects of Interviewing

Supervisors must be aware of one other aspect of interviewing. To put it simply, there are some things that an applicant cannot be asked. Fair employment laws apply to interviewing just as they apply to selection tests or application forms. The questions asked during an interview must not unfairly discriminate against any of the groups protected under Title VII, or under other legislation, and the questions asked must pertain to the applicant's ability to perform a specific job. The information concerning fair and unfair pre-employment inquiries given in table 2.2 (ch. 2) applies to interviewing, also.

Recommendations for Conducting Interviews

Most supervisors conduct employment interviews from time to time. The question is not whether to interview or not, but whether it will be done well or poorly. The problems discussed earlier in the chapter suggest several things that supervisors should and should not do in order to conduct effective interviews.

Be prepared. Before the interview, review all information that has been collected about the applicant (e.g., the resume, application form, results of the screening interview). You must know something about the applicant in order to ask intelligent questions during the interview. Avoid asking the applicant to merely repeat information contained in the resume or on the application blank. This is redundant and a waste of time. The applicant may also begin to wonder how effective you are as a supervisor if you merely ask for information you already have.

Spend a few minutes putting the applicant at ease. Don't jump right in to heavy questioning. Take a few minutes for small talk to build a relationship with the applicant. A few minutes spent putting an applicant at ease can pay off later in the interview. If applicants are anxious or uncomfortable, they may be reserved and not volunteer much information. On the other hand, if you take the time to make the applicants comfortable, they are more likely to be open and responsive to your questions.

Keep the job requirements in mind throughout the interview. The purpose of the interview is to gather information that will help predict how well the applicant would perform the job. By keeping the job requirements in mind, or even written down on a piece of paper in front of you, you are likely to be more objective and less likely to fall into the problems caused by halo error or stereotyping.

Maintain a balance between structured and unstructured questions. A certain amount of structure can increase the reliability, and perhaps validity, of the interview. Unstructured questioning can, however, uncover information that the structured questions would have missed.

Don't make decisions too early. If you allow yourself to make a decision in the first few minutes of the interview, you may miss some important information that could alter your decision. Unless the applicant quite obviously does not have the qualifications for the job, the decision should not be made during the interview. It is better to wait to draw any conclusions until you are back in your office and have an opportunity to review all of the information again.

Give the applicant an accurate picture of the job and of the organization. Sometimes supervisors paint too pretty a picture for the job applicant, especially if the applicant appears to be highly qualified. This may lead to the applicant accepting the job if it is offered; however, it may also cause the applicant, now the new employee, to resign if the job turns out to be something different than was expected. It is better practice to be as objective as possible in describing the job and the organization. It is better, on occasion, to have a good applicant decide against accepting a job than to have them quit soon after beginning work. This creates unnecessary costs for the organization in that the recruiting and selection processes must start all over again.

Give the applicant time to ask questions. The applicant must decide if he or she would really be satisfied in the job you have open and if she or he would like to work for your organization. The interview should be viewed as an exchange process rather than a one-way communication, with the interviewer asking all the questions. It is important that the interviewer find out about the applicant, but it is also important that the applicant find out about the job and the organization.

Let the applicant know what will happen next. After the applicant has finished asking questions, he or she should be informed of what will happen next. Most importantly, the applicant should be told when to expect a decision and who will be contacting him or her. There is nothing worse than leaving an interview without any idea whether or not the interviewer liked your qualifications; or when, or even if, you will be contacted. In this case, no news is *not* good news.

Close the interview on a positive note. Just as it is important to put the applicant at ease before the interview, it is important to do so, again, at the close of the interview. If the applicant is not hired, your interview may be the only contact he or she has with the organization. If a rejected applicant has had a negative experience in your interview, this may cause him or her to form an unfavorable impression of the organization. This may spread by word of mouth until the organization has gained the reputation of being a bad place to work. It is important, therefore, that applicants feel positive about their interviewing experience even if they are not hired. Keep in mind that primacy and recency effects apply to job applicants as well as to interviewers.

Summarize your thoughts immediately after the interview. It is important that you summarize and record your thoughts and impressions as soon as possible after the interview. Even if you were taking notes during the interview, it is a good idea to review them to make sure that they are accurate and complete. It is not necessary that a final decision regarding the applicant be made at this point, but it is important that the information collected during the interview be as accurate and complete as possible.

Once job applicants have been selected for employment, they must be socialized into their new jobs. This procedure is known as employee **orientation** and is one in which employees are provided with information about their new work environments that will help them to perform successfully.

Most people feel uncertain and anxious during their first few days or even weeks on a new job. These feelings could produce a negative impact upon job performance. A good employee orientation program can make employees more comfortable in their new surroundings and help them understand more clearly their new roles within the organization.

Orientation can be broken down into three stages.[18]

Stage 1: General Organization Orientation. General orientation is the responsibility of the personnel department, involving matters that pertain to all employees. Topics covered in general orientation would include company history, products or services offered, organizational objectives, organizational structure, and top-level managers.

New Employee Orientation

Stage 2: Job-Specific Orientation. The supervisor must take responsibility for job-specific orientation. This process provides the new employee with information specific to the department and job. Activities involved would include a tour of the department and work station, and introductions to co-workers. Topics covered would include explanations of important policies and rules, the relationship of the employee's job to other jobs, the job duties and expectations, the working hours, proper dress, and safety regulations. You should avoid overwhelming the new employee with information. Do not try to cover everything in a single day.

Stage 3: Follow-up. After the employee has been on the job between two weeks and one month, you should set aside time to meet again with that individual. This session should give the employee an opportunity to ask questions about anything that has happened or anything that is not yet clear. This session should also provide the opportunity to further clarify performance expectations. If there is any problem with the employee's performance, this should be discussed in a constructive manner with the employee.

The new employee orientation program is the responsibility of both the personnel department, for general information, and the individual supervisor, for job-specific information. An effective orientation program can reduce the amount of anxiety and frustration many new employees feel, and as a result, can make the employee feel more a part of the organization. It can also give new employees a clearer picture of exactly what you expect of them on the job. This can result in higher performance levels in less time than could be expected from an employee who did not have the benefit of an orientation program.

Summary

In order to ensure that the organization is neither overstaffed nor understaffed, the personnel department must plan for human resource needs on an ongoing basis. A skills inventory system may provide the needed information about current employees. Supervisors provide a great deal of input into both human resource planning and skills inventory systems by supplying information about job openings and job requirements, as well as information about employees.

A job analysis is an in-depth investigation of a job and of the type of knowledge, skills, and abilities that are required to successfully perform that job. A job analysis yields a job description and job specifications, both of which are particularly useful in the selection process.

Interviewing is a principal component of the selection process; however, there are several problems or interviewer errors common to this process. These include stereotyping, contrast effects, primacy and recency effects, emphasizing negative information, making early decisions, and the halo effect. Each of these types of errors decreases the accuracy of the information collected during the interview. Supervisors must be aware of these common errors and understand why they occur in order to avoid them.

Interviews can be classified as structured, unstructured, and semi-structured. The structured interview is very rigid and does not allow an interviewer the flexibility to probe into areas that are ambiguous or unclear. The unstructured interview is very flexible but it is difficult to use effectively unless the interviewer has had specialized training. The recommended form of interview is the semi-structured interview, which is a combination of the structured and unstructured forms.

Recommendations for interviewing are: to prepare in advance, to use the information collected during the early stages of the staffing process; and to concentrate upon collecting the appropriate (i.e, job-related) information during the interview. Avoiding the common interviewer errors is an important part of collecting useful information during the interview.

The chapter closes with a consideration of the new employee orientation process. Orientation consists of three stages: general orientation, job-specific orientation, and follow-up.

Key Terms

contrast effects (p. 58)
halo effect (p. 59)
human resource planning (p. 49)
job analysis (p. 52)
job description (p. 51)
job specifications (p. 51)
orientation (p. 63)
primacy effect (p. 58)
recency effect (p. 58)

recruiting (p. 48)
reliability (p. 54)
selection (p. 52)
semi-structured interview (p. 60)
skills inventory (p. 49)
stereotyping (p. 57)
structured interview (p. 60)
unstructured interview (p. 60)
validity (p. 55)

Questions for Discussion

1. In which activities of the staffing process are supervisors most involved?
2. What are the primary determinants of staffing needs? Explain.
3. What are skills inventories and how are they used?
4. Which recruiting methods are used most often for office/clerical and plant/service jobs?
5. Which recruiting methods are used most often for management positions?
6. What is the input of supervisors into the recruiting process?
7. What are job descriptions and why are they important in recruiting?
8. What is a job analysis? How is it performed?
9. How is a job analysis related to recruiting and selection?
10. How are the recruiting and selection processes related?
11. What is the importance of reliability and validity to the selection process?
12. Discuss the problems and errors common to the interview process. What can be done to minimize these problems?
13. Describe the different types of interviews. Which type has higher reliability? Which type has higher validity? Why?
14. Can you think of any recommendations for effective interviewing that were not mentioned in this chapter?
15. What is an example of a fair pre-employment inquiry with regard to age? Marital status? Dependents? Weight? Arrests? Handicaps?

References

1. H. Koontz, C. O'Donnel, and H. Weirich, *Essentials of Management* (New York: McGraw-Hill Book Co., 1982).
2. W. L. French, *The Personnel Management Process.* 4th ed. (Dallas: Houghton-Mifflin Co., 1978).
3. C. P. Sparks, "Job Analysis," in *Personnel Management,* ed. K. M. Rowland and G. R. Ferris (Boston: Allyn and Bacon, 1982), 78–100.
4. Griggs v. Duke Power Company, 3 FEP 175 (1971).
5. I. L. Goldstein, "The Application Blank: How Honest Are the Responses?" *Journal of Applied Psychology* 55 (1971): 491–492.
6. C. C. Kessler and G. J. Gibbs, "Getting the Most from Application Blanks and References," *Personnel* 52 (1975): 53–62.
7. C. Camden and B. Wallace, "Job Application Forms: A Hazardous Employment Practice," *Personnel Administrator* 28 (1983): 31–32, 64.
8. M. Rothstein and D. N. Jackson, "Decision Making in the Employment Interview: An Experimental Approach," *Journal of Applied Psychology* 63 (1980): 271–283.
9. E. A. Cecil, R. J. Paul, and R. A. Olins, "Perceived Importance of Selected Variables Used to Evaluate Male and Female Job Applicants," *Personnel Psychology* 26 (1973): 397–404.
10. J. C. Fair and C. M. York, "Amount of Information and Primacy-Recency Effects in Recruitment Decisions," *Personnel Psychology* 28 (1975): 223–238.
11. B. I. Bolstar and B. M. Springbett, "The Reaction of Interviewers to Favorable and Unfavorable Information," *Journal of Applied Psychology* 45 (1961): 97–103; T. D. Hollman, "Employment Interviewer's Errors in Processing Positive and Negative Information," *Journal of Applied Psychology* 56 (1972): 130–134.
12. M. D. Hakel, "Employment Interviewing," in *Personnel Management,* ed. K. M. Rowland and G. R. Ferris (Boston: Allyn and Bacon, 1982): 129–155.
13. H. G. Heneman, III, D. P. Schwab, D. L. Hewett, and J. J. Ford, "Interviewer Validity as a Function of Interview Structure, Biographical Data and Interviewee Order," *Journal of Applied Psychology* 60 (1975): 748–753.
14. E. C. Webster, *Decision Making in the Employment Interview* (Montreal: Industrial Relations Center, McGill University, 1964).
15. W. L. French, *The Personnel Management Process.* 4th ed. (Boston: Houghton-Mifflin Co., 1978).
16. E. Mayfield, "The Selection Interview: A Re-evaluation of Published Research," *Personnel Psychology* 17 (1964): 239–260; L. Ulrich and D. Trumbo, "The Selection Interview Since 1949," *Psychological Bulletin* 63 (1965): 110–116; D. P. Schwab and H. G. Heneman, III, "Relationship between Interview Structure and Interviewer Reliability in an Employment Situation," *Journal of Applied Psychology* 53 (1969): 214–217.
17. E. E. Ghiselli, "The Validity of a Personal Interview," *Personnel Psychology* 19 (1966): 389–394.
18. D. R. Mendenhall and C. W. Millard, "Orientation: A Training and Development Tool," *Personnel Administrator* 25 (1980): 40.

Sources of Information for Supervisors   Table 3.5

Information Required	Application Blank	Interview	References	Test	Other (Specify)
1. Work experience					
2. Education					
3. Skills and ability					
4. Dependability					
5. Ability to work with others					
6. Career plans					
7. Intelligence					

Supervisors need to have access to a variety of information about an applicant before an accurate selection decision can be made. The table lists several types of information that a supervisor faced with a selection decision would like to know about a candidate. For each type of information, choose the best source for obtaining that information. Indicate your decisions with a checkmark.

Exercise

Diagnosing Sources of Applicant Information

Questions

1. If you had to rely on only one of the sources of information listed in the table, which would you choose? Explain.
2. How useful is an application blank in gathering information upon which to base a selection decision?
3. How would you rate the validity and reliability of the application blank?
4. What recommendations would you make to the personnel department for making the application blank more useful in selection decisions?

Case

The Hiring Decision

Following are several resumes of individuals applying for the job of Administrative Assistant/Level 6, a position which you have recently advertised. The following is the job description that has been prepared for the position.

Job Description: Administrative Assistant/Level 6
This is a nonsupervisory position in the long-term planning department. The job entails collecting and analyzing financial, demographic, market, and industry information as well as preparing forecasts of the organization's environment for one, three, and five years into the future. These reports will be formally presented to a group of senior managers and/or the board of directors.

The position requires a college degree in business or a related field. The applicant should have a strong background in mathematics or financial/statistical analysis.

Follow these instructions.

1. Review the resumes and job description and prepare a set of questions that you would ask these applicants during an interview.
2. Based upon the information you have available, choose one of the applicants for the Administrative Assistant job. Be prepared to explain your decision.
3. Did you notice any problems with any of the resumes? How could each of these resumes be improved?

LUCY L. SWAN

307 Judith Drive
Charleston, Illinois 61920
(217) 266-2678

ACADEMIC PREPARATION

Eastern Illinois University
Master of Business Administration
Expected May 1987

Bachelor of Science in Business Administration
Majors: Marketing and Management
May 1985

OCCUPATIONAL PREPARATION

January 1982 to present

McMaster Advertising Agency
Charleston, Illinois 61920

Positions: Owner/Operator; Artist; Service Duties: Service accounts; head campaigns; investment advisor; photographic close-up shots; sculptural pottery.

November 1978 to Jan. 1982	Simpson's Products Company Mattoon, Illinois 62920
	Positions: Advertiser Duties: Total responsibility for layout of all ads for 16 stores; changing advertising/marketing throughout chain; handling co-op advertising subsidy.
Summer 1978	Sears, Roebuck and Company Mattoon, Illinois 62920
	Position: Product Representative Duties: Responsible for selling favorable Sears image to dissatisfied customers through Service Department.

ACHIEVEMENTS, HONORS, EXTRACURRICULAR ACTIVITIES

Dean's List Scholar, Eastern Illinois University, 1985 Who's Who Among Students in American Colleges and Universities
Charter Member, Graduate Business Association, Treasurer/Secretary, Eastern Illinois University, 1986
Member, Phi Chi Theta Business Honor Fraternity, Membership Chairperson, 1984
Member, American Marketing Association
Member, Society for the Advancement of Management

REFERENCES

Available upon request

CHARLES R. RODGERS

1274 South Empire
Starkville, Mississippi 39762
(601) 325-1799

ACADEMIC PREPARATION

Bachelor of Science
Mississippi State University
Major: Management
Grade Point Average: 3.15 on a 4.0 scale
Degree conferred: December 1987

Case continues . . .

Case (cont.)

Associate of Arts Degree--General Studies
Jones County Junior College
Ellisville, Mississippi 39437
Degree conferred: May 1985

OCCUPATIONAL PREPARATION

May 1985
to Dec.
1987

PRAT, Incorporated
Management Consultants

Position: Staff Consultant
Duties: Detail studies of client's process and labor
needs; Director of Process Definition Meetings;
Statistical analysis and research design.

July 1983
to May
1985

Milliken and Company
Textile Products Manufacturer
Meridian, Mississippi 39301

Position: Production Shift Manager, Brushing
Department
Duties: Motivation and supervision of machine
operators; Goal setting with employees; Administrative
activities including quality control, production and
personnel record keeping.

Summer
1982

Bonanza Sirloin Pit
Meridian, Mississippi 39301

Position: Cook
Duties: Grill cook as well as other miscellaneous duties
as required.

ACTIVITIES AND ORGANIZATIONS

Member, Sigma Alpha Epsilon Alumni Association
Gold Key Award for Leadership, Jones County
Junior College
House Manager, Sigma Alpha Epsilon Social Fraternity

PERSONAL DATA

Birthdate: May 25, 1960; Poplarville, Mississippi
Height: 6 feet; Weight: 185 pounds;
Health: Excellent

Marital Status: Single; willing to travel and relocate
Interests: Hunting, fishing, and spectator sports
NOTE: Paid for 75% of all college expenses through scholarships and
part-time employment

REFERENCES

Available upon request

SANDRA L. SUMMERS

365 Third Avenue
Tucson, Arizona 85712
(602) 298-9733

ACADEMIC PREPARATION

Bachelor of Science
University of Arizona
Major: Marketing Management
Degree conferred: December 1987

High School Diploma
College Preparatory Studies
Jefferson High School
Tucson, Arizona 85712

OCCUPATIONAL PREPARATION

Summer 1987	Wilson's Jewelers, Incorporated 3818 Hampton Street Tucson, Arizona 85712 Position: Cashier/Customer Service Duties: Responsible for checking customers out at cash register; and handling layaways, customer credit, and customer complaints.
Summer 1986	Memorial Hospital Tucson, Arizona 85712 Position: File Clerk/Secretary Duties: Handled filing system for the Credit Department and worked as secretary in the Nuclear Medicine Office.

Case continues . . .

Case (cont.)

Summer 1985	Kay Jewelers University Mall Tucson, Arizona 85712

Position: Sales Associate/Cashier
Duties: Responsible for sales of 14K gold jewelry and high-quality diamonds; handled customer layaways, accounts, jewelry repair, and customer assistance.

ACTIVITIES AND HONORS

Member, American Marketing Association
Secretary, International Relations Club
Member, Beta Gamma Sigma, National Business
Honor Society

PERSONAL DATA

Birthdate: November 19, 1963; Tucson, Arizona
Height: 5'4"; Weight: 117 lbs.; Health: Excellent
Marital Status: Single; willing to travel and relocate

CHRISTOPHER HARPER

1728 Ashford Lane
Ithaca, New York 14850
(607) 272-9901

ACADEMIC PREPARATION

Bachelor of Science
Ithaca College
Ithaca, New York 14850
Major: Management
Grade Point Average: 3.76 on 4.0 scale
Degree expected: December 1987

High School Diploma
Lincoln High School
Ithaca, New York 14850

WORK EXPERIENCE

June 1985
to
present

Computer Operator and Mail Clerk. Operated computer terminals in forwarding and address correction systems; updated student files in computer systems; sorted mail, and handled student and faculty problems.

April
1984–
July 1984

Retail Cashier and Customer Service. Responsible for running checkout terminal and arranging merchandise. In charge of customer service relevant to returns, exchanges, and other customer-related problems.

Nov.
1983–
Jan. 1983

Retail Sales, Cashier, and Customer Service. Sold cosmetics, accessories, and clothing; cashier for men's, juniors', and ladies' departments. Recorded charge account and layaway payments.

April
1983–
August
1983

Cashier and Host. Received orders, served customers, assisted in food preparation, and supervised waitresses.

ACTIVITIES, INTERESTS, HONORS

Member, Alpha Lambda Delta, Freshman
Honor Society
Member, Gamma Beta Phi, National Scholastic
Honor Society
Member, Beta Gamma Sigma, National Business
Honor Society
Member, Society for the Advancement of Management
President's List Scholar
Dean's List Scholar

PERSONAL DATA

Birthdate: April 19, 1964; Ithaca, New York
Height: 5'10"; Weight: 165 lbs.; Health: Excellent
Marital Status: Single

REFERENCES

Available upon request

Chapter 4

Theories of Motivation

Learning Objectives

After reading this chapter, you should:

1. be able to discuss the major theories of motivation.
2. know the difference between intrinsic and extrinsic motivation factors.
3. understand the difference between content and process theories of motivation.
4. be able to explain the multidimensional nature of motivation.
5. be aware of the various reinforcement schedules and know when each should be used.

Adam was really at a loss concerning what to do about Jill, one of the office workers he supervised. Jill was not pulling her weight compared with the effort given by his other employees. It wasn't that Jill's performance was unsatisfactory. Rather, it was as if Jill knew exactly what was considered the minimal level of acceptable performance, and made sure that she did no more and no less. It seemed that she knew how to perform well enough to keep from getting fired, but was not motivated to do any more.

Adam's other employees had always done more than he asked them. They were always willing to lend a hand when a coworker fell behind or an unexpected heavy workload arrived. Recently, however, everyone's morale seemed to be declining. Adam heard one employee say, "If she can get away with taking it easy, so can we." Adam was sure they were referring to Jill. He knew that a serious problem was developing and hoped he could think of a way to resolve it before it got any worse. It seemed that the only solution was to motivate Jill to put more effort into her work. He just wasn't sure how to begin.

One of the most frequently occurring and difficult problems you will face as a supervisor is that of motivating your employees—keeping them interested in, and working hard at their jobs. Maintaining high levels of motivation is difficult to accomplish because employees and situations are constantly changing. What motivated Jill a couple of months ago may not have much of an impact upon her now. Further, what motivates Jill right now may not be what motivates Bob, and this, in turn, may not be what motivates someone else, and so on.

Motivation is a very complex process. Often supervisors will try to find the single factor that seems to be most important to employees as a group (e.g., pay) and will use that factor in their attempts to motivate everyone. It would probably be more advantageous to look for several factors that are important to each individual. At any one point in time there are likely to be several elements motivating an employee, and these are likely to be different from those which motivate another employee. To further complicate things, these motivating factors are likely to change over time. To get the most from your employees (i.e., in order to motivate employees to perform at levels near their potential), you must thoroughly understand the motivation process. This chapter will discuss several important theories of motivation in preparation for a discussion of applied motivation in chapter 5.

What is Motivation?

Motivation is typically defined as what it takes to get someone to exert effort. As the Peanuts cartoon indicates, motivation can be thought of in terms of incentives. While incentives are important they represent only a part of the picture. You, as a supervisor interested in motivating employees within a complex work environment, need to consider the three dimensions of motivation as represented by the following sets of questions:[1]

What energizes behavior? What is it that causes an employee to be willing to exert effort on the job? What determines how much effort an employee is willing to exert?

© 1972 United Features Syndicate, Inc. Reprinted by permission.

What directs or channels behavior? Behavior must be energized, as well as channeled in appropriate directions; that is, it must be directed toward task accomplishment instead of other less productive activities.

What maintains behavior? We don't want to energize and direct behavior only to have to start the process all over again. Steps can be taken to see that employees maintain a certain level of performance once they have been energized and once that energy has been channeled in appropriate directions.

It is often helpful to classify motivation theories into the categories of content theories and cognitive theories.

Content theory is also referred to as **need-satisfaction theory.** Content theories can be used as a guide in determining the kinds of needs that are important to employees. These theories have very little to say about the cognitive, or thought, processes that individuals use to make decisions about their own behavior. Content theories focus upon what energizes behavior. The content theories discussed in this chapter are Maslow's Hierarchy of Needs and Herzberg's Two-Factor Theory.

Cognitive theory is also referred to as **process theory.** These theories focus upon (a) what channels behavior and (b) what maintains behavior. A cognitive theory considers the processes that individuals go through to decide whether they will put forth any effort at all, how much effort they will exert, and how long they will continue to put forth that level of effort. Because individuals are assumed to be rational, it is also assumed that they make decisions in order to maximize their own rewards. The cognitive theories considered in this chapter are: Adams' Equity Theory, expectancy theory, operant conditioning, and social learning theory.

Categories of Motivation Theory

Content theory focuses upon the needs that are important to individuals. These theories ask whether there exist identifiable categories of human needs and whether different needs produce different effects upon behavior. Most content theories in some way discuss two different kinds of needs or rewards: extrinsic and intrinsic.

Extrinsic rewards are usually tangible or material in nature, and are generally provided by someone else. Your employees depend upon you, as the supervisor, or the organization, as a whole, to provide such things as pay, good working conditions, fringe benefits, and good supervision. These are extrinsic rewards.

Content Theories

Figure 4.1
Simple model of
motivation

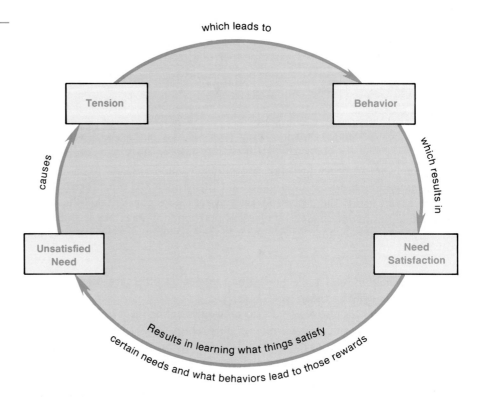

Intrinsic rewards are usually intangible or nonmaterial, and are provided by the individual to himself or herself. Your employees do not have to depend upon you to supply their feelings of accomplishment or self-esteem. When employees perform well, they give themselves these intrinsic rewards. Of course, there are things that you can do to place employees in more situations where intrinsic reward opportunities exist.

Figure 4.1 presents a simple model of motivation upon which content theories are based. A fundamental concept of content theory is the idea that unsatisfied needs serve as motivators; and, that once a need is satisfied it ceases to energize behavior. Unsatisfied needs cause individuals to feel tension, an uncomfortable sensation that they will attempt to alleviate. When these individuals engage in a correct behavior and are rewarded for doing so, the need is satisfied and the tension eliminated.

One important result of this process, according to the theory, is that some learning is likely to take place. The individual may learn that certain kinds of rewards satisfy certain needs. The next time that need is felt, the individual will know what to do to satisfy it. The individual also learns what behaviors lead to this reward. When that need is experienced again, the individual knows what behavior to engage in to get the desired reward. The following content theories are based, at least in part, upon this simple model of motivation.

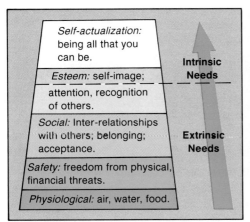

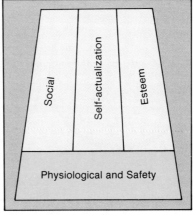

Figure 4.2

Figure 4.3

Figure 4.2
Maslow's hierarchy of
needs

Figure 4.3
Modified hierarchy of
needs

Maslow's Hierarchy of Needs

Maslow's Hierarchy of Needs identifies five major categories of needs in all people. Maslow has placed these needs into a hierarchical arrangement in which the lower-level, extrinsic needs are at the bottom and the higher-level, intrinsic needs are at the top.[2] Maslow's theory relies heavily upon the idea that the individual seeks constantly to fulfill unsatisfied needs. Individuals move systematically through the hierarchy from bottom to top, satisfying the lower-level needs first. The lowest level of unsatisfied needs determines the category of needs most important to the individual at any given point in time (see fig. 4.2).

If an individual has unsatisfied physiological needs (e.g., the need for food), it is not likely that this person will be concerned about some higher level of need (e.g., the recognition of others). Once physiological needs become largely satisfied, however, the individual will move up to the next level and begin trying to satisfy the need to feel safe or secure. This process continues until the person reaches the top of the hierarchy where, Maslow suggests, since it is impossible to completely satisfy the need for self-actualization, the person remains.

Several features of Maslow's theory are bothersome to its critics. First, the theory does not seem to accommodate individual differences. It seems unlikely that everyone progresses through the hierarchy in this precise step-by-step fashion. It seems just as probable that some people may skip some categories entirely, or that they move through the stages in different orders. It is difficult to argue with the placement of physiological needs—a hungry person is not concerned with higher-level needs. The same could be said of safety needs. It would seem to be far less predictable, however, which of the top three categories of need is likely to emerge once physiological and safety needs have been satisfied.[3] Figure 4.3 presents a slightly different hierarchy of needs that is, perhaps, more realistic than Maslow's. According to this model, when physiological and safety needs have been satisfied, there is no way to predict which category will emerge next. It is likely to differ from individual to individual.

Figure 4.4
A multidimensional model
of motivation

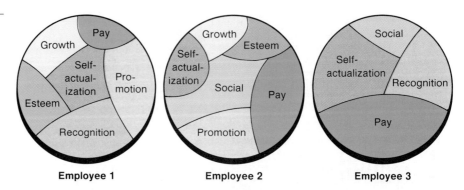

Employee 1   Employee 2   Employee 3

Another serious problem with Maslow's theory is that it does not regard motivation as multidimensional. Maslow's hierarchy cannot account for situations in which both extrinsic and intrinsic factors are important to, and are therefore capable of motivating, an employee. A more accurate, though more complicated, portrayal of motivation is given in Figure 4.4. The size of the area inside each circle represents the importance of the need to each employee. The importance of each need is likely to change over time.

The third problem with Maslow's hierarchy lies in its assumption that satisfied needs cease to motivate. This may be true for certain lower-level needs. For example, if you have just finished a big steak dinner including a very rich dessert, it is unlikely that I could motivate you by offering to buy you a lobster dinner. But consider some of the higher-level needs. How much recognition does it take before your need for recognition is satisfied and ceases to motivate? For some people, the satisfaction of certain higher-level needs (e.g., self-actualization, growth and development, the esteem of others) may serve to increase the importance of those needs.[4]

Herzberg's Two-Factor Theory

Two-Factor Theory (also known as Motivator-Hygiene Theory) divides motivational factors into two distinct categories: hygiene factors and motivators.[5] **Hygiene factors** are the extrinsic rewards gained from the job. Job security, pay, supervision, interpersonal relations, and working conditions are examples of hygiene factors. **Motivators,** on the other hand, are the intrinsic rewards gained from the job. Achievement, recognition, the work itself, responsibility, and personal growth are all motivators. According to the Two-Factor Theory, these two categories of needs are distinct, unrelated, and have different effects upon motivation.

Herzberg suggests that hygiene factors can only be used to prevent job dissatisfaction. Giving employees high levels of hygiene factors will not cause them to be highly motivated; they operate only as a kind of necessary base. An acceptable level of these hygiene factors is necessary to prevent high levels of job *dis*satisfaction, but even extremely high levels of these factors will not produce high motivation in the job.

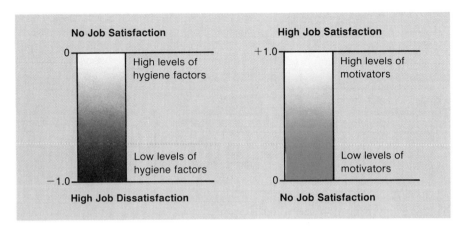

Figure 4.5
Herzberg's two-factor
theory

Motivators, on the other hand, can be used to bring about high levels of job satisfaction and motivation. A low level of motivators does not produce job dissatisfaction, however. If satisfaction levels could be accurately measured, and a range was established where -1.0 = high job dissatisfaction; 0 = neutral (i.e., neither satisfied nor dissatisfied), and; $+1.0$ = high job satisfaction and motivation, then Herzberg's theory would operate as shown in figure 4.5.

Two-Factor Theory suggests that employees must be given sufficient levels of extrinsic rewards (hygiene factors) in order to prevent them from becoming highly dissatisfied with their jobs. An adequate level of hygiene factors, alone, might be enough to keep employees coming to work and putting forth enough effort to keep from getting fired. Motivated employees, however, require a sufficient number of intrinsic rewards (motivators) to keep them that way.

Comparison of Maslow and Herzberg

The Maslow and Herzberg content theories have many similarities. Figure 4.6 draws a comparison between the two theories. Both include discussions of extrinsic and intrinsic rewards. Both seem to agree that while extrinsic rewards are necessary, supervisors should emphasize intrinsic rewards if they want to motivate their employees.

The differences between these theories do not make them contradictory. Instead, each seems to shed some additional light upon the motivational process. Both do a relatively good job of providing an answer to the question of what energizes behavior but neither ventures far beyond that question. To learn what channels behavior and what sustains behavior we have to consider the cognitive theories.

Figure 4.6
Comparison of the
Maslow and Herzberg
content theories of
motivation

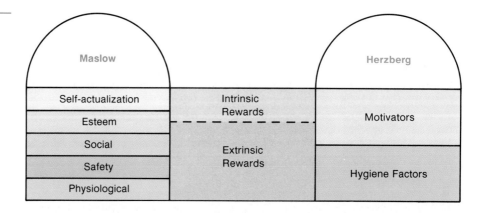

Cognitive Theories

Cognitive theory focuses upon decisional processes and expectations. These theories view individuals as capable of making evaluations of the current situation and of projecting that evaluation to include the expectation of future conditions. Individuals are also seen as having the ability to make decisions about their own behavior. The major cognitive theories discussed in this chapter are equity theory, expectancy theory, operant conditioning, and social learning theory.

Adams' Equity Theory

Adams' Equity Theory shifts the focus away from the types of rewards employees see as most important and instead, emphasizes the comparisons that employees make.[6] Employees compare the rewards they are receiving with the rewards they see others receiving. In doing this they are trying to determine whether they are being equitably treated by the organization, by the supervisor, or by both.

The two major components of equity theory are (a) inputs and (b) outcomes. **Inputs** are those things that an employee brings to the job: effort, experience, education, and training. **Outcomes** are those things that an employee gets from the job. Outcomes include any type of reward such as pay, promotions, fringe benefits, nice desk, or the particular treatment they receive from the supervisor. Employees compare their own ratios of outcomes to inputs with the ratios of others. A state of equity exists for the individual when he or she perceives the ratios to be equal.[7]

$$\frac{\text{Your Outcomes}}{\text{Your Inputs}} = \frac{\text{Other's Outcomes}}{\text{Other's Inputs}}$$

This perception is highly subjective on several counts. First, individuals decide which inputs and outcomes to consider. The inputs and outcomes you use when you make your comparisons are likely to be different than the ones someone else uses in making their comparisons. Second, individuals weight incomes and outcomes differently. Even though both you and I have decided to include experience in our inputs, I might consider it very important and weight it heavily, while you might assign it a much lower weight. Finally, an individual knows what his or her own inputs and outcomes are, but often can do no better than make an educated guess about those of others.

Examples should help to clarify this process of comparison. Assume that outcomes and inputs can be measured accurately and that they can range from low, to moderate, to high. Equity would exist in the following situations:

Perceived Equity of Reward

Employee A	Employee B		Employee C		Employee D
$\dfrac{\text{low outcomes}}{\text{low inputs}}$	$= \dfrac{\text{high outcomes}}{\text{high inputs}}$	or	$\dfrac{\text{moderate outcomes}}{\text{moderate inputs}}$	$=$	$\dfrac{\text{low outcomes}}{\text{low inputs}}$

These examples show that the balance of comparison is retained even in situations where one employee perceives that another is receiving more outcomes—as long as that other person is required to put more into the job in order to get these outcomes. A perception of equity does not require that the inputs and outcomes of others be equal to the individual's inputs and outcomes; it demands only that the *ratios* be equal.

Inequity exists when individuals perceive that they are either underrewarded or overrewarded in comparison with another person. When inequity is perceived, a state of tension is created in the individual; that is, the individual becomes psychologically uncomfortable and motivated to take some action that will reduce the inequity.

Example: Perceived Overreward

Employee A	Employee B		Employee C		Employee D
$\dfrac{\text{high outcomes}}{\text{low inputs}}$	$= \dfrac{\text{moderate outcomes}}{\text{moderate inputs}}$	or	$\dfrac{\text{moderate outcomes}}{\text{moderate inputs}}$	$=$	$\dfrac{\text{moderate outcomes}}{\text{high inputs}}$

Employee A feels overrewarded compared with Employee B.
Employee C feels overrewarded compared with Employee D.

Example: Perceived Underreward

Employee A	Employee B		Employee C		Employee D
$\dfrac{\text{moderate inputs}}{\text{moderate outcomes}}$	$= \dfrac{\text{moderate inputs}}{\text{high outcomes}}$	or	$\dfrac{\text{high inputs}}{\text{moderate outcomes}}$	$=$	$\dfrac{\text{moderate inputs}}{\text{moderate outcomes}}$

Employee A feels underrewarded compared with Employee B.
Employee C feels underrewarded compared with Employee D.

Not surprisingly, research suggests that most people can better tolerate high levels of overreward than they can underreward; there are some, however, who tend to become uncomfortable if overrewarded.

It is difficult to predict exactly what an employee will do when inequity is perceived. If underrewarded, employees might reduce their inputs to restore equity:

$$\frac{\overset{\text{moderate}}{\cancel{\text{high}}\ \text{outcomes}}}{\text{moderate input}} = \frac{\text{moderate outcomes}}{\text{moderate inputs}}$$

If overrewarded, employees might actually increase their inputs just so that equity can be restored:

$$\frac{\overset{\text{high}}{\cancel{\text{moderate}}\ \text{outcomes}}}{\text{high inputs}} = \frac{\text{high outcomes}}{\text{high inputs}}$$

It is important to remember that this is a very subjective and highly individual process. When you engage in an equity theory–type comparison, it is *your* perception of your own inputs and outcomes that you are comparing with *your* perceptions of some other person's inputs and outcomes.

While equity theory comparisons can be made on the basis of virtually any type of reward or outcome associated with the job, people seem to be most sensitive to differences in pay levels or salary increases. Two employees could receive the same amount of pay, and yet both could perceive inequity with regard to pay. For example, assume that you just hired a new female employee. She is highly skilled and highly motivated to perform up to her abilities. Assume further that she outperforms everyone else in the department during her first year on the job. A second employee has been in your department for several years and is a good performer, but is clearly not as good as the newly-hired employee. When salary increases are given, you give both employees a 15 percent raise, the highest in the department. The new employee may perceive inequity because she knows she has outperformed everyone else, yet received the same amount of salary increase as someone else who did not perform as well. The employee with seniority may perceive inequity because he received the same amount of salary increase as someone who had only been in the department for one year. Clearly, these two employees are using different input as the basis for their comparisons. The new employee appears to be considering effort only, while the senior employee seems to be giving much greater weight to years of service and to experience.

Equity theory comparisons make it extremely difficult to administer rewards. The example just given shows that two good performers, receiving exactly the same amount of reward, can still perceive inequity. As a supervisor, you must try to communicate your views of what inputs are most important. In other words, if employees know what areas of performance you consider to be most important (and which are the ones you will be considering in making reward allocation decisions), they are less likely to feel inequitably treated when the reward allocations are actually made. Everyone will be using the same set of inputs in drawing their comparisons. Without this information, however, they are free to consider whatever inputs they choose in making their comparisons.

© 1984 United Features Syndicate, Inc. Reprinted by permission.

Expectancy Theory

The expectancy theory of motivation, like equity theory, is based upon a subjective perceptual process. Underlying this theory are three specific types of perceptions about the work situation: performance expectancy based on effort, outcome expectancy based on performance, and valence, or value placed upon outcomes.

Effort → Performance Expectancy (E_1) The **effort → performance expectancy** variable represents the employee's perception of the relationship between effort and successful performance. "If I try, can I successfully perform?" An employee with a low E_1 is not likely to be highly motivated regardless of what else happens. That employee's perception is that success is improbable no matter how hard he tries, so why should he try? Even if you offered the employee a huge bonus for accomplishing some goal, it is unlikely that the employee would exert much effort trying to accomplish it.

Performance → Outcome Expectancy (E_2) The **performance → outcome expectancy** variable refers to the employee's perception of the relationship between performance and outcomes (or rewards). "If I do successfully perform, will I get the rewards I want?" Employees with low E_2 are not likely to be highly motivated even if offered a reward they desire very much because the employee does not see a very strong connection between successful performance and rewards. A high E_1 cannot make up for a low E_2. In other words, even if employees perceive that personal effort will yield successful performance, they still may not be motivated to perform if they do not perceive that a successful performance will yield any desired outcomes or rewards.

Valence is the value or importance that an individual attaches to an outcome or reward. Any job has outcomes attached to it. Those outcomes could come in the form of pay, fringe benefits, treatment from supervisors, challenge, or autonomy. Individuals are likely to value each of these outcomes differently. One of your employees might value pay and fringe benefits very highly, be neutral about treatment from supervisor, and actually attach a negative valence to increased challenge and autonomy. The next employee might value these outcomes in quite a different manner.

What is important is the net valence. Employees subjectively evaluate all of the outcomes attached to their jobs and come up with some overall estimation of

Figure 4.7
Simple expectancy theory
model

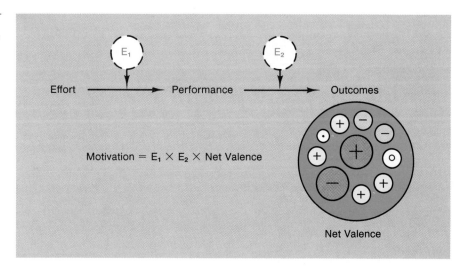

the desirability of the rewards being offered. Even if an employee had a high E_1 and a high E_2, motivation is likely to be relatively low unless positive outcomes are present in sufficient quality and quantity to produce a high net valence.

These three types of perceptions are combined in the simple model of expectancy theory shown in figure 4.7. The model suggests that employees must perceive high levels of E_1 and E_2 as well as a high positive net valence. This is the same as saying that employees must believe that if they put forth the effort, they can perform successfully; *and* that if they do successfully perform, they will be rewarded; *and* that when rewards are given, they will be the rewards that are the desired rewards. Examples will help to clarify expectancy theory.

JBS Manufacturing has just added two new clerical employees to the personnel department. These employees must now begin evaluating and making decisions about their own performances on the job.

Profile: Cara has been with JBS for twelve years and has worked in several different departments. One thing she has learned about the company is that it does not promise anything it cannot deliver. Her new boss told Cara that if she gets the departmental reports out on time each month, she can count on getting a big raise at the end of the year. Since Cara recently purchased a new house, she knows this additional money will really help. She has no experience with personnel reports, however, and is not even sure what reports need to be submitted.

Diagnosis

High Valence: Cara values money, especially with the added expenses of a new house.

High E_2: Her experience with JBS tells her that if JBS promises something, they'll deliver.

Low E_1: Cara is not sure what "successful performance" is. She is not sure that she can perform regardless of the amount of effort she puts forth.

Profile: Bob recently joined JBS after graduating from the local community college. Bob was confident of his ability to handle the work in the personnel department since he had taken several personnel courses and had majored in office administration. His manager told Bob that he was responsible for certain reports, and that if he got them out on time every month, he would receive a substantial salary increase at the end of the year. Since Bob had spent the last two years in school, he certainly felt he could use the additional money. He was not sure, however, that he could count on receiving a big raise even if he was able to get the reports out on time. He had worked for a manager several years ago who always promised things, but never delivered.

Diagnosis

High Valence: Bob has not had much income for the past two years because he has been in school full time.

High E_1: Bob is very confident of his ability to handle the job.

Low E_2: Bob is unsure that he will receive the promised rewards even if he successfully performs the job.

Operant Conditioning

Operant conditioning, also called instrumental learning or behavior modification, is based upon the Law of Effect which states: Behavior that is followed by a desired consequence tends to be repeated, while behavior that is followed by an undesired consequence tends to be eliminated.[8]

Operant conditioning involves the use of several types of reinforcement. Reinforcement is the term used to describe the administering of a consequence (desirable or undesirable) for a behavior in order to either strengthen or eliminate that behavior. Both positive reinforcement and avoidance learning cause behavior to be strengthened, thus making the behavior more likely to recur. Extinction and punishment are techniques used to reduce or eliminate a behavior, thus making the behavior less likely to recur.

Positive Reinforcement

In an occupational setting positive reinforcement takes place when an employee is given a valued reward for a behavior that the supervisor wants to encourage. Positive reinforcement strengthens behavior; hence, the employee is likely to continue to exhibit that behavior in the future in order to continue receiving the reward. If your secretary does an exceptional job preparing an important report, you might positively reinforce that individual with praise or time off. If the secretary values the reward you choose, he or she is likely to do an exceptional job on the next report. Generally, the less time that expires between the behavior and the reinforcement, the stronger the effect will be.

Avoidance Learning

Avoidance learning also strengthens behavior. In an occupational setting, avoidance learning is demonstrated when an employee engages in a desirable behavior, from the point of view of the supervisor, and does so in order to avoid an undesirable or unpleasant consequence. For example, an employee might make every effort to be at work on time in order to avoid receiving a reprimand from you.

Extinction

Extinction is a technique used to reduce the likelihood of a behavior recurring by withholding a positive reward every time that behavior occurs. For example, a small child says a "bad word." The parents, thinking it's cute, respond by laughing and giving the child attention. This is positive reinforcement; they have just made the child more likely to say that word again. Realizing their mistake, they begin to ignore the child everytime the child says the word. This is an attempt to extinguish the behavior. For a time, the behavior will continue. The child has learned to expect the positive reinforcement of increased attention after saying the bad word. Over time, the child will realize that the positive reinforcement is no longer forthcoming for that behavior, and the frequency of the behavior will decrease. Eventually, the behavior may disappear entirely. The use of the extinction technique, in this case, would have been successful.

Extinction works if you control the reward that someone gets for engaging in an undesirable behavior. For example, a student who behaves badly in a classroom is probably getting attention and, therefore, positive reinforcement from the other students. The instructor is not likely to be successful using extinction in that situation because the other students control the rewards.

Punishment

Punishment involves the administration of an undesirable consequence or the withholding of a desirable consequence. In situations where you do not control the rewards associated with an undesirable behavior, the use of punishment may be necessary. In the classroom situation earlier described, the instructor would not accomplish anything by using extinction to change the student's behavior. Extinction would only work if the other students were to ignore the student's antics. Then there would be no reward associated with the behavior and the behavior would eventually be eliminated. But for the instructor to succeed in stopping the behavior in the context of an appreciative class of students, punishment may be the only recourse. A verbal reprimand in front of the class could constitute a sufficiently undesirable outcome to stop any future recurrences of that particular behavior.

There are dangers associated with the use of punishment.[9] Punishment may lead to undesirable side effects. If the punishment causes the employee to become anxious or embarrassed, that person may feel the need to do something to "get even" with the one who administered the punishment. Retaliation could take many forms ranging from stretching a break or lunch hour to sabotage (e.g., destroying important documents).

Proponents of operant conditioning recommend the use of the positive reinforcement and extinction techniques, as opposed to avoidance learning and punishment. It has been suggested, however, that punishment can be used effectively in organizational settings.[10] The key is to administer the punishment objectively, impersonally, and consistently. Every time a particular undesirable behavior occurs, it is punished in the same way. In addition, the initial punishment must be strong enough to offset any reward the employee might get from some other source.

Schedules of Reinforcement

There are five schedules of reinforcement according to which rewards and punishments may be administered. Table 4.1 describes each of these reinforcement schedules, dividing them into two major categories: continuous schedules and partial schedules.

Continuous Reinforcement Schedule

Continuous reinforcement means that a reward is administered after every correct behavior or a punishment after every undesirable behavior. A piece-rate system of production is an example of a continuous schedule of reinforcement. Every time employees complete a piece of work (e.g., make a toaster or a widget), they earn a certain amount of money. Continuous reinforcement results in fast learning; however, if the reinforcement stops, fast forgetting or extinction occurs, also.

Four types of partial reinforcement schedules may be used. Under any **partial reinforcement** system, reward or punishment is given on the basis of some predetermined set of rules other than simply supplying the reinforcement each time a correct behavior takes place. Two are based upon time; these are called interval schedules. The other two are based upon the number of correct behaviors exhibited; these are called ratio schedules.

Table 4.1   Schedules of Reinforcement

Type of Schedule	Description	Example
Continuous	Reinforcement is administered after every correct behavior.	Every time a subordinate is late for work, he or she receives a verbal reprimand from the supervisor.
Partial		
Fixed Interval	Reinforcement is administered after some fixed period of time.	Salary checks are issued at the end of every month.
Variable Interval	Reinforcement is administered after varying periods of time based upon some average time period.	Supervisors check subordinate's work five times per week, on average. The time period between checks varies.
Fixed Ratio	Reinforcement is administered after a certain number of correct behaviors.	A bonus is paid to a computer salesperson after every fifth computer is sold.
Variable Ratio	Reinforcement is administered after a certain number of correct behaviors on average. The exact number of correct behaviors required between reinforcements varies.	A bonus is paid to a computer salesperson after every fifth computer sold, on average. A bonus might be paid after 5 sales, then after 10, after 5 again, then after 2, etc.

Fixed Interval Schedule

Under a **fixed interval reinforcement** schedule, rewards are systematically administered after a fixed period of time. Many people on a salary are paid once a month or once a week. Unfortunately, under this schedule, it sometimes becomes difficult for employees to associate their performance levels with the reward. (Recall the perception associated with E_2 of the expectancy theory of motivation.) Rewards may seem to be more closely associated with time than with performance level. Employees may believe that, once they meet some minimal acceptable performance level, they will receive the same level of reward regardless of their level of performance.

Variable Interval Schedule

Under a **variable interval reinforcement** schedule, rewards are administered after some period of time but the length of that period of time is varied. This schedule would not be effective in administering wages or salary. If the average pay period was thirty days, then payment on a variable interval schedule might result in a check being issued, for example, once after thirty days, then after forty-five days, then after fifteen days, and so on. A variable interval schedule is more effectively used to administer other types of rewards, such as praise of an employee's good performance.

Fixed Ratio Schedule

Under the **fixed ratio reinforcement** schedule rewards are administered after a specified number of correct behaviors. For example, every time a repair technician successfully repairs ten washing machines, he or she receives a bonus. Since the reinforcement is based upon the performance of correct behavior, then behavior reinforced on this type of schedule is likely to be learned relatively quickly. Once learned, the behavior is more likely to recur than behavior learned under an interval-based reinforcement schedule.

Variable Ratio Schedule

A **variable ratio reinforcement** schedule is one that administers a reward on the basis of some average number of correct behaviors. This means that the number of correct behaviors between reinforcements is constantly changed. A good example of a variable ratio reinforcement schedule is a Las Vegas slot machine. The machine might pay off after 1000 plays, and then again after 450 plays, and so on. People watch for the machines that have been played a large number of times without a payoff. Then they begin playing these machines in the hope that the reinforcement is close at hand. Individuals are motivated to continue playing these machines (sometimes for hours) because they are never sure when the payoff will come.

Variable ratio schedules of reinforcement result in learning that is relatively permanent. If an employee's behavior is reinforced under a variable ratio schedule, it is difficult for that person to predict exactly when reinforcement will occur. Performance must be high enough to qualify for the reinforcement when it comes, but since they do not know when it will come, employees have no alternative but to continue to maintain that high level of performance.

There is no question that operant conditioning is a very powerful technique for modifying behavior. A great deal of learning takes place when we are reinforced, whether by reward or by punishment, for certain behaviors. Reinforcement cannot account for all learning that occurs in organizational settings,

© 1983 King Features Syndicate, Inc. World Rights Reserved.

Social Learning Theory

however. Operant conditioning requires that a person actually engage in a behavior and that a reward or a punishment for that behavior actually be given. This is a very time consuming and costly way to learn, since we all make mistakes.

Social Learning Theory

Social learning theory assumes that it is possible for learning to take place on a vicarious basis. **Vicarious learning** does not require that the individual engage in the behavior and receive reinforcement for it in order for meaning to become attached to the behavior. We learn vicariously when we observe someone else engage in the behavior and receive the reward or punishment for it. One of your employees may observe you rewarding Sam with the afternoon off for accomplishing a difficult goal. That employee may think "If I perform well, the boss will reward me, also." A great deal of learning about which behaviors to display and which to avoid in work settings occurs on this vicarious basis.

Social learning theory can be tied to expectancy theory. When employees form perceptions, particularly of E_1 and E_2, they generally use two sources of information: direct experience, through operant conditioning; and indirect experience, through vicarious learning. How you, as supervisor, administer rewards will have an impact, not only upon the employee who receives the rewards, but also upon the other employees who observe or are made aware of your behavior.

Motivation is a very complex process. Each of the theories discussed in this chapter can give rise to useful suggestions of ways to motivate employees. It is important that you understand each of these theories. The next chapter will integrate these theories and provide some practical advice for motivating employees.

Summary

A theory of motivation can be classified as a content theory or a cognitive theory. Content theories focus upon what energizes behavior and include Maslow's Hierarchy of Needs and Herzberg's Two-Factor Theory. Content theories suggest that the first step in motivating employees is to determine which rewards are most important to *each* employee. The variety of rewards that content theories discuss may be classified into two categories: intrinsic and extrinsic. Extrinsic rewards are external to the individual; the individual must depend upon someone else to administer these rewards. Examples are pay, physical working conditions, and treatment by supervisor. Intrinsic rewards are internal to the individual; the individual provides these types of rewards to himself or herself for good performance. Examples of intrinsic rewards are feelings of accomplishment, growth and development, self-esteem, and self-actualization. Most content theories would agree that both of these categories of rewards are important to motivation.

Cognitive theories focus upon the mental process that individuals engage in when making decisions about their behavior. These theories, which include Adam's Equity Theory, Expectancy Theory, Operant Conditioning, and Social Learning Theory, are concerned with what channels or directs behavior, as well as what sustains or maintains behavior.

Equity theory suggests that individuals compare their rewards with those of others. This comparison process includes a consideration of the level of input (e.g., effort) as well as the level of output (e.g., rewards). Supervisors must treat employees equitably. This generally means that rewards are closely tied to performance levels. Expectancy theory suggests that employee expectation is an important determinant of motivation; that is, the employee must not only be offered important rewards, but must also believe that successful performance will bring those rewards.

Operant conditioning and social learning theory are both based upon the Law of Effect. This law states that rewarded behavior will tend to be repeated, and behavior which is punished or which is not rewarded in any manner will tend to disappear. Operant conditioning is concerned with the direct application of rewards and punishments, while social learning theory suggests that learning takes place, as well, through the observation of the application of rewards and punishments to others.

Key Terms

avoidance learning (p. 84)
cognitive theory (p. 82)
content theory (p. 74)
continuous reinforcement (p. 89)
effort → performance expectancy
  (p. 85)
extinction (p. 88)
extrinsic rewards (p. 77)
fixed interval reinforcement (p. 90)
fixed ratio reinforcement (p. 91)
hygiene factors (p. 80)
inequity (p. 83)
inputs (p. 82)
intrinsic rewards (p. 78)

motivation (p. 76)
motivators (p. 80)
need-satisfaction theory (p. 77)
operant conditioning (p. 87)
outcomes (p. 82)
partial reinforcement (p. 89)
performance → outcome expectancy
  (p. 85)
process theory (p. 77)
social learning theory (p. 93)
valence (p. 85)
variable interval reinforcement (p. 91)
variable ratio reinforcement (p. 91)
vicarious learning (p. 93)

Questions for Discussion

1. Explain the difference between an intrinsic reward and an extrinsic reward.
2. Is money an extrinsic or intrinsic reward?
3. What kinds of needs cease to motivate once they are satisfied? What kinds of needs continue to motivate even after they have begun to be satisfied?
4. What can supervisors do to avoid the problems associated with equity theory? Be specific.
5. Discuss as many reasons as you can for the existence of E_1 problems, E_2 problems, and valence problems.

6. Should supervisors emphasize extrinsic or intrinsic rewards? Explain.
7. Can punishment be used effectively in work settings? If so, under what specific conditions is it likely to be successful? If not, why not?

References

1. T. R. Mitchell, "Motivation: New Directions for Theory, Research, and Practice," *Academy of Management Review* 7 (1982): 80–88.
2. A. H. Maslow, *Motivation and Personality* (New York: Harper and Row, Publishers, 1954).
3. E. E. Lawler and J. L. Suttle, "A Causal Correlation Test of the Need Hierarchy Concept," *Organizational Behavior and Human Performance* 7 (1972): 265–287.
4. C. P. Alderfer, "A New Theory of Human Needs," *Organizational Behavior and Human Performance* 4 (1969): 142–175.
5. F. Herzberg, B. Mausner, and B. Snyderman, *The Motivation to Work* (New York: John Wiley and Sons, 1959).
6. J. S. Adams, "Toward an Understanding of Inequity," *Journal of Abnormal and Social Psychology* 67 (1963): 422–436.
7. G. S. Leventhal, T. Weiss and G. Long, "Equity, Reciprocity, and Reallocating Rewards in the Dyad," *Journal of Personality and Social Psychology* 13 (1969): 300–305.
8. E. Thorndike, *Animal Intelligence* (New York: Macmillan Co. 1911).
9. A. Bandura, *Principles of Behavior Modification* (New York: Holt, Rinehart, & Winston, 1969).
10. R. D. Arvey and J. M. Ivancevich, "Punishment in Organizations: A Review, Propositions, and Research Suggestions," *Academy of Management Review* 5 (1980): 123–132

Exercise

Diagnosing Motivational Problems

Write a short case describing a situation in which an employee has either an E_1 problem, an E_2 problem, or a valence problem. Include in your description what might be done to correct the motivational problem.

Exercise

Balancing Individuality and Equity

Chapter 4 has emphasized the importance of individual differences, recognizing that people value rewards differently. This suggests that supervisors may have to use different rewards to motivate different employees. Equity theory, however, suggests that if you treat people differently, they may perceive that they are being inequitably treated. How do you reconcile these two ideas? Write a response to this question and be prepared to share it with the class.

Case

The Maintenance Department

Kelly Long was pleased that Bud Albers had accepted his job offer of Senior Repair Technician in the maintenance department. Kelly had been supervisor of this department for the past twelve years. Until recently, the company had not been willing to pay the kind of salary that it took to hire the most highly qualified repair technicians. Prior to that time Kelly had been forced to hire technicians with little formal training. Most of these people had received their training on the job. Many of them were largely self-taught.

Kelly did not complain about his employees. They were a good bunch. They just did not have the advanced technical training to take care of complex jobs quickly and efficiently. They got things done, but they sometimes took much longer than Kelly thought was necessary.

Bud was the first of the "new breed" of repair technician. He had an associate degree from the local junior college and had taken some additional classes from State University. In the interview, Kelly asked Bud some rather technical questions. It was obvious that Bud really knew his stuff. From some of Bud's answers, it was clear that he knew substantially more than Kelly did in a number of areas. Kelly was excited about the prospect of having such a highly trained employee in his department.

During the first couple of weeks, the older employees were polite to Bud, but they did not seem to open up to him. Bud did not appear to notice, however. He had buried himself in his work, determined to learn all there was about the organization, its policies, and the machinery he was responsible for maintaining. After about three months, Bud knew the machinery inside and out. It seemed he could tell what was wrong with the machinery by the sound it was making. Kelly was amazed at Bud's ability to determine the problem and repair the machinery. Often, he would have something repaired before the older employees could decide what was wrong with it.

At the end of Bud's first six months of employment, Kelly planned to call Bud into his office to tell him what a great job he had been doing. His thoughts were interrupted by the arrival of Ned Smith, a long-time employee in the department. Ned had a few complaints. "I think you should know, Kelly, most of us are pretty upset with that new employee you hired," he said. "The word is out that he was hired at a much higher salary than most of us are getting, and some of us have been here for ten years!

Besides, this guy thinks he's a real hotshot. I think he gets a kick out of showing up the older employees. He's never made any attempt to eat lunch with us or to join the departmental bowling team, or anything, for that matter. It appears to us that he thinks he's too good to associate with us. He just does his work and goes home.''

''I didn't know anyone was unhappy with Bud,'' Kelly responded. ''I knew that he seemed to stay on his own pretty much, but that didn't appear to be a problem. Let me have a talk with Bud and see what he has to say. I'll get back to you in a couple of days.''

Later that day, Kelly ran into Bud in the break room. ''Kelly, I think I'm going to start looking for another job. You've given me the freedom to do my job the way I think it ought to be done, and I'm certainly well paid. I don't think I could do better anywhere else, as far as salary goes. The problem is, I'd like to work with people who are interested in improving themselves, and not just in getting their checks on Friday. The employees in your department do a pretty good job. They can fix just about anything if they're given enough time. They're just not interested in learning or developing new skills.''

Kelly didn't know what to say. It seemed that no one in the maintenance department was very happy right now. Kelly had received no hint of any existing problem until Ned came to see him earlier that day. Now it seemed he had a serious problem on his hands. He hated to lose Bud, but at the same time, his departure could solve the problem with the older employees.

Questions

1. What do you see as the primary problem in this situation?
2. What motivational theories can be used to diagnose this situation?
3. What factors would you use to motivate Bud?
4. What factors would you use to motivate Ned?
5. Could Kelly have done something to prevent this situation from occurring?
6. What should Kelly do now?

Chapter 5

Applications of Motivation Theory

Learning Objectives

After reading this chapter, you should:

1. recognize a number of constraints that make the application of motivation theories difficult.
2. understand what it takes to use money as a motivator.
3. be able to explain the task design, or job enrichment, process.
4. understand how goals can be used to motivate employees.
5. be able to differentiate job context from job content.
6. be able to develop your own motivational strategies for specific situations.
7. understand the relationship between Theory X–Theory Y characteristics in people and the motivational strategies used.

Lisa was worried about one of her employees. Sarah was obviously very bright and well trained, having received a degree in English from State University just last spring. Recently, Sarah appeared to have become somewhat bored and uninterested in her work. Her performance was still acceptable, but it just was not what Sarah was capable of doing. Lisa was concerned that if something was not done, she might lose Sarah.

Lisa had hired Sarah five months ago as Administrative Assistant, Level 6. This was a higher grade than most new employees were hired into, but given Sarah's education, Lisa felt it was appropriate. Sarah's work for the first three months was outstanding. Lisa's boss had even commented about Sarah's good work. Yet for the past two months, Lisa had heard Sarah say things like, "You don't need a college degree to handle this job. The work is really quite simple and at times very repetitive."

In an attempt to motivate Sarah and improve her morale, Lisa had been able to talk her boss into allowing her to give Sarah an unscheduled pay raise after only four months on the job. This seemed to help for a couple of weeks, but now Sarah seemed as uninterested as ever.

Just today, a new problem had emerged. Lisa had overheard two of her other employees talking. The comments made suggested that many of the other employees felt that Lisa was showing favoritism to Sarah.

Lisa did not know what to try next. She remembered from her college course in supervision that it was important to treat employees as individuals. She had tried to do that with Sarah. Now, not only is Sarah still unmotivated, but the other employees are upset.

Chapter 4 provided a discussion of several major theories of motivation. An understanding of the ideas included in these theories is a necessary prerequisite to learning how to effectively motivate employees. While theories are instrumental in simplifying and integrating what is known about certain phenomena, they do not provide a complete picture. You have already learned that motivating employees is a complex process. In order for a theory to be useful, it must simplify concepts and even ignore some variables. Most situations are just too complex to include all the variables in a single theory. It is not a big surprise, therefore, to find that you cannot just pull a theory out of a textbook and apply it on the job. Theories provide a framework within which you can work; they can guide you, but often cannot tell you precisely what you need to do in a particular situation.

The focus of this chapter is on the application of motivation theories. Certain variables which constrain, or limit, a supervisor's ability to use some of the ideas were introduced in chapter 4 and will be discussed in this chapter. Two additional theories of motivation will be considered, and some potential problems in motivating employees will be examined. The chapter will conclude by offering a number of motivational strategies that a supervisor might use.

Understanding Employees

Most theories of motivation have at least one thing in common. They all seem to imply that if you want to be able to motivate your employees, you must know each of them well enough to know which rewards are most important to each person. It is easy to say, "Don't use the same motivational technique on all of your employees." It is quite another matter to determine exactly what each employee wants to get out of the job.

What Do Employees Want From Their Jobs?		Table 5.1
	Supervisors	**Subordinates**
1. Good working conditions	4	9
2. Feeling "in" on things	10	2
3. Tactful discipline	7	10
4. Full appreciation for work done	8	1
5. Management loyalty to workers	6	8
6. Good wages	1	5
7. Promotion and growth with company	3	7
8. Sympathetic understanding of personal problems	9	3
9. Job security	2	4
10. Interesting work	5	6

Reprinted, by permission of the publisher, from "What Makes a Good Job?" by Lawrence G. Lindahl, in *Personnel,* January 1949, p. 265. © 1949 American Management Association, Inc. All Rights Reserved.

What Do Employees Want from Their Jobs?

An interesting study was performed a number of years ago, the purpose of which was to find out exactly how much supervisors knew about what their employees wanted from their jobs.[1] Partial results of this study are shown in table 5.1. Workers in several organizations were asked to rank, in order of importance to them, the ten job factors listed in the table. The immediate supervisors of these workers were asked to rank order the same list but were instructed to evaluate the ten items in terms of how they thought their employees would rank them.

The numbers suggest that the supervisors who responded to the survey did not have a clear idea of which factors the employees thought were most important. The two factors ranked highest by employees (full appreciation for work done and feeling "in" on things) are both intrinsic factors. Supervisors ranked these two factors eighth and tenth, respectively. On the other hand, supervisors ranked extrinsic factors (good wages and job security) in first and second place. In other words, these two factors were seen by the supervisors as being most important to their employees. Employees ranked these factors fifth and fourth, respectively. These supervisors were likely to have offered good wages and job security to employees who wanted full appreciation for the work done and to be included in decision making.

While this study was performed some time ago, it still suggests that supervisors may need to put greater effort toward making sure that they fully understand the aspects of the job that are most important to each of their employees. It is probably a mistake to assume that you know what your employees value today, even though you were successful in motivating them in the past. As has been pointed out in previous chapters, an individual's needs are constantly changing. We continually add and subtract different types of needs for our total "bundle of needs." Not only do the specific needs that we consider important undergo change over time, but we constantly change the weight or degree of importance that we place upon each of those needs. This change complicates things considerably. A fair question at this point would be, "How do I find out what things are most important to my employees?"

Information-Gathering Strategies

Three general strategies can be used to gather the information that will help you to answer this question. Those strategies are communication, observation, and surveys.

Communication

The communication strategy requires that you listen carefully to what your employees say to you or to others, and that you ask questions to clarify, in your own mind, what things are most important to each employee. Consider the following examples of comments made by employees:

> **Comment:** "There really isn't much challenge to this job once you learn it. It seems like I do almost the same thing every day."
> **Diagnosis:** This employee apparently places a high value on challenging work and the challenge is not being met. This person may have high needs for growth and development compared with other employees.
> **Comment:** "Every time I do a really good job on some assignment, my supervisor gives me more responsibility and more difficult assignments. The pressure is about to get to me."
> **Diagnosis:** This employee is being rewarded with more challenging assignments and increased responsibility. While these might be motivating for some people, this employee apparently does not value these factors very highly.

In both examples, it is fairly clear what rewards are, or are not, important to the individual. One employee values challenging work, while the other does not. The supervisor needs to provide more challenge and variety in the work assignments of the first employee and needs to stop presenting so much challenge to the second. In addition, the supervisor needs to communicate with the second employee to determine what specific rewards that individual most highly values.

Observation

Observing how employees react in various situations is a strategy that will often provide clues to what these individuals want to get out of their jobs. Consider the following:

> **Example:** You have just finished assigning a challenging task to Tom who responds with little enthusiasm. Later, you notice that Tom is making progress, but he is doing only enough to get by.
>
> **Diagnosis:** Tom does not seem to value difficult or challenging tasks. This is not what it takes to motivate this employee. You should engage in further discussions with Tom to find out what factors are most important to him.
>
> **Example:** You have just finished telling Alice that she received the highest pay raise in the department. She tells you that she really appreciates that, but is concerned that she is not being given enough opportunity to use her skills and abilities.
>
> **Diagnosis:** Pay is probably important to Alice; however, she also has a need for challenging work that is not being met. You should try to assign other duties to Alice—some of your own work, perhaps, such as that report the boss wants but you haven't had time to do yet. This added responsibility may satisfy Alice's need for challenging, interesting work.

Surveys

An obvious way to find out what things are important to your employees is to ask them. A short survey, or questionnaire, can be completed anonymously and serves as a way of uncovering important information about your employees' feelings or problems that they might be experiencing but about which they are reluctant to talk to you directly.[2] Even though you lose the ability to identify individuals with anonymous surveys, the problems revealed through the answers to questions can be further pursued using the techniques of communication and observation. Best results are achieved with a survey if it is made a standard practice. If employees are suspicious of the survey, you are not likely to get open, honest responses. Once employees get used to the idea of responding to a short questionnaire once or twice a year, they may become less suspicious and provide honest responses.

**Understand-
ing Yourself**

You may succeed in determining what your employees want from their jobs. Then you must be able and willing to provide these rewards. There will be various constraints placed upon your ability to give rewards; these will be discussed later in this chapter. For the moment, attention is focused upon your willingness to provide various rewards.

As people grow and develop, basic behavioral patterns, attitudes, and beliefs become established. When you get to know a person well, you can predict how they will react in a certain situation because you are familiar with their patterns of behavior. Obviously, no one behaves exactly the same way in every situation; however, there is enough stability in behavior across situations and across time that we can generally predict how someone is likely to react under certain conditions.

Collectively, these stable behavioral patterns, attitudes, and beliefs form the foundation for the much broader, and much more generalized, views of the world which many people come to hold. Adhering to a world view may result in problems in the work situation, or it may not, depending upon the specific nature of that view and the degree of flexibility that the view allows. McGregor's Theory X–Theory Y provides an explanation of this problem.[3]

Theory X—Theory Y Supervisors

Theory X–Theory Y is concerned with the way supervisors or managers view their employees. A supervisor with a **Theory X** view of employees believes that (a) most employees dislike work and will avoid it if they can; (b) since employees dislike work, they must be closely controlled and even threatened with punishment in order to get them to perform, and; (c) most employees have little ambition, want to avoid responsibility, and therefore, prefer to be closely controlled and told exactly what to do.

Supervisors with a **Theory Y** view of employees believe that (a) most employees actually enjoy work; (b) most employees are motivated by autonomy and the opportunity for self-control; (c) not only do employees accept responsibility, but many actually seek increased responsibility; and, (d) most employees possess relatively high levels of imagination and creativity and are willing to apply these talents toward solving organizational problems.

Some people have developed Theory X views of others and some have learned to have Theory Y views. Many more maintain views with characteristics of both types. The implication of this theory is that your view of employees will, at least in part, determine the motivational strategies you employ. For example, a Theory X supervisor is more likely to emphasize such extrinsic factors as pay and working conditions. Often these types of rewards make it easier to exert close control over the employee. A Theory Y supervisor is more likely to emphasize such intrinsic factors as challenging work, responsibility, and autonomy. These rewards facilitate self-control in the employee. At least part of the reason that the employee exerts more effort is because the work itself is enjoyable. External control from the supervisor is not as necessary under such conditions.

Interaction with Employees

While the assumptions of Theory Y may appear to be more correct or pleasant than those of Theory X, that distinction cannot be either fairly or accurately made. Some employees may prefer to be told what to do and to be closely controlled because such regulation gives them a sense of security. These employees, who may be said to have Theory X characteristics, may feel uncomfortable working under a supervisor who has a strong Theory Y view of people. The opposite work situation is also likely to create problems; employees with Theory Y characteristics are more likely to feel some dissatisfaction with a Theory X supervisor than with one whose views are more similar to their own.

Supervisors who can judge the characteristics of their employees and then match their own styles to their employees will be effective supervisors. Unfortunately, it is often difficult for a person with strong Theory X views to behave in a Theory Y manner, and vice versa. If you hold very strong Theory X or Theory Y views, it may be difficult for you to behave any differently toward your employees. If your style does not match the characteristics of your employees, you are not likely to be successful in motivating. The exercise at the end of this chapter will help you to examine your assumptions about employees.

In attempting to motivate employees, supervisors may try to improve job context, job content, or both. **Job context** refers to the extrinsic factors associated with a job, similar to Herzberg's hygiene factors. **Job content** refers to the intrinsic factors associated with the work itself. These are similar to Herzberg's motivators. The section to follow will examine specific issues related to improving job context and job content.

Motivating Employees

Job Context

Money is typically thought of as an extrinsic reward or hygiene factor. In order to use money in an effective way to motivate employees, the monetary reward must be made **contingent** or dependent, upon performance. In other words, money must be given only after some objective or specified level of performance has been reached.

Money as a Motivator

The decision to use a monetary reward as a motivator should rest upon the assumption that the individual both values money highly and perceives that increased effort will result in increased monetary rewards. Oftentimes, the level of rewards given must be significantly higher than that received by employees at lower performance levels or else money will not motivate. Consider what would happen if a group of employees were evaluated as poor, average, and excellent performers after which these percentage salary increases were given:

Poor Performers	5%
Average Performers	6.5%
Excellent Performers	8%

If the evaluation process has been done accurately and these employees have been appropriately classified as poor, average and excellent performers, this would be an excellent opportunity to increase motivation. In this case, however, the opportunity has been missed since the manner in which monetary rewards were administered does not adequately differentiate between these assessed levels of performance. What incentive do the poor performers have to become average performers? A difference of 1.5 percent is not likely to excite many people. If their annual salary is $20,000, this would amount to an extra $300 a year or an extra $25 per month! The same is true of average performers. Why would they want to become excellent performers? It might be more desirable to them to simply hold back effort, continue to be average performers, and forego the small additional salary associated with doing an excellent job. In this example, money has not been made highly contingent upon good performance. Even poor performers got relatively high salary increases. Who is likely to be unhappy with the situation described? The poor performers? No, they are probably being overpaid. The average performers? No, they are probably being paid about what they deserve. The excellent performers are most likely to be the unhappy ones. They are not being paid much better than average employees. Equity theory comparisons made by the excellent performers are likely to leave them psychologically uncomfortable.

If money is going to motivate performance, it must be made highly contingent upon performance. Great care must be exercised in evaluating employees' performances and relatively large differentials must exist in the amounts of monetary reward given to employees who achieve different levels of performance.

Money is probably most often thought of as an extrinsic reward; it enables you to buy material, tangible things. But because money has symbolic value for many people, it may also be considered to be an intrinsic reward. Take, for example, the highly-paid executive who makes more than a million dollars a year. It is hard to believe that they need a large salary increase so that they can purchase more. On the other hand, it is likely that these executives place great importance upon a large salary increase because of its symbolic value. The executive may interpret a salary increase as a statement of personal worth or contribution to the organization. Many of us look at money in both ways. We need the additional money to buy essentials but we also consider the amount of the pay or salary increase to be the organization's way of saying, "Here's what you are worth to us."

Highest-Paid U.S. Executives

Table 5.2

Name/Position	Organization	Total* Annual Compensation
1. T. Boone Pickens, Jr. *Chairman & President*	Mesa Petroleum	$4,223,000
2. Barry Diller *Senior Executive Vice-President*	Gulf & Western	2,866,000
3. Thomas D. O'Malley *Vice-Chairman*	Philbro-Salomon	2,514,000
4. John H. Gutfreund *Chairman*	Philbro-Salomon	2,379,000
5. Frank D. Trznadel, Jr. *Senior Vice-President*	Comdisco	1,602,000
6. Clifton C. Garvin, Jr. *Chairman*	Exxon	1,350,000
7. Howard H. Kehrl *Vice-Chairman*	General Motors	1,269,000
8. Donald E. Peterson *President*	Ford Motor	1,229,000
9. Lee A. Iacocca *Chairman*	Chrysler	1,195,000
10. Anthony R. Hamilton *Chairman*	Avnet	1,049,000
11. John R. Opel *Chairman*	IBM	1,034,000

*Does not include other long-term forms of compensation, such as stock options.
Source: Based on *Business Week,* May 6, 1985, "Executive Pay: Who Made the Most,"
pp. 78–100.

Because of its symbolic value, money may also serve to supply us with other intrinsic rewards. A salary increase may provide an individual with feelings of self-esteem, recognition, and achievement or accomplishment. The point is, it is probably a mistake to look at monetary rewards only as extrinsic in nature. The size of the reward, by itself, as well as its amount in comparison with those given other employees, may hold intrinsic importance for many individuals.

Other Extrinsic Rewards

Money is not the only extrinsic reward available to supervisors to use in motivating employees. Other extrinsic rewards that could be given include promotions, status symbols, special awards, fringe benefits, good working conditions, job security, interpersonal relations, and time off. These rewards vary considerably in the amount of the reward that can be administered, the frequency with

Dunagin's People *by Ralph Dunagin. Copyright © 1984 by and permission of News America Syndicate.*

DUNAGIN'S PEOPLE

"IT MAY NOT BE A LIFETIME JOB, BUT IT WILL SEEM LIKE IT."

which the reward can be administered, and again, the importance of the reward to different individuals.[4] For example, there is little flexibility in the amount and frequency with which promotions may be given. Fringe benefits lack this same flexibility and, typically, are not under the control of supervisors. Status symbols (e.g., a large desk, private office, large name plate) and special awards (e.g., certificates, plaques) may be highly flexible in amount administered, but cannot be administered frequently or employees will tire of them.

Job Content

Chapter 4 defined intrinsic rewards as rewards that individuals give to themselves for good performance. Feelings of achievement or of self-actualization are two such rewards. Work that is routine and repetitive, or work that does not present much of a challenge, provides limited opportunity for employees to give themselves intrinsic rewards. Similarly, work situations within which employees are not permitted much control offer fewer opportunities to satisfy intrinsic needs than situations in which employees have some degree of influence. As such, employees will enjoy greater opportunity to receive intrinsic rewards if their work is challenging and interesting, and if they have been allowed to have some control over their work. Three very practical motivational strategies may be implemented to provide employees with increased opportunity to gain intrinsic rewards. These are: task design, goal setting, and quality circles.

Task Design

Task design, also referred to as **job enrichment,** focuses upon those changes which must be made in order to increase the intrinsic motivational properties of the work itself. It attempts to determine what steps can be taken to make work more challenging and interesting for employees and to give them more control over their work.

Typically, task design makes an effort to give employees more autonomy and responsibility. This could be accomplished, for example, by allowing employees to have a greater say in what happens on the job. They could be given the authority to decide when to take breaks, to make changes in the way their jobs are performed, or to check for and correct their own mistakes.

Feedback, in the form of evaluation or corrective information, is an important element in making tasks intrinsically motivating. The more quickly this information is supplied, the greater its effect is likely to be. In other words, feedback should be given as soon as possible after the successful or unsuccessful job performance. In order for employees to be able to give themselves an intrinsic reward, they must perceive that they have performed effectively. When you tell employees that they have done a good job, you are providing them with an opportunity to feel a sense of accomplishment or to feel recognized.

It is equally important to the task design effort to make the work activity itself, as interesting and challenging as possible. This is most often achieved by giving employees a more identifiable portion of work to do. Instead of having workers perform highly specialized jobs, constituting only a small part of the entire process, they are assigned larger portions of the job. For example, instead of some workers attaching electric cords to toasters while others install the electrical elements as they pass by on an assembly line, workers might be assigned to a team that is responsible for building a toaster from start to finish. People are likely to get more meaning and more intrinsic motivation from building an entire toaster than they would from merely attaching a cord to, or installing the element in, one of these appliances.

Quality Circles

Another way to make work more intrinsically motivating is to organize quality circles. **Quality circles** are small groups of about eight to fifteen employees, all of whom work at similar jobs. As a quality circle, this group meets voluntarily to identify and solve problems, develop new work methods, and improve the productivity and quality of work. A decision to form a quality circle is based upon the assumption that employees are closest to their work and, therefore, are best suited to solve work-related problems and develop ideas to increase productivity and efficiency. The organization must show its commitment to quality circles by providing work time for the group to meet, by supplying financial support, and by accepting the ideas and suggestions developed by the group.[5]

Supervisors are usually the appointed leaders of the quality circles. This role is critical to quality circle success; supervisors must provide an open, participative environment in which group members feel free to suggest ideas and voice objections without fear of reprisal or criticism.[6]

Goal Setting

Research on goal setting has identified several characteristics of goals that have an effect upon employee motivation and productivity.[7] These goal characteristics include: difficulty, clarity and specificity, acceptance, participation in goal setting, and feedback about goal achievement. Goals which are difficult, yet attainable, serve as a stimulus or challenge to employees. **Goal clarity** and **goal specificity** make it clear to employees exactly what is expected of them. It has been noted that an individual who is unsure of the supervisor's definition of "successful performance" are likely to have a low E_1 and, therefore, a low level of motivation. Adequate goal clarity and specificity may also serve to increase employees' confidence and, as a result, their willingness to exert effort toward accomplishing their goals.

Goal acceptance can be defined as the degree to which employees view their goals as appropriate or legitimate. Employees with high levels of goal acceptance are likely to be highly committed to accomplishing their goals. There are two primary ways to increase your employees' goal acceptance. First, the goals must be appropriate for the job of each employee. For example, it would be inappropriate for the dean of the college to make research and publishing the goals of his or her secretary. Clearly, these activities are not among those that most secretaries would consider appropriate for their jobs. Second, by allowing employees to help set the goals that they are to accomplish, goal acceptance will often increase. Many employees become much more highly committed to goals if they have helped to set them than if those goals were handed to them by a supervisor.

Employees who have been allowed to participate in the setting of their own goals may feel a greater sense of control over their work. Such participation provides a sense of ownership of the job. If employees are simply handed the goals they are to accomplish, they may feel controlled and may come to feel more like a piece of equipment than an important member of the organization.

Constraints upon Theory Implementation

Unfortunately, the ideas contained in motivational theories cannot always be implemented in work settings. A variety of individual and organizational constraints can make the implementation of a motivational technique very difficult.

Supervisor and Employee Constraints

Particular characteristics of the employee and of the supervisor can act as constraints upon the implementation of motivational techniques. The employee's individual needs, personality, experience, and ability may limit the success of these techniques in some situations; the beliefs and values of the supervisor may produce the limitations in others. Some supervisors find it difficult to give employees freedom on the job and to allow them to participate in goal setting and decision making. It may be that these supervisors have trouble administering praise and recognition to employees. Others may have a hard time distributing the more extrinsic rewards (like pay) in such a way that those rewards serve as motivators for employees. These supervisors may find it more comfortable to administer such rewards in an across-the-board fashion, giving all employees similar amounts, rather than attempt to distinguish among the levels of individual performance.

Organizational Constraints

A number of organizational characteristics may limit a supervisor's flexibility in implementing motivational techniques. These include the constraints imposed by budgets, policies, organizational structure, technology, and unions.[8]

While budgets are necessary to guide supervisors in expending organizational resources, they usually limit supervisors' flexibility in administering rewards. This is particularly true for monetary rewards. It is not uncommon for a supervisor to be unable to give an excellent employee the pay raise the individual deserves because there is not enough money in the budget.

Some organizations adhere to the policy that no employee may receive more than a specified amount or percentage raise during any one-year period. If, as a supervisor, your salary increase recommendations have to be approved by your boss, your flexibility may again be limited. A manager will sometimes establish a range for salary increases and be reluctant to deviate from this range.

Let's take Mary's situation as the example. Mary was an excellent employee in her first year with the organization. After finishing Mary's performance evaluation, her supervisor requested that she receive a 12 percent raise, and sent the appropriate form to his boss for approval. The supervisor's boss returned the form with a note saying he would not approve such a high raise for any clerical employee. A request for a 10 percent raise met with the same results. Finally, the boss reluctantly approved an 8 percent raise for Mary. This amount was only about 2 percent more than was given to employees who, clearly, were only average in ability. While Mary continued to be one of the supervisor's best performers, she never again worked at the level of performance that she had achieved during her first year.

Organizational structure can also function as a constraint upon a supervisor's activity. Organizational structure refers to the relationships among members of the organization in terms of authority and responsibility. A principal feature of any organization's structure is its degree of centralization. **Centralization** refers to the degree to which people at lower levels of an organization have the authority to make decisions and use their own judgment. Organizations are said to be centralized if top management makes most of the important decisions and then issues directives for supervisors to follow. Organizations in which people at lower levels are allowed to make important decisions on their own are said to be decentralized. Supervisors in centralized organizations are not likely to have a great deal of flexibility in administering rewards. They are either told what they can and cannot do, or are required to get upper management's approval before their ideas can be implemented.

Technology refers to the process used to produce the commodities or services that the organization has to offer. Obviously, an automobile manufacturing plant and a hospital have very different technologies. Some technologies are very inflexible; that is, the work must be performed in a specific manner and cannot be changed. Supervisors may be able to do very little to enrich these jobs or make them more intrinsically motivating. On the other hand, some technologies are more flexible and may allow some form of job enrichment to be implemented.

The presence of a union can also limit a supervisor's flexibility in implementing motivational techniques. Most unionized organizations operate under a labor contract which specifies pay rates, how pay raises may be earned, and how discipline or punishment may be administered. Supervisors have no choice but to adhere to the contract. Some unionized plants do not even conduct performance evaluations of their employees because pay rates under a labor contract are usually tied to seniority rather than performance level.

Motivational Strategies

The discussion of constraints should not have provided the impression that supervisors are in a hopeless situation when it comes to implementing motivational theories and concepts. Constraints are simply part of a realistic picture of the supervisor's role and are part of what makes the task of motivating employees so complex.

It could happen, unfortunately, that you, as a supervisor could diagnose an employee's motivational problem and feel very confident that you know the best solution, only to find that you cannot implement your ideas because of some organizational constraint.

Such obstacles are part of the facts of organizational life and are best minimized by developing as much flexibility in your motivational strategies as possible. The following are suggestions designed to guide you in developing effective motivational strategies.

Get to know yourself. Determine whether you have a bias toward intrinsic or extrinsic rewards. Are you a strong Theory X or Theory Y supervisor?

Develop ways of increasing your flexibility. If you find that you have strong Theory X views and are uncomfortable administering praise, then work on it! The fact that you learned your Theory X or your Theory Y view suggests that you can also learn to become more flexible in your beliefs and behaviors.

Analyze your own situation. Make sure that you understand which rewards you control and which rewards you do not. If it is not clear to you, for example, whether you can reward a high-performing employee with an afternoon off, schedule a meeting with your boss to talk about it. You need to know which rewards you are permitted to use for acknowledging good performance.

Use the rewards you do control. You will not always control all important rewards so you must use the ones you do control to your best advantage. To achieve this, rewards must be administered equitably, though not necessarily equally, and on a highly contingent basis. Administering rewards on a noncontingent basis (such as the situation in which everyone gets a raise no matter how they have performed) will reduce the E_2 levels of those employees. They may come to feel that they do not have to perform in order to get the rewards.

Get to know your employees. You have to know which types of rewards are most important to each employee. You also need to know your employees well enough to recognize when they have changed the way they value certain rewards.

As much as possible, make rewards contingent upon successful job performance; that is, differentiate levels of rewards based upon levels of performance. When rewards are administered on a noncontingent basis, employees learn to expect the rewards but do not learn what they need to do in order to be rewarded. You and your employees should hold a common definition of the term "successful performance." Your employees must be told what is expected of them and should be assured that you are both willing and able, in terms of your authority, to differentiate rewards based upon levels of performance. Do not ever promise or even imply that an employee might get some reward unless you know that you can, in fact, deliver that reward.

Be continuously aware of employees' E_1 expectancies. As you will recall, these E_1 problems may be expected to arise when employees do not know what is expected of them; when they lack the ability or skills to successfully perform; or when they lack confidence in their own abilities to perform. In the effort to alleviate such problems, or prevent them from occurring, you may find that you need to set some clear and specific goals for employees; provide additional training for those employees, or move them into a job for which they are more qualified, or; engage in coaching and confidence building in order to increase those individuals' motivation.

Treat employees equitably. Equity comparisons can generate real problems since they are so subjective. Many employees will not resent differentials in rewards when those rewards are based upon clear differentials in performance. The more objective the performance criteria used in making reward allocations, the easier it will be to justify these decisions to employees. Not all supervisors are fortunate enough to have established an objective measure of employee performance. Under these circumstances, you as supervisor should strive to be as impartial and objective as possible and to make it obvious to your employees that you are attempting to do so.

A great many factors must be considered in choosing an appropriate motivational strategy for an employee. The theories discussed in chapter 4 as well as the ideas presented in this chapter are intended to provide a background of information that may be helpful in making those choices. It will still be your responsibility to know your employees, diagnose each situation, and, ultimately, select the most effective motivational strategy for that particular situation.

Summary

This chapter has focused upon some possible applications of the motivation theories presented in chapter 4. It is critical that supervisors learn how each employee values various rewards. While this is sometimes difficult, it can be accomplished through communication, observation, and surveys.

Some supervisors hold very strong beliefs about employees. These beliefs may influence them in the selection and use of specific motivational strategies. Theory X supervisors want to closely control employees and tend to emphasize extrinsic rewards. Theory Y supervisors prefer to allow employees more freedom and tend to emphasize intrinsic rewards. Supervisors must be able to use both extrinsic and intrinsic rewards in motivating employees.

Money is commonly considered to be an extrinsic reward; however, it has intrinsic properties as well. Many people view a pay raise as a symbol of their accomplishments or their worth to the organization. In order to effectively use money as a motivator, it must be made highly contingent upon performance.

Task design, or job enrichment, is a method of making jobs more intrinsically motivating. Often, this is achieved by giving employees more freedom or autonomy on the job, allowing them to participate in setting goals and making decisions, and providing immediate feedback about their performances. Effective goal setting may also increase employees' intrinsic motivation by clarifying their expectations and providing them with increased challenge.

Several constraints associated with the implementation of motivational theories were discussed. These include such individual constraints as the abilities, needs, personality, and experience of the employee, the beliefs and values of the supervisors, and such organizational constraints as budgets, company policies, corporate structure, technology, and unions.

Finally, some general suggestions for selecting a motivational strategy were offered.

centralization (p. 112)
contingent (p. 105)
feedback (p. 109)
goal acceptance (p. 110)
goal clarity (p. 110)
goal specificity (p. 110)
job content (p. 105)

job context (p. 105)
job enrichment (p. 109)
quality circles (p. 109)
task design (p. 109)
technology (p. 112)
Theory X (p. 104)
Theory Y (p. 104)

1. Explain Theory X–Theory Y.
2. How do you think Theory Y employees would react to working for a Theory X supervisor? What could be the reaction of Theory X employees to a Theory Y supervisor? Be specific.
3. What do you recommend for a supervisor who finds that his or her department consists of equal numbers of employees with Theory X and Theory Y characteristics?
4. What specific steps could be taken to enrich the job of a keypunch or data entry operator? A supermarket checker?
5. Is task design or job enrichment likely to work for everyone? Why or why not? What types of people might not respond to job enrichment?
6. How can employees be motivated through goal setting?
7. What constraints do supervisors face in applying extrinsic rewards? Intrinsic rewards?
8. Should supervisors always be concerned about the motivational levels of their employees? Can you think of any situations where motivation does not really matter?

1. L. Lindahl, "What Makes a Good Job?" *Personnel* 25 (1949): 263–266.
2. R. B. Dunham and F. J. Smith, *Organizational Surveys: An Internal Assessment of Organizational Health* (Glenview, Ill.: Scott, Foresman, & Co., 1979).
3. D. McGregor, *The Human Side of Enterprise* (New York: McGraw-Hill, 1969).
4. D. A. Nadler, J. R. Hackman, and E. E. Lawler, III, *Managing Organizational Behavior* (Boston: Little, Brown, & Co. 1979).
5. E. Yager, "Examining the Quality Control Circle," *Personnel Journal* 58 (1979): 684.
6. S. Ingle, "How to Avoid Quality Circle Failure in Your Company," *Training and Development Journal* 36 (1982): 57–59.
7. E. A. Locke, K. N. Shaw, L. M. Saari, and G. P. Latham, "Goal Setting and Task Performance: 1969–1980," *Psychological Bulletin* 90 (1981): 125–152.
8. C. C. Pinder, *Work Motivation: Theory, Issues, and Applications* (Glenview, Ill.: Scott, Foresman, & Co. 1984).

This exercise is designed to provide you with the opportunity to examine your own views of employees. Your scores on the following statements will determine where you fall on a Theory X–Theory Y continuum. Respond in terms of how you would actually behave, not in terms of what you think the text or your instructor would say is a correct response. There are no correct or incorrect answers. Circle a number on each of the scales to indicate your response.

1. A supervisor must watch subordinates carefully to make sure that they perform.

1	2	3	4	5
Agree Strongly	Agree	Can't Decide	Disagree	Disagree Strongly

2. Most subordinates can be trusted to perform on their own.

1	2	3	4	5
Agree Strongly	Agree	Can't Decide	Disagree	Disagree Strongly

3. Most subordinates prefer to be told exactly what to do.

1	2	3	4	5
Agree Strongly	Agree	Can't Decide	Disagree	Disagree Strongly

4. Most subordinates want to learn and grow and develop.

1	2	3	4	5
Agree Strongly	Agree	Can't Decide	Disagree	Disagree Strongly

5. Subordinates will not perform without some supervisory pressure.

1	2	3	4	5
Agree Strongly	Agree	Can't Decide	Disagree	Disagree Strongly

6. Subordinates should be allowed to participate in making important decisions.

1	2	3	4	5
Agree Strongly	Agree	Can't Decide	Disagree	Disagree Strongly

7. Supervisors should be careful that they are not too soft on their subordinates.

1	2	3	4	5
Agree Strongly	Agree	Can't Decide	Disagree	Disagree Strongly

8. Supervisors should make their subordinates' jobs as interesting and challenging as possible.

1	2	3	4	5
Agree Strongly	Agree	Can't Decide	Disagree	Disagree Strongly

9. Supervisors should retain control by making all the important decisions themselves.

1	2	3	4	5
Agree Strongly	Agree	Can't Decide	Disagree	Disagree Strongly

10. Few subordinates are highly motivated to work.

1	2	3	4	5
Agree Strongly	Agree	Can't Decide	Disagree	Disagree Strongly

Compute your score by adding up the numbers you have circled. Find your score on the graph below.

Theory X   Theory Y

10   20   30   40   50

Note: Items 2, 4, 6 and 8 Are Reverse Scored ($1 = 5, 2 = 4, 3 = 3, 4 = 2, 5 = 1$).

Jim was excited about his new position as supervisor of Campus Recruiters for JBS Corporation's personnel department. While he had only about a year's experience in supervising the work of others, he had majored in personnel management in college and was glad to be working in his field at last. He felt fairly confident about his supervisory ability and was eager to put his training to work.

His new assignment was to supervise five campus recruiters who spent much of the year traveling to college campuses across the country recruiting for a variety of positions within JBS. During a single campus visit a recruiter might look for accountants, computer programmers and analysts, financial analysts, chemical and electrical engineers, and general management majors for JBS's Management Trainee Program. Often, this required the recruiter to spend from three to five days interviewing applicants. It was not unusual for the recruiter to travel immediately to another campus for another three to five days of interviewing. Recruiters were on the road almost continuously during the months of October, November, December, March, April, and May. These were the months just prior to fall and spring semester graduation. During the rest of the year, recruiters were on the road an average of three days out of the week.

During discussions with his new boss, the personnel director for JBS, Jim made it clear that he thought additional recruiters were needed to do a good job recruiting the many campuses with which JBS had contact, and the many positions for which the recruiters typically interviewed. While the personnel director seemed to agree with Jim, he said that he did not think that additional recruiters would solve all of the morale and motivational problems in the campus recruiting department. He suggested that Jim become familiar with the department and its methods of operation before making any big changes. Jim agreed and busied himself with learning all he could about the department and its employees.

Jim found that the backgrounds of the campus recruiters were very similar. All had college degrees in personnel management and had no experience when hired by JBS. One employee had been in the department for five years while another had only nine months experience in the department. The others had been campus recruiters for about three years. Three of the recruiters were women, and all were between the ages of twenty-three and thirty. None were married.

The campus recruiters were given adequate expense accounts, were allowed to stay in first-class hotels when traveling, and were provided with company cars. In comparing salary levels of JBS recruiters with other firms in the area, Jim found JBS to be quite competitive. In fact, throughout the company's history, JBS had hired new recruiters at about $1,000 more than other local companies. None of this information seemed to suggest to Jim any particular reason for the sagging morale and decreased motivation of the recruiters. He decided to meet with the recruiters individually in order to get to know them and to, hopefully, gain some insight into the department's problems.

None of the recruiters said anything to Jim during the meetings that suggested any reason for the problem. Most spoke favorably of JBS and of the personnel department. All stated that they had chosen personnel as a career field and were happy to be getting the experience that their jobs were providing. Each mentioned the goal of becoming a personnel director in the future.

After the interviews, Jim was even more convinced that the major cause of the morale and motivation problems was that of overwork. The addition of three more campus recruiters would alleviate much of the stress that the present recruiters seemed to be experiencing and would reduce the physical fatigue that resulted from such a demanding travel schedule. Jim also felt that the contributions of these recruiters were often overlooked. He decided to initiate a Campus Recruiter of the Month Award to recognize the recruiter who returned from a recruiting trip with the largest number of qualified applicants. Jim felt confident that he had solved the problem as he put his recommendations into a memorandum for the personnel director.

Questions

1. Do you think Jim has identified the underlying causes of the morale and motivational problems in the campus recruiting department? What is your assessment of the situation?
2. Do you agree with Jim's recommendation for additional campus recruiter positions? Why or why not?
3. Do you agree with the strategy of the Campus Recruiter of the Month Award as Jim has proposed it? Do you see any potential dangers with this strategy? Will it increase the motivation of the recruiters?
4. What would you recommend to the personnel director if you were the supervisor of the campus recruiting department?

Chapter 6
Supervisory Leadership

Learning Objectives

After reading this chapter, you should:
1. be able to define leadership.
2. be aware of the five bases of power.
3. understand the relationship between bases of power and leadership style.
4. be able to describe the five major leadership styles.
5. understand the advantages and disadvantages of the major leadership styles.
6. be aware of the situational variables that influence a supervisor's leadership style.
7. understand what supervisors can do to develop a motivating work climate.

Joan slid into a booth in the coffee shop across the street from the company where she worked. She wanted to have a leisurely cup of coffee and relax before starting the drive home. It had been a hard week, yet in reflecting upon all that had taken place, Joan could not help feeling that she had gotten a great deal accomplished.

Several problems had arisen and the work load had been unexpectedly heavy, but Joan had gotten everything resolved before the close of business today. She decided that the reason she had managed to take care of all the problems was because of her decision to use a more participatory leadership style with her employees. Instead of making decisions and telling them how to solve problems, she had given them some guidance and direction and let them solve the problems themselves.

Just then Joan overheard the voices of three of her employees in the booth behind her. One of them was saying, "I don't know what's come over Joan. It's not like her to ignore problems like that. It's a good thing that we all chipped in to cover for her."

Another employee replied, "Yeah, but I'm not going to do that again. It's not my job to make those kind of decisions. That's what Joan gets paid to do. If I'm going to make supervisory decisions, then I want to get paid for it."

These comments took Joan completely by surprise. Apparently her new participatory style wasn't working as well as she thought.

While it may be quite easy to decide whether or not individuals are good leaders, it is more difficult to determine what those people do that makes them good leaders. Certain types of people come immediately to mind when considering the general notion of good leadership. A U.S. president, a corporate executive, a coach, a teacher, or a senator or representative are a few examples. What is it about these people that makes others think of them as good leaders? The relevant behavior and activities of good leaders must be identified in order to learn anything from a study of leadership.

This chapter provides a working definition of leadership, as well as a discussion of the sources of power from which leaders may draw. Five major leadership styles are described and the situational variables that determine when a particular leadership style is most appropriate are discussed.

Leadership may be defined as "the use of power and influence in order to accomplish a task."[1] According to this definition, individuals may be good leaders because of the power they possess or because they are able to influence the behavior of others. Several reasons can account for the ability of a person to exert power or influence over others. A person may be given authority by the organization and, thus, enjoy leadership status on the basis of position within that organization. A supervisor is more likely to be considered a leader than an employee who does not supervise the work of others.

Individuals may be considered leaders because of some special skill or talent, or because of the particular information or knowledge they possess. For example, assume that you are responsible for putting this chapter into a word processing system with which you are not familiar. A person with the knowledge to operate this system would probably be able to influence your behavior, regardless of that person's formal position. You are willing to be influenced by that person because of the expertise or knowledge he or she possesses.

Coach Paul "Bear" Bryant: A charismatic leader

Photo courtesy University of Alabama Sports Information Office

A person may be considered a leader due to that person's ability to control rewards and punishments, although that ability is somewhat related to position within the organization. Under these circumstances a person has power because he or she can administer both rewards and punishments to others. If you value the rewards or cannot escape the punishments, your behavior can be influenced.

Finally, a person may be considered a leader simply on the basis of personality or interpersonal attraction. You may be willing to follow or be influenced by a person you admire. The great football coach Paul "Bear" Bryant serves as a good example of this type of leader. While he certainly had a measure of control over rewards and punishments, Bryant's ability to lead grew out of the respect and admiration of those who followed him.

"The Bear"

A farmer's son from Arkansas, who got his nickname from wrestling a bear, became the winningest coach in college football in 1981 when his University of Alabama Crimson Tide beat the University of Auburn Tigers. Comments from former players, assistant coaches, and even the governor of Alabama add to the legend of Coach Paul "Bear" Bryant.

"He'd go into a staff meeting and he'd never have to say 'Let me have your attention.' He had it. You respected him and you liked him. You didn't do it because you were scared of him. Although I was a little scared of him." *New Orleans Saints Head Coach Bum Phillips, assistant coach under Bear Bryant at Texas A & M.*

"This must be what God looks like." *George Blanda, quarterback for Bear Bryant at the University of Kentucky.*

"I'm glad he never ran against me for governor." *George Wallace, governor of Alabama.*

Even Bryant, himself, provides some insight into his effect upon people. "I'm just a plow hand from Arkansas. But I've learned how to hold a team together. How to lift some men up, how to calm down others, until finally they've got one heartbeat, together, a team."

Source: "Not Your Average Bear," *Time,* 27 December 1982, 80; "No. 1, and Still Counting," *Time,* 7 December 1981, 68.

Bases of Power

Bases of power may be thought of as those qualities and characteristics of both personality and situation that enable people to become leaders. The most widely-known model of power bases was developed by French and Raven.[2] According to this model, there are five bases of power: reward, coercive, legitimate, referent, and expert.

Reward power When you are able to provide something an employee wants, you have **reward power** over that employee. If you control salary increases or promotional opportunities, you will probably have some influence over the behavior of those employees who value these rewards. If you do not control rewards your employees value, you will need to rely upon one of the other sources of power.

Coercive power When you can administer punishments to employees, you have **coercive power** over them. Employees will comply with your requests because they wish to avoid punishment.

Legitimate power When employees feel that you have the right to influence their behavior, you have **legitimate power.** Employees may feel that, because you are their supervisor, you have the right to issue orders and to expect those orders to be obeyed. This has nothing to do with your knowledge or expertise, or your control over rewards and punishments. This source of power derives only from the position that you occupy in the organization.

Referent power When employees admire you because of your personality, reputation, or charisma, you have **referent power.** Employees are willing to be influenced by you because of your interpersonal attraction for them.

Expert power When you have information, expertise, or knowledge that employees value or need, you hold **expert power** over them. Employees are willing to be influenced by you, in this case, because you are a recognized expert in a particular area.

A leader may derive power from any or all of these sources. In fact, it may be a mistake to rely too heavily upon any single source of power. For example, supervisors who rely too heavily upon legitimate, reward, or coercive power may find that problems in relationships with employees start to develop. Most people do not like to feel controlled. When you withhold rewards or threaten punishment in order to influence the behavior of an employee, it is quite likely that this person will feel controlled and, perhaps, react defensively. Many situations call for the exercise of legitimate, reward, or coercive power, or some combination of these. You will be a more effective leader, however, if you develop the other sources of power, as well.

Current leadership theories tend to focus upon the use of particular sources of power for particular situations. These theories attempt to characterize the type of behaviors that are most appropriate for leaders to exhibit under certain sets of circumstances. These behaviors can be classified into two broad categories: initiating structure behaviors and consideration behaviors.

Categories of Leader Behaviors

Initiating Structure Behaviors

Initiating structure behaviors are those which involve setting performance standards, providing information about and guidance in the performance of tasks, and encouraging employees to perform to their capacities. In other words, leaders who display initiating structure behaviors are usually attempting to lend structure to their employees' work efforts.

Leaders are practicing initiating structure behaviors if they

1. emphasize output or quantity of work.
2. set high performance standards or goals.
3. emphasize the quality of work.
4. schedule the work to be done.
5. provide information and guidance on how to perform tasks.
6. assign specific tasks to specific employees.
7. encourage employees to perform up to their capacities.
8. emphasize the importance of meeting deadlines.
9. criticize poor performance.
10. make decisions without consulting employees.

Consideration Behaviors

Consideration behaviors are those which give help to employees and emphasize mutual trust and respect in relationships.

Leaders are engaging in consideration behaviors if they

1. encourage employees to participate in making decisions that affect their jobs.
2. allow employees to perform their jobs the way they think best.
3. treat employees as equals.
4. are friendly and approachable to employees.
5. compliment employees in front of others.
6. reward employees for good work.
7. try to resolve conflicts between employees.

8. try to create a pleasant climate in which to work.
9. keep employees informed about what is going on in the organization.
10. encourage employees to communicate openly about problems.

Leader Behaviors Compared

A great deal of research has been performed in the attempt to determine whether one style of behavior is more effective than the others.[3] Unfortunately, the findings are confusing and contradictory. Some studies have found that leaders who exhibit initiating structure behaviors were more effective, while other studies have determined that the opposite is the case. These inconclusive findings have prompted researchers to suggest that effective leadership style is, perhaps, dependent upon situational variables. Changing situations, therefore, call for changes in leadership style. The most widely accepted leadership theories today suggest that a good leader is one who can exhibit the style of behavior that the situation requires. These theories are called contingency, or situational, theories; they suggest that there are times when the most effective leadership style is one that incorporates both initiating structure and consideration behaviors.

Leadership Styles

Figure 6.1 has combined the two classes of leader behaviors to produce five major leadership styles. These are the laissez-faire, directive, supportive, participative, and achievement-oriented styles of leadership.

Laissez-Faire

A **laissez-faire** leader displays low levels of both initiating structure and consideration behaviors. To others, it might appear as if this type of leader has little interest in the performance of the work group. Employees are probably given the freedom to make most decisions under this form of leadership.

Directive

A supervisor with a **directive** leadership style displays high levels of initiating structure behavior and low levels of consideration behavior. This leader would make most, if not all, decisions for the work group and would make sure that these decisions were carried out by the employees.

Supportive

A **supportive** leader displays a high level of consideration behavior and a low level of initiating structure behavior. Such a leader is most concerned with creating or maintaining warm, open interpersonal relations and avoiding conflict.

The self-confidence of the supervisor is the final supervisor-related variable that will be discussed. If supervisors are confident, even in uncertain situations, they are likely to diagnose the situation and exhibit the appropriate leadership style. On the other hand, if supervisors lack confidence when they find themselves in uncertain situations, they are likely to revert back to their dominant leadership style, regardless of what the situation seems to require.

Employee-Related Variables

Obvious employee-related variables are the training, education, job knowledge, and experience of the employee. The higher the existing levels of these variables, the less appropriate is a leadership style using high levels of initiating structure behaviors. These employees know how to perform the task. They do not need a directive leader to tell them what they already know.

Another important employee-related factor is the employee's need for independence or **autonomy.** Employees with a high need for autonomy are likely to react negatively to a leader who displays high levels of initiating structure behaviors. These employees are likely to feel unnecessarily closely controlled when working under a directive leader. On the other hand, employees with low needs for autonomy are likely to respond more favorably to directive leadership. These individuals might feel uncomfortable under a supportive or laissez-faire leader because of the high degree of freedom and lack of structure that typically result.

Employees' tolerance of ambiguity is another employee-related factor to consider. Tolerance of ambiguity is a phrase that refers to how well employees are able to deal with uncertainty in their jobs. Employees with a high tolerance of ambiguity are likely to work better under a participative, supportive, or even laissez-faire leadership style. Employees with a low tolerance of ambiguity prefer a directive leadership style because they would rather be told what to do and how to do it.

The employee's understanding of, and identification with, organizational goals constitutes another employee-related variable. Employees who understand the organizational goals are likely to be knowledgeable about what needs to be accomplished in order to achieve those goals. They do not need a directive leader telling them what to do. In addition, if employees identify with organizational goals, this means that they are committed to accomplishing those goals. They do not need a directive leader trying to closely control their activities in the effort to ensure that the activities are consistent with organizational goals. Employees with a high degree of understanding of, and identification with, organizational goals are likely to perform better under a supervisor who minimizes initiating structure behaviors.

A final employee-related factor is the extent to which employees have become accustomed to a particular leadership style. If you happen to replace a person who has been giving directive leadership to a group of employees for some time, and you begin using a highly participative style, it may take your employees some time to become comfortable with your unfamiliar style of leadership. If you have the flexibility that allows you to exhibit the style that best suits the situation, you may want to exhibit a directive style at first, and then begin slowly to vary your leadership style.

Organizational Variables

Several organizational factors should be considered when attempting to determine the most appropriate leadership style. The first of these relates to the dominant leadership style of the organization as a whole. Sometimes an entire organization will appear to practice a dominant style of leadership; that is, most supervisors and managers seem to exhibit very similar leadership behaviors. Most likely this is because top management uses a particular style with their employees. These employees emulate their top management bosses by using the same style with those whom they supervise, and so on. The presence of such an established method of leadership can create pressure for you to exhibit the same style, even if it is not the best approach to use in that situation. If the organization has a very dominant style, you may be viewed with some suspicion if you try to use another. An organization that uses a very dominant directive style of leadership may consider the supervisor who prefers a participative or supportive style to be too soft on the employee and, therefore, not a very good supervisor. This is a most undesirable situation in which to find yourself, particularly if you are prevented from using the leadership style most effective for the situation. Nevertheless, it is a situational variable that you should consider in protecting your career within an organization.

The size of the work group should influence your leadership style. The larger the work group, the more difficult it becomes to use a more consideration-oriented style. You simply may not have to time to include employees in decision making when you supervise a large work group.

The geographic distribution of your employees in the work place will also influence your leadership style. The farther apart from each other that your employees are placed in the work environment, the more difficult it becomes to use a consideration-oriented leadership style. Again, there simply may not be enough time for you to allow employees to participate in decision making. If your employees are situated in a single physical location, you will be able to use a more supportive or participative style.

Another organizational factor to consider is work group effectiveness, or the degree to which your employees manage to cooperate and work together as a team. The higher the level of work group effectiveness, the more appropriate it becomes to use consideration-type behaviors. On the other hand, if work group effectiveness is low, then you will probably need to exhibit a directive style of leadership to ensure that the work gets done correctly, as well as on time.

The nature of the work or of the particular task at hand should also be examined on a situational basis. Sometimes a problem may be so complex or unusual that only the supervisor will have sufficient knowledge or information to

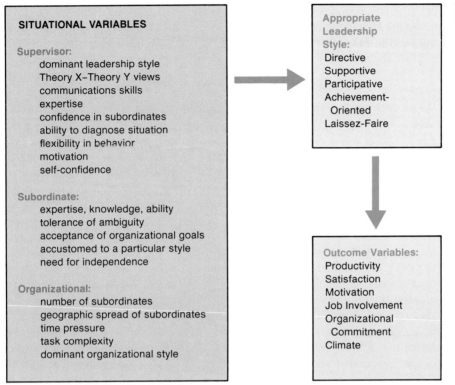

SITUATIONAL VARIABLES

Supervisor:
   dominant leadership style
   Theory X–Theory Y views
   communications skills
   expertise
   confidence in subordinates
   ability to diagnose situation
   flexibility in behavior
   motivation
   self-confidence

Subordinate:
   expertise, knowledge, ability
   tolerance of ambiguity
   acceptance of organizational goals
   accustomed to a particular style
   need for independence

Organizational:
   number of subordinates
   geographic spread of subordinates
   time pressure
   task complexity
   dominant organizational style

Appropriate
Leadership
Style:
Directive
Supportive
Participative
Achievement-
   Oriented
Laissez-Faire

Outcome Variables:
Productivity
Satisfaction
Motivation
Job Involvement
Organizational
   Commitment
Climate

Figure 6.2
The leadership process

properly deal with it. In such a situation, the directive style would be most appropriate. If employees possess the knowledge and experience to deal with the problem, however, a more participative style is likely to be the most effective.

The last organizational factor is that of time pressure. If you are facing a very close deadline, you may not have enough time to use a supportive or participative leadership style. In this case, a directive style may be necessary just to get the work out on time.

Each of these situational variables has been considered individually. To do so presents a somewhat unrealistic picture since any situation you face as a leader is likely to include more than one of these variables. It is relatively easy to decide upon the appropriate leadership style when you examine these variables one at a time. It becomes a much more difficult process when all of these variables are considered as a group, as shown in figure 6.2.[5] That, however, is exactly what you have to do. Several variables in one situation may call for a supportive style; several others may call for a directive style. The problem, in this case, is to determine which of these variables is most important. Say, for example, that the size of the work group is small and centrally located, there is no time pressure, and the organization does not have a dominant leadership style. A supportive or participative style would seem to be appropriate. If, however, you are also aware that your employees are not able to tolerate much ambiguity or uncertainty in their work, then a more directive style could be best, regardless of the presence of any other variables.

Advantages and Disadvantages of Leadership Styles

While each leadership style has particular characteristics that make it useful, each has certain accompanying disadvantages, as well. In the process of diagnosing the situation, determining the most appropriate leadership style, and then engaging in those types of leader behaviors, both advantages and disadvantages should be kept in mind. For example, while a situation may clearly call for a directive leadership style, certain employees may react negatively to this style. They may become defensive or feel pressured, producing a negative impact upon their productivity. Other employees may become unusually careful and stop using their own initiative or creativity. The directive style may make them feel as if they are being closely watched and controlled and that they don't want to take any chances of making errors. On the other hand, a supportive style may be interpreted by some employees as weakness on the part of the supervisor. These employees may then take advantage of the supervisor by restricting the effort that they put forth. This example is intended to demonstrate that while it may be possible to diagnose the situation and display the right leadership style, it is important to be prepared to face the costs that can be experienced with the use of any particular leadership style. Table 6.1 compares the five major leadership styles.

Recall that chapter 4 explained how, according to social learning theory, a great deal of learning takes place on a vicarious basis. A particular leadership style is usually selected for a particular employee in a particular situation. Other employees, however, are likely to be present and to observe your behavior toward this employee; therefore, it is important to keep in mind that a leadership style displayed in one situation for a certain employee could have an effect upon other employees who observe these behaviors. Some additional communication and explanation may be necessary to make it clear to the other employees why you behaved as you did.

Suppose you supervise the work of five employees. Four of the five have been on the job for some time, know exactly what to do, and have been performing consistently at high levels. Without knowledge of any other existing situational variables, it is unlikely that a highly directive style would be appropriate for this group of employees. This information suggests that a supportive or even a laissez-faire style would be more effective. The fifth employee, however, has just joined your department. The work is relatively complex and this employee has been having some difficulty learning how to perform the job. Clearly, a directive style

Comparison of Five Major Leadership Styles

Table 6.1

Leadership Style	Advantages	Disadvantages
Directive	Highly efficient Saves time Gets quick results Appropriate when subordinates do not have necessary information, skills, experience, etc., and when subordinates cannot tolerate ambiguity or uncertainty	May restrict upward communication Subordinate's knowledge and expertise not included in decision making May result in negative effect upon subordinates with high needs for achievement and recognition
Participative	Information and expertise of subordinates included in decision making Subordinates more committed to goals and plans they helped to create Higher degree of freedom for subordinates Subordinates feel like they are an important part of the organization Appropriate when subordinates have a high need to participate and when a great deal of information is needed to make a highly accurate decision	Time consuming May result in a loss of control for leader May cause resentment if ideas and suggestions of subordinates are consistently ignored
Supportive	Establishes friendly, open working environment Builds trust and respect between leader and subordinates Should motivate subordinates who lack self-confidence	Some subordinates may interpret supportiveness as weakness and hold back effort Can be frustrating for subordinates with high needs for achievement
Achievement-Oriented	Subordinates likely to peform nearer their capacity Focus subordinates' attention upon results Subordinates with a relatively high need for achievement are likely to be highly motivated	May cause some subordinates to feel too much pressure for performance

Table 6.1
(cont.)

Comparison of Five Major Leadership Styles

Leadership Style	Advantages	Disadvantages
Laissez-Faire*	Frees up the leader for other tasks Allows subordinates to use their own initiative and judgment Develops subordinates	May create a climate of apathy and distrust among subordinates with low needs for autonomy

*Some authors define the laissez-faire leadership style as an absence of leadership, indicating a lack of concern for both performance and relationships. When defined in this manner, it is difficult to conceive of a situation where this style might be effective. If, however, this style is defined as consisting of low levels (not zero levels) of both initiating structure and consideration behaviors, the laissez-faire style may be appropriate in certain situations (i.e., those in which the task is highly structured, in which the task is interesting and challenging, or in which subordinates identify with organizational goals, and have the skill, experience, and motivation to work independently).

would benefit this situation. But put this into the larger context. You have four employees who do not need direction, so you will be emphasizing consideration behaviors with them. You have another employee who needs a directive style in order to bring that individual's performance to an acceptable level. How will it affect the new employee to use a supportive or participative style on the other four? A supportive or participative style may be viewed by some employees as a form of reward, especially if the work itself is not particularly enjoyable or interesting. If the new employee views encouragement from the leader and the opportunity to participate in decisions as important rewards, that individual may perceive some degree of inequity. The other four employees are receiving rewards that this person is not. In order to use a directive style with this employee while using a supportive style with the others, the new employee must clearly understand your reasons for using two different leadership approaches.

Developing a Motivating Work Climate

Styles of leadership can have a very strong impact upon the climate or atmosphere of the work group. **Climate** refers to employees' perceptions of the work environment. Climate is a difficult concept to define precisely, but it can be thought of as the personality of an organization or department.

Organizations, as a whole, typically have an identifiable organizational climate. Because of the strong influence of individual leadership styles, however, each division, department, or work group is likely to have an identifiable climate of its own, as well.

Keep in mind that virtually everything you say or do in your supervisory role will communicate to your employees. An important part of developing a motivating work climate is managing these communications so that the messages are interpreted as you intend them. For example, a supervisor who chews out an employee in front of other employees is conveying the message that the climate of this work group is punishing or risky. If employees make mistakes, they can expect to get punished for them. On the other hand, a supervisor who is supportive and encouraging when mistakes are made is creating an entirely different climate. Employees in this environment are likely to feel more comfortable using their own initiative because they aren't worried that they will be punished if they make a mistake. The employees in this work group are likely to be more highly motivated because they have been given increased autonomy in their work and have had trust in them displayed by their supervisor.

In the Introductory Incident, Joan was attempting to increase employee participation in the effort to increase motivation. That message did not come across as Joan intended. Her attempt to take a more participative leadership approach was perceived as laissez-faire by her employees. Joan probably should have communicated more openly with her employees about her intention to begin using a more participatory leadership style. Without this communication, employees perceived that Joan suddenly did not care much about problems at work. If this misinterpretation continues, the climate is likely to develop into one of apathy and distrust.

It is difficult to prescribe the specific characteristics of a "good" or "motivating" climate. As with leadership theories, a contingency view must be taken. What is a good climate in one set of circumstances may not be the best climate in another situation. Supervisors need, first, to determine the type of climate they want to create, and then must engage in those leader behaviors that are consistent with that type of climate.

Virtually everything a supervisor does has some effect upon the climate of the work group. The factors most likely to have an impact upon climate are reviewed.

Motivational strategies The climate of the work group is likely to be influenced by the chosen motivational strategies of the supervisor. An emphasis upon extrinsic rewards, intrinsic rewards, or some combination of rewards will each produce different climates. When extrinsic rewards are emphasized, employees often feel controlled. Extrinsic rewards tend to "push" employees to perform, and intrinsic rewards "pull" employees to put forth effort. Both types of rewards are important to most employees.

Systems of reward When it is obvious to employees that rewards are contingent upon performance and when those rewards are administered equitably, this often produces an exciting, motivating climate. When rewards are administered on the basis of seniority or some other factor that has no relationship to the quality of performance, then employees come to expect these rewards just because they have remained members of the organization. Although these employees may feel a strong sense of security in their jobs, they are not likely to be highly motivated to perform well.

Methods of administering discipline or punishment Supervisors who administer discipline in a manner that makes employees feel embarrassed or threatened are likely to damage the climate of the work group. Discipline can be administered effectively by making it as impersonal, objective, and as consistent as possible.

Degree of freedom given employees to participate When employees are allowed to participate in making the decisions that affect their jobs, they are likely to become committed to seeing that these decisions are carried through to successful completion. They are likely, also, to feel as if they are a part of the organization, and not just another one of the organization's resources to be used in accomplishing goals.

Degree to which employees are informed of the plans and activities of the organization It is hard for employees to feel they are an important part of the organization when they find out about organizational plans and activities after they have occurred.

Degree to which supervisors create and enforce rules, procedures, and policies If organizational goals are designed to make employees feel closely controlled and to limit initiative and creativity, then the supervisor should create a large number of rules, procedures, and policies, and enforce them to the letter. On the other hand, if it is important that employees feel free to use their own judgment and initiative, then few rules, procedures, and policies should be created.

Nature of communication The nature of the communication between supervisor and employees influences work group climate. When the communication is that of orders, directives, and commands, employees get the impression that they are not important members of the organization. Once again, they are likely to feel closely controlled and this feeling tends to stifle initiative and creativity. When communication takes the form of advice, information, and encouragement, employees are likely to respond with high motivation and commitment.

Degree to which the supervisor shows concern for employees Concern can be demonstrated in a number of ways. Supervisors who take the time to help employees with personal problems are likely to create a climate of concern. Take the owner of a relatively large manufacturing company who frequently walks through the plant and calls line employees by their first names. Such actions seem insignificant and are easily overlooked or forgotten, but, over time, the effects of these little considerations build up and come to exert a strong positive influence upon the work group climate.

Supervisor's primary base of power If a supervisor continually operates from a single base of power, the climate of the work group will be affected. Supervisors who operate from a legitimate, a reward, or a coercive power base are likely to create climates that are cold and impersonal, in which employees do not feel free to use their own judgment and initiative when problems arise. Supervisors who operate predominantly from referent or expert power bases are likely to create climates in which employees are willing to put more into their work than their job descriptions specify. Problems that don't seem to be the responsibility of any particular person may be shouldered, voluntarily, by employees who admire and respect their supervisors.

Many more supervisory behaviors could have just as great an impact upon the work group climate as those identified in this chapter. It is up to the supervisors to determine the most appropriate climate for their own work groups; they must engage in whatever leader behaviors will create this climate in the perceptions of employees.

Summary

Leadership is defined as the use of power and influence in order to accomplish a task. The five bases of power that leaders may draw upon are: reward power, coercive power, expert power, legitimate power, and referent power. Part of being an effective leader is knowing which source of power to use in a particular situation.

Two categories of leader behaviors were identified: initiating structure behaviors and consideration behaviors. On the basis of these two categories of behaviors, five major leadership styles were identified. These are the laissez-faire, supportive, directive, participative, and achievement-oriented styles of leadership. In order to determine the most appropriate leadership style for a given situation, the supervisor must be able to diagnose situational variables. These situational variables were categorized into supervisor-related factors, employee-related factors, and organizational factors.

Work group climate was defined as the personality or atmosphere of the work group. Virtually everything that a supervisor does and says has an effect upon the climate of the work group. Supervisors must be aware of the potential of their words and actions to affect employees and must make every effort to engage in those behaviors that are consistent with the type of work group climate they want to create.

Key Terms

achievement-oriented (p. 127)
autonomy (p. 129)
bases of power (p. 124)
climate (p. 134)
coercive power (p. 124)
consideration behaviors (p. 125)
directive (p. 126)
expert power (p. 124)

initiating structure behaviors (p. 125)
laissez-faire (p. 126)
leadership (p. 122)
legitimate power (p. 124)
participative (p. 127)
referent power (p. 124)
reward power (p. 124)
supportive (p. 126)

Questions for Discussion

1. Other than the ones discussed in this chapter, what situational variables do you think are important to consider when choosing a leadership style?
2. Why do you think it is difficult for some people to be flexible in exhibiting various leadership styles? What can be done to help these people become more flexible?
3. Could the argument be made that the "one best leadership style" is the one in which the leader displays both a high task orientation and a high relations orientation? Explain.

4. What can supervisors do to develop and use referent power? The other sources of power?
5. Describe a situation in which a directive style of leadership would be the most effective style to use. A participative style? A supportive style? An achievement-oriented style? A laissez-faire style?
6. Explain the difference between organizational climate and work group climate.
7. What can supervisors do to develop a motivating work climate?
8. What are the advantages and disadvantages associated with a directive leadership style? A supportive style? A participative style? An achievement-oriented style? A laissez-faire style?

References

1. F. E. Fiedler, "A Contingency Model of Leadership Effectiveness," in *Advances in Experimental Social Psychology,* Vol. 1, ed. L. Berkowitz (New York: Academic Press, 1964).
2. J. R. P. French and B. Raven, "The Bases of Social Power," in *Group Dynamics,* ed. D. Cartwright and A. F. Zander, 2nd ed. (Evanston, Ill.: Row, Peterson, 1960), 607–623.
3. S. Kerr, "Theories and Measures of Leadership: A Critical Appraisal of Current and Future Directions," in *Leadership: The Cutting Edge,* ed. J. G. Hunt and L. Larson (Carbondale, Ill. SIU Press, 1977), 9–45, 51–56.
4. P. Hersey and K. H. Blanchard, *Management of Organizational Behavior,* 4th ed. (Englewood Cliffs, N.J.: Prentice-Hall, 1982).
5. R. Tannenbaum and W. H. Schmidt, "How to Choose a Leadership Pattern," *Harvard Business Review* 36 (1958): 95–101.

Exercise
Diagnosing Situational Variables

Below are listed the five major leadership styles. For each, list as many situational variables as you can for which that style of leadership would be appropriate.

1. Directive
2. Supportive
3. Participative
4. Achievement-oriented
5. Laissez-faire

As he was driving home, Ron reflected upon his first month as a supervisor with JBS Manufacturing. He felt things had gone well, in general, but he was a little concerned with his apparent lack of acceptance by some of his employees. Ron speculated that this was a typical reaction to the changes he had made in the department. People are just naturally resistant to change, and things are quite a bit different now than when Charlie was in charge, Ron thought. He tried to reassure himself that these employees would come around once they got used to the changes.

The cutting department had been supervised by Charlie Seymour until his retirement last month. There had been a big office party and all of the employees in the department had chipped in to buy Charlie a rather expensive gift. Charlie had supervised the department for the past nine years. He had been extremely well-liked by all of his employees and, judging by the amount spent upon his retirement party, it seemed JBS thought highly of him, as well.

After replacing Charlie, Ron had looked over the performance reports from the past five years. While productivity in the department had been adequate during this time period, it was certainly not close to reaching the level that Ron thought it should have reached. For one thing, Ron had noticed that several employees seemed to run out of materials at the same time and spent what Ron considered to be an excessive amount of time retrieving replacements.

By the end of the second week on the job, Ron had made a number of changes in the way departmental work was performed. Most of this change resulted from the hiring of a new person whose job was to walk around the department and serve as a "gopher." When one of the cutters needed a tool or more material, this person would "go fer it." This allowed the cutters to stay at their stations and continue working instead of shutting down their machines and going to get these things themselves. Ron announced that each cutter should be able to increase the amount of his output by at least 10 percent because of the addition of the "gopher."

One week after implementing this change, Ron looked eagerly at the performance reports. Productivity in the department had improved only 4 percent. Ron decided to send a memo to all employees thanking them for the increase in productivity, but intended to make it clear that he expected even more improvement. He had also decided to talk to a few of the employees to see how they felt about the department and the way Ron was supervising it.

Later that afternoon, Ron went for his customary walk around the department. He stopped at Pete Stallworth's station and asked how things were going. Pete was young, married, and he and his wife had just had twins. He seemed excited about the changes Ron had made.

"You know, Ron, I had asked Charlie more than a year ago to hire a gopher. I was able to increase my output by a little over 13 percent last week! The bonus that JBS

Case continues . . .

Case (cont.)

pays for output over the standard is extra money in my pay envelope that really helps. It helps me keep my mind on my job, too. I used to hate having to interrupt what I was doing to go get materials myself.''

"Great," Ron replied. "Keep up the good work." Still he wondered why departmental productivity showed only a 4 percent increase when Pete had managed to increase his output by more than 13 percent.

Ron walked over to Tom Burgess, one of the older employees in the department. Tom had been with JBS ever since graduating from high school twenty-two years ago and had been in the cutting department for the last seven years. "How's it going Tom?" Ron inquired.

"Pretty good, Ron—except I never seem to be able to find that new guy you just hired when I'm about to run out of materials. I think I can go get them myself much quicker than if I waited around for that guy. Charlie never thought it was necessary to have a gopher for us. If you had asked me before you hired that guy, I'd have advised you against it.''

"Well, just give it some more time, Tom," Ron replied. "I think it will work after we all get used to it.''

Ron walked back to his office and pulled out the individual productivity reports. Pete's output had gone up the most, increasing by 13.4 percent. Tom's was the lowest. It had actually gone down 3 percent! The performances of the other employees were scattered between these two extremes. After looking at the report for some time, he noticed that the younger employees, as a group, had done better than the older employees, and wondered what might account for this.

Ron decided that he would try to motivate the older employees by posting the productivity reports on the departmental bulletin board each week. When the older employees see how much better the younger employees are performing, they'll have to try to keep up, Ron thought as he pulled his car into the driveway of his house.

Questions

1. Why do you think that some of the employees in the department did not respond positively to Ron's changes? Why did some, like Pete, respond very well?
2. How would you analyze Ron's leadership style? Is this the leadership style that the situation requires?
3. What would you have done differently if you had taken over the department after Charlie's retirement?
4. Assume that you have just taken over the department from Ron. What would you do?

Chapter 7

Authority, Responsibility, and Delegation

Learning Objectives

After reading this chapter, you should:

1. be able to differentiate among authority, responsibility, and accountability.
2. understand the difference between formal and informal authority.
3. be able to explain how informal authority is developed.
4. understand the delegation process.
5. recognize why some supervisors are reluctant to delegate.
6. recognize why some employees are reluctant to assume responsibility.
7. understand the relationship between authority and responsibility.
8. be able to discuss the benefits of delegation.
9. be aware of the relationship between delegation and decentralization.
10. be able to present several ways of achieving successful delegation.

Several supervisors from the payroll department at JBS Manufacturing had gathered around Helen's desk, as they always did after work. Helen enjoyed these few minutes with the other supervisors. It gave her a chance to compare notes with them and to talk over common problems. These informal meetings had been the source of several good ideas which Helen had been able to implement in her work group.

Tonight, Bob was complaining that his employees just didn't seem to want to accept any responsibility. "I've got my hands full with my own work, yet I spend half of my day checking on my employees and often helping them get their work out," he said. I end up doing work myself that my employees ought to be doing. I can get the work done more quickly and better, much of the time if I just go ahead and do it, rather than take the time to explain what needs to be done to them. Of course that means I'm here after hours quite a few nights trying to catch up on my own work."

Helen found Bob's remarks interesting. It was common knowledge that Bob's employees complained that Bob tried to do everything himself. His employees felt that Bob didn't trust them to get the work done on their own, or to handle important assignments. Helen wondered how Bob and his employees could differ so much in their perceptions of the situation. Bob seemed to want his employees to assume more responsibility, yet he thought they were trying to avoid it. Bob's employees seemed to want more responsibility, yet they thought that Bob was reluctant to give it to them.

Authority may be defined as the right to make decisions, to perform certain activities, or to direct others in the performance of activities leading to the accomplishment of organizational objectives. Implicit in this definition is the idea that a person who has authority also has the power to influence the behavior of others.

The five bases of power discussed in chapter 6 are closely related to authority.[1] Many people tend to equate authority with organizational position or with the ability to reward and punish. From this perspective, supervisors are regarded as having the right to act or to issue orders to others and to expect that these orders will be carried out. A supervisor who has authority, therefore, has the power to use penalties and rewards to see to it that the necessary activities are performed. This source of authority, called **formal authority,** is what sustains the legitimate, reward, and coercive bases of power.

Another source of authority within an organization is called **informal authority.** Informal authority is a term that has derived from Subordinate Acceptance Theory.[2] This theory suggests that supervisors can have as much authority as their employees will allow them. According to this view, authority exists when employees allow themselves to be directed; that is, supervisors have authority when employees accept them as authorities. Informal authority is what forms the foundation of the expertise and referent bases of power.

The notion of **subordinate acceptance** is an important one for supervisors to consider. Two supervisors in identical jobs at the same level in the organization have the same amount of formal authority. Even so, the amount of **real authority,** or total authority of each can be very different. For example, figure 7.1 Supervisor A and Supervisor B are in identical jobs at the same level in the organization. What a diagram of organizational structure cannot show is that Supervisor

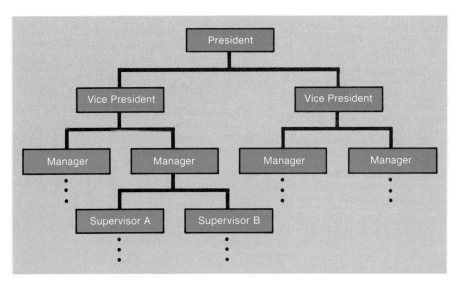

Figure 7.1
Representation of formal authority

B has a great deal more real authority because of the subordinate acceptance source of informal authority. Since the figure represents only formal authority, or the authority of organizational position, we do not know from this depiction of authority that Supervisor *B* has taken steps to increase the amount of informal authority. Assume that this is exactly what Supervisor *B* has done, and that, because of these efforts, employees are now more willing to accept Supervisor *B's* authority. Assume also, that Supervisor *A* has relied primarily upon the formal authority measures of reward and punishment to direct employee activities. Supervisor *A's* employees may comply with *A's* orders, but they are unlikely to do much more; instead, they will probably do as little as is required either to avoid punishment or to attain reward. Supervisor *B's* employees are more likely to be willing to put forth effort beyond the minimal acceptable level of performance because they more readily accept Supervisor *B's* authority (see fig. 7.2).

The amount of real authority that a supervisor has is a function of both formal and informal authority. In effect:

Real authority = Formal authority + Informal authority

Supervisors who develop their informal authority will have a great deal more real authority than supervisors who rely solely upon their formal authority.

In order to develop informal authority supervisors must promote and encourage a willingness, on the part of employees, to submit to supervisory attempts to influence behavior. Tannenbaum suggests that this is best accomplished by allowing employees to have more influence.[3] In other words, supervisors can, themselves, achieve more control or influence over employees by allowing those employees to exert more control. On the surface, this sounds a bit like circular logic, yet the principle on which this idea is based is not unlike that which underlies the notions of employee participation or the use of consideration behaviors

Figure 7.2
Effect of differences in
real authority on
performance

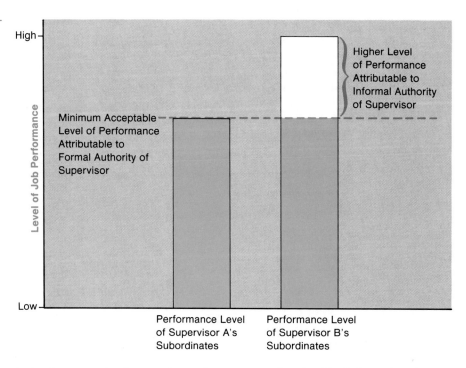

by leaders; namely, that employees become more involved in their work and more receptive to influence attempts by supervisors when the employees, themselves, have some control over their jobs.

The same author further asserts that many supervisors and managers are mistaken in assuming that the amount of authority or control in an organization is fixed or that there is only so much authority available in an organization. If this were the case, no one could gain any authority without someone else giving up or losing some. Tannenbaum disagrees, arguing that it is possible to increase the amount of authority within an organization, and that every individual could, potentially, gain authority at the same time.[4]

This can be accomplished, he explains, by allowing employees to exert more control. The supervisor does not lose authority to employees; instead, employees become more willing to be influenced by a manager who has given them some control over their work environments. The following is a list of activities that supervisors could engage in to increase their informal authority:

1. *Allow employees to participate* in important decisions that will affect their working environment.
2. *Do not rely solely upon a single source of power.* Particularly, do not use strictly legitimate, reward, or coercive power to influence the behavior of employees. Instead, increase the use of the referent and expert bases of power.

3. *Listen to employees.* Show interest in their ideas and suggestions. If employees believe that you are receptive to their ideas, they are more likely to be receptive to your attempts to influence their behavior.
4. *Encourage open communication.* Employees must believe that you are interested and willing to listen to their ideas and problems. Otherwise, they are not likely to make the effort to communicate with you on a regular basis.
5. *Display confidence and trust in employees.* First you must be reasonably sure that your employees are willing and capable workers, and so will perform successfully if given the opportunity to do so. If employees feel that you trust them to perform their jobs without close supervision, they will be more willing to be influenced by you.
6. *Keep employees informed about departmental and organizational plans and objectives.* Employees who are not kept informed about the activities of their department or organization may feel left out or isolated. Employees who are aware of what is going on in their organization are likely to feel more like an important member of that organization and, as such, are more likely to be willing to submit to supervisory authority.

Responsibility and Accountability

Responsibility and accountability are closely related to authority. Authority was defined as the right to make decisions or to take action. **Responsibility** is the obligation to perform that results from accepting authority. When you have the authority to take certain actions, you are also responsible for seeing to it that the actions are performed correctly.

Accountability, though very similar to responsibility, is a distinct form of obligation. Responsibility may be thought of as a self-perception of duty where accountability can be seen as more closely related to the perceptions of others. If you know that you have authority over certain activities, you feel responsible for making sure that they are performed correctly. Accountability, on the other hand, tends to be linked with the rewards and punishments administered *to* those who are responsible for particular tasks *by* those in authority. Your manager should hold you accountable for those activities for which you are responsible. If the activities are performed well, there may be some reward; similarly, if the activities for which you are responsible are not performed correctly, you may receive some form of punishment or have the reward withheld. An understanding of authority, responsibility, and accountability provides background useful in the consideration of the process of delegation.

Delegation

Delegation may be defined as the process by which supervisors assign a portion of their work to employees. Not only are specific jobs or tasks assigned in the delegation process, but to those assignments is attached the authority necessary to get them accomplished.

Advantages of Delegation

The advantages of delegation are several:

1. The primary reason that supervisors delegate to employees is to free up managerial time for dealing with more important matters.[5] Delegating creates more time for supervisors to actually supervise, rather than using it perform more technical tasks.
2. Delegating tasks reduces the job pressure of supervisors. It allows them to focus upon fewer and more critical tasks, and to do a better job on those.
3. Delegation may result in better job performance or decision making.[6] Many times employees are closer to the problem or have more experience in dealing with it. The expertise of the employee may be greater than that of the supervisor, in certain situations. If you, as supervisor, have not been as closely involved in certain activities as your employees, it makes sense to delegate relevant matters to them.
4. Delegation will often speed up decision making. Since employees do not have to get the supervisor's approval or wait for the supervisor's decision, those decisions will often be made more quickly. Valuable time is often lost while employees first seek the advice of their superiors before making a decision.
5. Delegation may increase the initiative and motivation of employees. Employees who need challenge, responsibility, and achievement are likely to respond positively to new tasks, decision-making opportunities, and the challenges that result from delegation.
6. Delegating tasks or decision-making responsibility may encourage the development of employees. One of the best ways to develop an employee is to assign a task or problem and allow that individual to generate a plan for dealing with it.
7. Delegation may result in increased job involvement and organizational commitment on the part of employees. If important tasks and decisions are delegated to employees, it is likely that they will feel more involved with their work and with the organization. Employees actively involved with the organization are more aware of organizational aims and are better able to see how their own jobs fit in with the broader workings of the organization.

Supervisor Reluctance to Delegate

Despite the advantages of delegating, many supervisors remain reluctant to do so.[7] This reluctance may be attributable to one or more of the following reasons:

1. *Inability to plan.* Many supervisors get so caught up in day-to-day activities that they are unable to plan activities in advance. Time must be set aside to plan work activities in order to facilitate delegation.
2. *Belief that only the supervisor can do it properly.* Some supervisors are reluctant to delegate to employees because they believe that they can perform the work better than those employees. If employees actually lack the ability,

then delegation is not appropriate in the first place. More often, this belief is simply the perception of supervisors. Even if employees do not currently have the skills, the supervisor may save time in the long run by taking time, now, to train them.[8]

3. *Insecurity of supervisor.* Some supervisors feel that if employees perform too well on tasks, they will become a threat to the supervisor's own advancement.

4. *Feeling that employees are already too busy.* Before employees are delegated additional tasks or decision-making responsibilities, their present workloads should be carefully analyzed. The supervisor should not feel reluctant to delegate additional activities to employees, however, particularly if those activities will contribute to their development.

5. *Unwillingness to let employees make mistakes.* Supervisors must be willing to allow employees to make mistakes when they undertake new activities. These mistakes should be turned into learning experiences for the employees. The long-run gains made toward employee development normally outweigh, by far, the mistakes made initially.

6. *Fear of losing control.* Some supervisors are reluctant to "let go," and hold tight to an apparent need to be on top of everything. These supervisors face a real danger of becoming overburdened with decisions to be made and tasks to be performed.

In the Introductory Incident, Bob was reluctant to delegate to his employees. It is difficult to determine, on the basis of the information provided, why this was the case. One might assume, however, that Bob was simply caught up in day-to-day operations and so, had never taken the time or made the effort to delegate to employees. Bob might find that if he took the time, now, to delegate certain activities and would teach the employees how to perform those activities, he would have more time for his own work, in the long run.

Employee Reluctance to Accept Delegation

Just as some supervisors are reluctant to delegate, some employees are reluctant to accept delegation. Typical reasons for this reluctance on the part of employees include the following: (a) they may be afraid that they will be criticized or punished if they fail; (b) they have been given no incentive for accepting additional responsibility; (c) they may be genuinely happy with their present situation and want to avoid change, or; (d) they may have low needs for challenge, achievement, or recognition.

Unfortunately, no clear answers to these problems have been discovered. It is clear, however, that when employees accept additional responsibility it means that they will have to work harder. There must be some reward making it worthwhile for employees to accept additional responsibility. Reward does not necessarily have to be immediate or of the extrinsic type, such as a salary increase. It could be given in the form of increased recognition, increased opportunity for promotion, or more challenging, motivating work. The kind of reward given is likely to differ depending on the characteristics of the individual in line for a reward.

It is important, also, that supervisors take the time to communicate with employees about the increased responsibility and what it is likely to mean. Otherwise, employees may perceive only that the supervisor is piling more work on top of them. Employees should perceive delegation in terms of development and increased opportunity. Just as important, supervisors must create a climate supportive of employees who want to try new things and stretch their abilities and knowledge. Employees must not be afraid of being punished for mistakes or they will not be willing to accept new responsibilities. Supervisors who have taken the time to develop both formal and informal authority should find their employees more receptive to increased delegation.

The Delegation Process in Action

The delegation process consists of three basic steps: assigning responsibility, giving authority, and demonstrating accountability.

Assigning Responsiblity

The supervisor assigns responsibility to the employee by giving the employee a task to perform or a decision to make. For example, the supervisor might place an employee in charge of preparing a report on the status of the organization's accident prevention program.

Giving Authority

The supervisor gives the employee the necessary authority to carry out assigned responsibiliites. For example, the supervisor might give the employee the power to require other departments to submit information concerning their accident rates and the specific actions they have taken to reduce accidents.

Demonstrating Accountability

The supervisor holds the employee accountable for results by creating an obligation to perform in the mind of the employee. Typically, accountability is demonstrated through the use of rewards and punishments. For example, when the accident prevention program is not completed on time, the employee receives a somewhat lower performance rating. Implicit in the delegation process is the idea that the employees' performances on delegated activities will be considered in their performance evaluations.

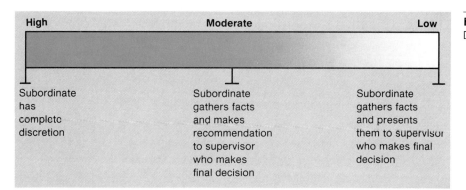

Figure 7.3
Degrees of delegation

Making Delegation Effective

Supervisors can do several things to increase the effectiveness of delegation.[9] First, delegation should be viewed as a matter of degree; that is, the amount of discretion or control employees are allowed can fall within a broad range (see fig. 7.3). In some cases, employees may be given complete freedom to take action, and in others, be permitted only to gather information and present it to the supervisor for a final decision. The amount of discretion given to any individual will be determined, in large part, by that employee's experience and ability to deal with the immediate problem or activity.[10] You, as supervisor, will have to make a determination, not only about whom to delegate an activity to, but what degree of delegation is most appropriate.

When assigning tasks or decisions to employees, you should take great care to clarify the associated goals and priorities. Make sure the employee clearly understands what results are expected. You may find it helpful to get together with the employee to set some goals for the project, including the time frame within which the task must be accomplished or the decision made. Future conflicts or disagreements about what was to be accomplished may be prevented by putting these goals in writing.

When delegating authority, be as specific as possible. Take great care to explain to employees exactly what they do, and do not, have the authority to do. A management principle known as the **Parity of Authority and Responsibility Principle** is one that should guide your behavior in supervisory situations. This principle states that the degree of responsiblity placed upon an employee and, therefore, the extent to which that individual may be held accountable, should equal the degree of authority that individual is accorded. Put more simply, employees should be given enough authority to accomplish their tasks, but not more than is required. At the same time, employees should not be held accountable for activities that they had insufficient authority to accomplish.

Table 7.1	Tips for Effective Delegation
	1. Identify which activities or decisions to delegate
	2. Select the right employee
	3. Clarify goals, priorities, and results expected
	4. Clearly define authority and responsibility
	5. Establish controls
	6. Monitor progress

Supervisors should continually monitor the progress of employees as they work toward completing delegated tasks. This does not mean that you should spend all of your time checking up on employees. This would erase all you have gained from delegation. Not only would it take up the time you have gained by delegating to employees, but it might also make employees uncomfortable to have you watching them so closely. It is important to monitor employees' progress, but you can accomplish that without standing over their shoulders. It may be possible to build some sort of control mechanism into the delegation process. At the same time that objectives and goals are set and agreed upon, you can agree upon the type and timing of the progress reports that the employee will make to you. The more objective the information contained in these reports, the less time you will have to spend checking upon employees. If your aim is to help employees to develop, then the key is to specify *what* you want accomplished, not *how* it should be accomplished. Allow employees to develop their own methods for achieving the desired results. You will need to make sure that communication channels are kept open so that you become aware very quickly of any problems that the employee cannot handle. You should not, however, rush in at the first sign of trouble. Give the employee an opportunity to deal with the problem first.

Success in the delegation process depends largely upon your ability to communicate effectively with your employees. Employees must have a clear understanding of their responsibilities, the extent of their authority, and the results that they are expected to achieve. If you are delegating to an employee for the first time, you may need to spend much more time communicating with this person than you would someone with whom you have previously worked. You will need to take extra care to ensure that authority, responsibility, and results are understood and accepted. You may also want to communicate with any others who may be affected by this employee's activities. These people may need to be told that the employee has been given some additional authority so that they can be prepared to be cooperative when that individual begins the assigned activities. This is especially important when you are granting the employee the authority to do things not normally done by a person in such a position.

One other principle of management deserves mention at this point. The **Principle of Absoluteness of Responsibility** states that responsibility cannot be delegated, meaning that supervisors cannot escape responsibilty for activities by delegating them to their employees. As a supervisor, you are still ultimately responsible for the completion of activities, even if you have delegated those activities to employees.

The extent to which a supervisor delegates authority is closely related to the degree to which the organization is centralized or decentralized in terms of authority. Delegation has been defined as the process by which a supervisor or manager assigns authority to a lower level in the organization. Remember that decentralization refers to the degree to which authority has been assigned to lower levels throughout the organization. The greater the amount of authority assigned at lower levels, the more decentralized the organization. The more that authority is retained by top-level managers, the more centralized the organization.

Three features of an organization indicate the degree to which it is decentralized. In general, decentralization increases as (a) a greater number of decisions are made at lower levels in the organization; (b) more important decisions are made at lower levels in the organization, and; (c) superiors do less checking on the decisions made at lower levels. **Decentralization** may be viewed, therefore, as the change in organizational decision making that takes place when all supervisors and managers within that organization take part in the delegation process. If most managers in an organization delegate a large number of important decisions and activities, the organization tends to decentralize.

The advantages of decentralization are similar to the advantages of delegation, except that these advantages are enjoyed on an organization-wide basis rather than within one department or work group, only. The organization becomes more responsive and reacts more quickly to both threats and opportunities because decisions can be made at lower levels. Employees do not have to send information up to superiors and wait for a response. Decentralization generally results in a better trained, more highly motivated work force because employees participate more in, and have more control over, their jobs.

Summary

Authority is defined as the right to make decisions, to perform certain activities, or to direct others in the performance of activities, leading to the accomplishment of organizational objectives. As such, authority is closely related to power. Supervisors need to develop as many of the five bases of power as possible. There are likely to be negative outcomes associated with the long-term use of legitimate, reward, and coercive power.

Formal authority arises from the position held within an organization and is related to the legitimate, reward, and coercive bases of power. Informal authority stems from the degree to which employees are receptive to the supervisor's use of authority or influence and, therefore, is more closely associated with the expertise and referent power bases. The amount of real authority that any supervisor has is a product of both formal and informal authority.

Authority, responsibility, and accountability are closely related. Responsibility may be thought of as the self-perceived obligation to perform that results from accepting delegated authority. Accountability has to do with the idea that the performance of delegated activities will be monitored and that rewards and punishments will be administered on the basis of that performance. All three are important to the process of delegation.

Delegation is the process by which supervisors assign a portion of their work to employees. It requires that specific tasks or decisions be assigned to employees, that those employees be granted the necessary authority to perform those tasks, and that they then be held accountable for the results. While there are a number of recognized advantages to delegation, many supervisors are reluctant to implement that process, just as many employees are reluctant to accept delegation. Supervisors must plan their delegation activities carefully in order to ensure their effectiveness.

Key Terms

accountability (p. 145)
authority (p. 142)
decentralization (p. 151)
delegation (p. 145)
formal authority (p. 142)
informal authority (p. 142)
Parity of Authority and Responsibility
    Principle (p. 149)

Principle of Absoluteness of
    Responsibility (p. 150)
real (total) authority (p. 142)
responsibility (p. 145)
subordinate acceptance (p. 142)

Questions for Discussion

1. Define and differentiate among the following terms:
   a. authority
   b. responsibility
   c. accountability
2. Describe the delegation process.
3. Why are some supervisors reluctant to delegate authority to employees?
4. Why are some employees reluctant to accept delegation?
5. What can supervisors do to make delegation as effective as possible?
6. What are the advantages and disadvantages of delegation?
7. Explain centralization and decentralization.
8. When should an organization be decentralized?
9. Explain the Parity of Authority and Responsibility Principle.
10. Explain the Principal of Absoluteness of Responsibility.

References

1. J. R. P. French and B. Raven, "The Bases of Social Power," in *Group Dynamics,* ed. D. Cartwright and A. F. Zander, 2nd ed. (Evanston, Ill.: Row, Peterson, 1960), 607–623.
2. C. I. Barnard, *The Functions of the Executive* (Cambridge, Mass.: Harvard University Press, 1938).
3. A. S. Tannenbaum, "Control in Organizations: Individual Adjustment and Organizational Performance," *Administrative Science Quarterly* 7 (1962): 236–257.
4. Ibid.
5. H. K. Baker and S. R. Holmberg, "Stepping Up to Supervision: Mastering Delegation," *Supervisory Management* 26 (October 1981): 17–18.

6. J. G. Lagges, "Role of Delegation in Improving Productivity," *Personnel Journal* 58 (1979): 776–779.
7. E. Raudsepp, "Why Supervisors Don't Delegate," *Supervision* 41 (1979): 12–15.
8. S. Dowst, "Delegate Like a Pro to Gain More Time," *Purchasing* 86 (1979): 97.
9. D. Arthur, "Guidelines for Effective Delegation," *Supervisory Management* 24 (1979): 9–13.
10. A. E. Brill, "Delegation: It's Harder than It Looks," *Journal of Systems Management* 30 (1979): 36–37.

Recall that chapter 6 examined leadership from a contingency perspective, and suggested that particular situations call for particular leadership styles. It is also possible to view the process of delegation from a contingency perspective. In other words, some situations call for no delegation, some situations call for a little delegation, others call for high levels of delegation. List situational variables calling for:

Exercise

How Much to Delegate?

1. Low levels of delegation
2. Moderate levels of delegation
3. High levels of delegation

Bill has been a supervisor in the order processing department at JBS Manufacturing for about six months. In this job he supervises seven clerical employees as they process customer orders and supplier invoices for payment. Eight such work groups comprise the order processing department. Once an employee learns the account codes and special forms that JBS uses, the work required is relatively simple. The only difficult part of the job is making sure that transactions are recorded in the correct accounts. If a sale is recorded in the wrong account, someone from the accounting department catches it at the end of the month and a request for a sales correction form is sent to Bill's department. This form authorizes the removal of the sale from the incorrect account and its transfer to the correct account number.

By the end of six months, Bill had learned his job well. In fact, he had his employees so well trained that they seldom came to him with any questions and he quite often found himself with nothing to do for a large part of the day. About a month ago he told his boss that he was available to take on some additional assignments. He specifically asked for something that he could really get his teeth into. Bill had been going to night school to complete his degree and had recently taken some advanced management courses. He felt that his current job wasn't providing enough of a challenge.

This morning Bill's boss called him into his office and asked if Bill would be interested in a special assignment. It seemed that not all of the department's work groups were operating as well as Bill's. One problem was that turnover was relatively high in the department. For example, in Bill's own group of seven employees, he could expect to have to replace at least two of them during the course of the year. These jobs did not pay very well and many people used them as kind of a stepping stone while waiting to get into school or while looking for a better job.

The special assignment Bill was given was to develop a training program for the clerical employees. The department manager reasoned that all new employees could go through this program during their first few days on the job and that this might reduce the number of incorrectly recorded sales. By training the employees very soon after they were hired, the problem of high turnover would not greatly affect these results. As it was now, it seemed that employees would leave just as they were beginning to know the job and just as their error rates were decreasing. Then a new employee would be hired, and the error rate would rise dramatically once again.

Bill said that this sounded like a project he would really enjoy, and asked when it should be completed and what the program should involve. The boss responded by saying, "Bill, this is your project. I need it to be completed within two months, but the particulars are up to you. I know you've been after me to delegate more responsibility to you, so here you are. My only objective is to lower the error rate in the department. Whatever you want to include in this training program is fine with me, as long as you accomplish that objective."

Bill said that it all sounded good to him and left to begin preparing some notes. On his way out, he asked if the boss would prepare a memo to the other supervisors and employees in the department informing them of his assignment. Bill felt that the distribution of a memo would encourage the cooperation of the others should he find he needed their information or assistance.

The next morning all order processing department employees received the following memo from the department manager:

Interoffice Memorandum

From: George Wilcox, Manager Order Processing Department

To: All Departmental Employees

Re: Special Assignment to Bill Hailey

Yesterday, Bill Hailey agreed to take on a special project in addition to his regular duties. This project involves the development and implementation of a training program for newly-hired employees in our department. Bill has complete authority for this project. Please give him your full cooperation.

For the next two weeks, Bill busied himself collecting information about the other work groups in the department. He found that each work group used its own set of forms and procedures. While all of the work groups performed such activities as billing customers and paying suppliers, each work group dealt with its own set of products. Differences in supplier terms and methods of handling different kinds of products made it difficult to standardize work in the department. While this discovery promised to make things a little more difficult than he expected, Bill still felt confident that he could develop a good training program. He decided to talk with all of the other supervisors to get their ideas on what the training should include. It soon became evident, however, that they didn't want to talk with Bill about the project. Many expressed doubts about the venture, as a whole. Others just seemed too caught up in day-to-day activities to give Bill any time.

After two months, Bill had completed his assignment. He had put together a two-day series of lectures, slide presentations, a short movie, and a walking tour of the plant. Topics covered everything from company history to the basic manufacturing process. Following is the outline for the training program:

New Employee Training Program Schedule

DAY 1

8:00–9:30: Registration, coffee, Welcome from Manager George Wilcox, Order Processing Department.

9:30–10:30: Slide presentation on the history of JBS Manufacturing Company

Case continues . . .

Case (cont.)

10:30–10:45:	Coffee break
10:45–12:00:	Walking tour of JBS facilities
12:00–1:30:	Lunch in JBS cafeteria
1:30–3:00:	Lecture by Manager, George Wilcox, Order Processing Department. Topic: "Activities of the Order Processing Department and Their Relationship to Other Departments."
3:00–3:15:	Coffee break
3:15–4:30:	Movie on the products produced by JBS and the types of customers served
4:30–5:00:	Question-and-answer period with Bill Hailey

DAY 2

8:00–12:00:	On-the-job training. New employee will sit with a current employee in his or her future department and observe work methods
12:00–1:00:	Lunch
1:00–4:00:	Continue to observe work methods
4:00–5:00:	Question-and-answer period with Bill Hailey

Bill presented his proposal to his boss, who said it looked great and should be implemented as soon as possible. It soon became obvious that the department manager very much enjoyed talking with the new employees during the course of the training program. In fact, he asked Bill if he could rearrange the schedule to give him more than the hour and a half that the proposal specified.

Three months after the implementation of the new training program, Bill and George met to discuss the progress made. There had been no change, whatsoever, in the error rate of the department. Apparently the new training program had not had any effect upon the problem.

Questions

1. What is your analysis of the case? What went wrong here?
2. What errors in delegation were made by George Wilcox?
3. Did Bill Hailey make any errors in accepting delegation?
4. If you were George Wilcox's replacement, what would be your next move to correct the situation?

Chapter 8

Communicating with Employees

Learning Objectives

After reading this chapter, you should:

1. be aware of the major factors influencing the perceptual process.
2. understand how perception influences communication.
3. be able to discuss the major barriers to effective communication.
4. be aware of several categories of nonverbal cues.
5. recognize the importance of providing feedback.
6. understand how to provide constructive feedback.
7. be able to describe how to listen more effectively.
8. understand the significance of the grapevine as an organizational system of communication.

7:30 A.M.   Tony, a supervisor in the finishing department at JBS Manufacturing arrives early to work in order to finish a memo to his superior.

7:50 A.M.   Tony finishes the memo and places it in the organizational mail system. He then heads for the cafeteria to get cup of coffee before his employees arrive for work.

7:55 A.M.   Tony runs into one of his employees, who asks Tony to explain the company policy on leaves of absence.

8:00 A.M.   Tony arrives back at his desk where another of his employees is waiting with a question about the work assignments for the day.

8:25 A.M.   Tony receives a phone call from his boss asking if Tony can make a department supervisors' meeting scheduled for that afternoon.

8:45 A.M.   The morning mail arrives at Tony's desk. Among the contents is a letter from an old college friend, productivity reports, inventory reports, financial statements, the company newsletter, and an announcement regarding the company golf tournament.

9:30 A.M.   Tony receives another call from his boss who asks Tony to prepare a special report on the efficiency of some new equipment recently installed in Tony's department.

9:37 A.M.   An employee walks in to Tony's office complaining about a coworker who is not pulling his weight. Tony promises to speak with the employee.

9:52 A.M.   Tony places a call to the company supply department to see what has been holding up the supplies he ordered last week.

10:08 A.M.   A production management class from the local university arrives for a tour. Tony walks around the plant with them, explaining the manufacturing process and answering questions.

10:26 A.M   Tony begins writing the efficiency report that his boss requested.

10:41 A.M.   Tony takes a break from preparing the report and walks out among his employees. He stops and asks Tom how the work is going. Tom replies that everything if fine; however, something about his tone of voice and facial expression suggests to Tony that something is bothering Tom. Tony makes a mental note to spend some time with Tom when he isn't so busy.

11:07 A.M.   When Tony gets back to his desk, one of the other supervisors is waiting to talk with him about a problem employee. Since Tony has been with JBS for twelve years, the other supervisors often come to him for advice. Tony listens to the problem and then suggests that he talk with the personnel manager.

11:30 A.M   Tony calls Bob, one of the other supervisors, and arranges to meet him for lunch to discuss how to handle the new quality control procedures.

Communication is an extremely important aspect of any supervisor's job, yet it is one that tends to be taken for granted. It is easy to become complacent about communicating, but complacency is what causes problems to arise. Most supervisors could improve the effectiveness of their communications if they took more time to plan them.

The Introductory Incident highlights the amount of time each day that supervisors spend communicating. Research has suggested that managers spend between 50 and 70 percent of their time engaged in some form of communication.[1] If this figure is at all accurate, communication is a topic that deserves a great deal of attention. This chapter will focus upon several of the forces or processes that are known to reduce the effectiveness of communication. Several specific communication activities will also be discussed. These activities will include nonverbal communication, listening, and providing feedback.

© 1984 King Features Syndicate, Inc. World Rights Reserved.

Many problems of communication stem from problems of **perception.** The words that we use in messages and the ways in which we receive and interpret messages are filtered through our perceptions. Since everyone perceives the world in ways a little different from everyone else, messages are often interpreted in ways that were not intended by the senders of those messages.

Perception

The common characteristics of the perceptual process can be divided into the two categories of external influences and internal influences.

External Influences

External influences upon the perceptual process have to do with the physical properties of objects. In effect, the brightest, loudest, most colorful, and biggest objects tend to be noticed. An object much different from, or contrasting greatly with, objects surrounding it will tend to be noticed. For example, advertisers typically use a great deal of color in their advertisements. On a magazine page filled with full-color advertisements, however, a simple black and white advertisement may be the most noticeable. In the army, recruits are taught to move very slowly across an open field in order to avoid detection. A fast-moving object or quick movement is very noticeable against a stationary background.

In the communication process, an awareness of physical factors can be useful in increasing the likelihood that a message will be received. The manipulation of physical factors cannot, however, ensure that the message will be perceived. Organizational life is full of stimuli that constantly bombard the individuals working within that system. People talking, office noises, and written messages are but a few examples of that stimuli. We cannot process all of the information that we are exposed to and have no alternative but to screen some of it out. Internal factors and external factors, together, operate to sort out those messages and objects which are perceived from those which are screened out. This process of screening out some stimuli, while allowing others to penetrate our perceptions, is called **selective perception.**

Internal Influences

Internal influences consist of our beliefs, values, and needs. This form of influence can be summed up in the old saying, "you see what you want to see and hear what you want to hear." Basically, we all tend to notice things that are consistent with our beliefs, values, and needs. Perhaps you drive down a stretch of highway every day on your way to school or work. How many of the billboards along that stretch of highway can you describe in any detail? Most of us could not even name the product or brand advertised on more than one or two. Those that we tend to notice usually have some association in our minds with a product or service that interests us particularly. Though we have been exposed to all of the billboards, we perceive only those that are somehow related to a strong belief, value, or need.

A perceptual problem related to this notion of internal influences is called **perceptual set,** and occurs when we see what we expect to see. We prepare ourselves to see something, and we see it whether it is really there or not. Authors often wrestle with this problem when they proofread. They are so familiar with the material that it becomes difficult to spot errors even though they seem obvious to someone else. As they read a sentence they see the word that they intended to write down instead of the one that is actually there in print. A similar process occurs in verbal communications. We tend to hear messages that are consistent with our values and beliefs, or that are related to some need. In a room full of people at a party, for example, you are likely to hear someone talking about a subject you find interesting while you easily ignore messages about other topics. You are more likely to hear a message that is consistent with your beliefs than one that conflicts with your beliefs. Messages containing information in contradiction with our beliefs and values make us uncomfortable, so we very often screen them out.

A somewhat different perceptual problem is called **closure,** occurring when we fill the gaps in the information that we receive. When we get a message that is incomplete, we often fill in the unknowns ourselves, unconsciously supplying the information that we might expect to be there or would like to be there. For example, an inteviewer tends to fill those gaps with information consistent with the rest of what was learned in the interview. If a supervisor interviews a very good applicant and later finds that some information is missing, that supervisor is likely to stop those gaps with positive information. The reverse happens for the applicant with poor qualifications. Since what is known of the applicant's qualifications place that individual in an unfavorable light, we are likely to assume that the qualifications about which we know nothing are equally poor.

The Basic Communication Process

If you were to construct a simple model of the communication process, it could look like the one in figure 8.1. This model incorporates a sender, whose function is to **encode** a message; a medium, that will **transmit** the message; and a receiver, who takes in and interprets, or **decodes,** the message. The accuracy of both the encoding and decoding processes depends heavily upon the perceptual process.

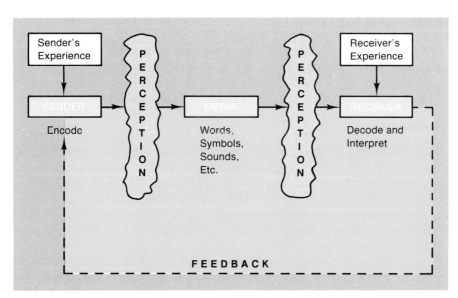

Figure 8.1
The basic communication
process

Your perceptions will influence the words and symbols you choose to include in your message, just as the receiver's perceptions will influence the way in which the message is received and interpreted.

As a message sender, you use your experience and perceptions as the basis for deciding what words and symbols to include in a message. You are likely to choose words that have special meaning for you, or that you interpret in a particular manner. Communication problems arise when senders simply assume that others are interpreting words and symbols as they do. As message senders, we need to become aware of the way in which our personal experiences and perceptions can influence the words, facial expressions, and gestures that we use in communicating with others. We need to be aware, as well, that receivers have had a different set of experiences and might perceive the world in ways different from each other and from ourselves.

Similarly, receivers have no alternative but to receive and interpret messages in light of their own experiences. As receivers of messages, we have a tendency to try to make those messages fit, or be consistent with, other information we have received. If it cannot be neatly pigeonholed in one of our existing categories of information, we may have difficulty interpreting the message. Some suggestions for minimizing these problems will be given later in the chapter.

Nonverbal Communication

The nonverbal elements of a message have more of an impact upon receivers than the verbal portions. Research suggests that only about 7 percent of a message is transmitted by words.[2] The remaining 93 percent is communicated through such **nonverbal cues** as tone of voice, body motion, gestures, and facial expression. Recall a time when someone told you something that seemed inconsistent with their tone of voice or facial expression. Which message did you believe? Most people tend to believe the nonverbal message when it conflicts with the verbal message.

The following categories of nonverbal cues have been identified: environment, proxemics, postures, gestures, facial expressions, head/face/eye behavior, and vocalics.[3]

Environment

The **environment** is the setting in which the communication takes place. The features of environment relevant to communication include room color, temperature, lighting, furniture, and time elements. Particular colors have been found to be associated with different moods.[4] The color red has been found to generate an exciting, stimulating mood in many people, while blue creates a secure, comfortable mood. Orange creates a distressed, disturbed mood in some people, and yellow has been known to produce a cheerful mood. Black has been found to create an unhappy or melancholy mood in some, but a powerful, masterful mood in others. The effects of these colors may vary with different individuals. For example, it has also been shown that the color red produces a protective, defending mood in some people, but a defiant or hostile mood in others.

There is little doubt that color has the potential to affect the moods of people. Supervisors must be aware of this potential and try to analyze the environment in advance of communications. For example, if you must provide constructive feedback to an employee who has been having performance problems, it might not be a good idea to do so in an orange or red room. If the communication takes place in a blue room, on the other hand, chances may be improved that the message will be interpreted by the employee as you intended, and that the communication will bring about the desired effect.

Temperature, lighting, furniture arrangement, and attractiveness of surroundings have relatively obvious effects upon the communication process. If you sit behind your desk and require an employee to sit in a chair in front of your desk, the furniture arrangement may impair the communication. The desk is a symbol of power and status and it stands between you and the employee. It is difficult for employees to be uninfluenced by this furniture arrangement. If you want the employee to communicate openly it might be a better idea to eliminate such symbols from view and, therefore, eliminate them as potential influential factors in the discussion. Instead, you might come around from behind your desk and sit beside the employee in a similar chair or, perhaps, hold the meeting in the cafeteria over a cup of coffee.

Dim lighting could make the environment seem intimate and personal, while strong light may cause the employee to be less open during communication. Temperatures either too high or too low can make the employee uncomfortable to the point that communication is impaired.

Time elements require a bit more explanation. There are three time elements of which supervisors should be aware.[5] These are: how long an employee must wait to see the supervisor, how much time the supervisor devotes to the meeting with the employee, and how frequently the supervisor communicates with the employee. Each of these three elements gives the employee a message. It can be very uncomfortable for employees to go long periods of time without any interaction with their supervisor. Most employees interpret in negative terms this absence of communication with their supervisor. They could easily feel that they have done something wrong, or that the supervisor does not view them as very important. Employees are likely to perceive the situation similarly if they are forced either to wait for long periods of time before they can get in to see you, or if you cut the meeting short.

It requires little expenditure of time or effort to stop and talk with employees, even if you have nothing of importance to say. Your attention lets employees know that you haven't forgotten about them and keeps the lines of communication open. When real problems or questions develop, employees will be more likely to bring them to your attention if you have already invested a little time showing them that you are approachable. A casual conversation with an employee on a busy day might seem like a poor use of time; however, it may pay off in the long run in terms of keeping communication channels open.

Proxemics

Proxemics refers to the physical location of individuals relative to the physical location of others. Research has found that status differences are emphasized by physical distance and minimized by closeness.[6] If you minimize the physical distance between yourself and an employee, it may increase the openness of the communication by reducing the effects of status differences. You should be aware, however, that not everyone will feel comfortable with this reduction of space. Proxemics research has identified four interpersonal space zones.[7] Intimate distance ranges from physical contact to eighteen inches; personal distance ranges from eighteen inches to four feet; social-consultative distance ranges from four to eight feet; and public distance is greater than eight feet. Intimacy is increased as the space between people is decreased; thus, unless you already have a close personal relationship with an employee, reducing the space to the intimate or personal range could make the person uncomfortable.

Postures

Postures, as a category of nonverbal communication, has to do with general body movements. Certain body movements, such as crossing one's arms or legs, or leaning backward, away from the other person, can be interpreted as dislike or as a lack of receptivity. It is possible that your messages are being filtered out or distorted if an employee holds these postures while you are talking. You might be better off waiting until another time to communicate with the employee. Other postures indicate openness or accessibility. These include any open stances, particularly involving the arms and legs.[8]

Gestures

Gestures are highly noticeable and relatively easy to interpret correctly. Gestures which indicate boredom, such as tapping a finger or pencil, or ones that suggest hostility, like clenching the fists, are easily noticed. Communications are not as likely to be effective when employees exhibit such gestures during that process of interchange. Supervisors must always be aware of the gestures of their employees and use them as guides in deciding whether the intended message has been received and interpreted accurately.

Head/Face/Eye Behaviors

Head, face, and eye behaviors convey a wide variety of nonverbal messages. Two of the more obvious head behaviors are head nods and head shakes. Head nods are said to indicate positive feelings or receptivity, whereas head shakes are interpreted as reflecting negative feelings or a lack of receptivity. Lowering the head and looking up, as if peering over one's glasses, and cocking the head slightly to one side indicates rejection or suspicion.[9]

Increased facial activity usually accompanies attempts to persuade people.[10] People seeking approval tend to smile more frequently.[11] Aside from the effect of the smile upon communication, facial expression may provide some insight into which employees have strong needs for approval or recognition and which do not as actively seek such feedback.

Eye contact is a very informative nonverbal cue. People tend to avoid eye contact when they wish to avoid communication, when they dislike the other person, or when they are trying to deceive the person. People tend to try to establish eye contact when they want to communicate and tend to be more receptive when messages are accompanied by eye contact.

Vocalics

Vocalics refers to characteristics of the voice, such as pitch, volume, quality, and rate of speech. For example, boredom is indicated by a moderate volume and rate of speech, with little variation in pitch (i.e. a monotone). Nervousness or excitement is indicated by a fast rate of speech, high volume, and high pitch. We often add things to our messages, unintentionally, through vocalics. Speakers who are unsure of their information or who are sending a message that they know contains inaccurate information will often speak loudly and quickly.

An awareness of these nonverbal cues can be of obvious help to supervisors in interpreting the messages they receive from employees. They can be just as helpful in sending messages. As noted, people tend to believe the nonverbal message when the verbal and nonverbal cues do not agree. Supervisors need to be aware of these nonverbal cues so that they can make every effort to send the same messages on both the verbal and nonverbal levels. Many cues are sent because we are not aware of their presence. For example, nonverbal cues indicating boredom or impatience, given off whenever an employee enters your office, may eventually damage your relations with that employee. Supervisors will very often be completely unaware that they sent these nonverbal cues. Later, they wonder what is wrong with the employee as they begin to notice that relations have deteriorated. A simple awareness and planning of communications that includes nonverbal cues can substantially increase the effectiveness of communications within an organizational setting.

Providing **feedback** to employees is one of the most important communication activities that supervisors perform. While supervisors give feedback, informally, almost on a daily basis, there are other occasions in which feedback takes on a more formal nature. Such occasions might include the performance evaluation feedback interview and counseling sessions. Formal feedback may be given during participative goal setting, as well. Generally, feedback is information provided to employees for their use in improving their performances; it may also be used to encourage and motivate employees. Often, however, feedback includes some information about what the employee has done incorrectly or about elements of performance that need improvement. It can be difficult to provide feedback in such a manner that it stays constructive and results in better performance. Unfortunately, many styles of giving feedback end up producing de-motivation and defensiveness on the part of the employee. The key to providing constructive feedback is to increase the receptiveness of the employee. If employees are not receptive to the feedback, they may not receive the message at all, or may receive a distorted version of the message.

Constructive
Feedback

Several characteristics identify **constructive feedback;** it is immediate, objective, specific, and corrective.

Feedback tends to have greater impact if it is given immediately after the behavior. Recall that the immediacy of reinforcement was identified in chapter 4 as a basic principle of operant conditioning. The closer the reinforcement to a behavior, the stronger will be the effect of the reinforcement on future behavior of that kind. Positive feedback is a reward or reinforcer for many people. Negative feedback, while not a reward, should follow soon after the behavior, also. If there is a behavioral or performance problem, negative feedback promptly administered gives the employee the opportunity to correct that behavior immediately. The faster the problem is corrected, the more quickly the employee can increase his or her contribution to the organization.

In order for feedback to be constructive, it must be objective or descriptive as opposed to evaluative. The word "you" should be avoided.[12] When an employee hears "you made a mistake on that assignment," that individual may very well become defensive and stop receiving, altogether, the message that is being sent. Those messages should not be evaluative. They should deal with specific behaviors that the employee can control. Feedback should focus on the work, rather than upon the person. It makes little sense to be critical of things the employee cannot control. For example, before criticizing an employee for being late with a report, it pays to determine why the report was late. It could be that necessary information from another department was not received. To be critical of employees for things beyond their control is likely to damage supervisor-employee relations.

Feedback must be specific, dealing with particular behaviors or particular areas of performance. It might be very good advice to tell an employee to be more cooperative, but that advice provides the employee with no real information. It is not clear what it means to be more cooperative. When you have finished providing constructive feedback, employees should know exactly what they must do and how to go about doing it.

Constructive feedback is designed to be helpful or corrective. It is not a good idea to provide feedback when you are angry or under stress because it is difficult to be objective in those emotional states. Any feedback given under such conditions is likely to be perceived by the employee as a personal attack or reprimand and seldom results in improved performance.

Listening

Listening has been defined as the process by which spoken language is converted to meaning in the mind.[13] This definition includes more than just hearing what is said. According to this definition, listening does not take place until a verbal message has been received and some meaning has been derived from that verbal message. As senders of messages, we want to take steps to ensure that the message is interpreted as we intend it to be; that is, we want to make sure that the meaning derived from the message is the meaning we transmitted. This will entail planning the communications, taking the experience and perceptual set of the receiver into consideration, and noting any display of nonverbal cues. On the other hand, as receivers of messages, we must take steps, as well, to ensure that we receive the meaning that was intended by the sender. Many misunderstandings between supervisor and employee can arise because of misinterpreted messages (see table 8.1).

While a great deal has been written about the sending portion of the communication process, it has been only recently that listening has received some of the attention it deserves. The concept of **active listening** places upon the listener, or receiver, the responsibility for receiving the message that the sender intended. Communication cannot occur until understanding has been transmitted from sender to receiver. It is incorrect to assume that the sender must shoulder all of the responsibility for transmitting the message and ensuring that it is received. Active listening places a demand upon receivers in the communication process, as well. There are several things that supervisors can do to become active listeners.

To be an active listener you must first understand the sender's message, and then use feedback to demonstrate that you are interested in what the sender has had to say. This technique can be extremely useful in dealing with an employee who is angry or upset. Active listening techniques include restatement, summarization, and response to nonverbal cues.

Missed Meanings in Supervisor-Employee Communications   Table 8.1

What the Boss Said . . .	What the Boss Meant . . .	What the Employee Heard . . .
"We've got to develop better housecleaning habits around here."	Maybe I should ask my boss if we can hire someone to clean up around these machines so the workers won't have to stop and do it.	Drop whatever you're doing and clean up this mess right now!
"Your performance was not what I expected it to be last month."	Your performance was okay for the first month on the job, but I know you can do much better.	If you don't improve your performance next month, you're fired!
"Yes, I know we need to talk about the changes you've suggested for your department, but I just don't have time right now."	My boss just called me and told me to bring the Clark report to his office immediately.	Don't bother me with any of your hair-brained ideas. I've got more important things to do!

Restatement

From time to time, feed back some of the message that you have received so far. **Restatement** gives the sender a chance to make corrections if you have made incorrect interpretations. Restatement also shows the sender that you are interested in what is being said and encourages the employee to continue communicating openly. If the employee is angry or upset, then responding objectively with a restatement of the facts may give the employee a chance to cool off. If you emphasize the objective facts of the situation, it may cause the employee to focus upon them rather than more emotional issues.

Example

"If I understand what you are saying, you feel that we made the wrong decision."

Summarization

As was the case with restatement, if you summarize what has been said from time to time, senders will get the chance to correct anything you have interpreted incorrectly. It also gives senders a chance to hear their own messages. Senders may wish to revise or retract some of what they have said after hearing the message spoken by someone else.

Example

"So far you have told me that the shipping department is not forwarding bills of lading to you and this has prevented you from completing your monthly reports."

Response to Nonverbal Cues

Since much of the content of any message is made up of nonverbal cues, feedback to the sender should include your interpretation of these cues to ensure that this interpretation is a correct one.

Example 1

"You have agreed to accept this assignment, however, the tone of your voice suggests that you may be somewhat reluctant."

Example 2

"You have agreed to these objectives but your facial expression indicates that you're unsure about something. Is there anything you would like to discuss with me?"

Example 3

"Judging from the way you said that, you're pretty angry about what has happened."

All active listening techniques are designed to provide the sender with opportunities to correct or revise what has been said. They are also supposed to encourage the sender to continue talking and providing information. The quotes just given as examples illustrate that the feedback is very objective in nature. You evaluate neither the sender nor the message. If you do, the sender is likely to become defensive and stop communicating openly. When the sender is angry or upset, active listening can bring perspective to the situation, allowing the person to look more objectively at the facts. Table 8.2 lists several other suggestions for becoming a better listener.

Two other areas of organizational communication are important for supervisors to understand. These are (a) the reasons why employees do not openly communicate and (b) the grapevine system of communication.

Why Employees Do Not Communicate

It is very important that employees not feel reluctant to initiate communication with their supervisors. Employees are often closer to day-to-day operations than supervisors and, as a result, often become aware of problems or opportunities before their supervisors. Employees may also discover better ways of performing work activities. Unless you have created a climate in which your employees feel comfortable about communicating upward, however, employees may not share this information with you.

How to Listen More Effectively

Table 8.2

1. *Do not try to anticipate* what the sender is going to say. If you are anticipating, you are not listening. Concentrate upon the verbal and nonverbal messages. Are these messages consistent?

2. *Do not evaluate the sender.* We often base our interpretations of the accuracy of a message upon some characteristics of the sender. Source credibility is defined as the believability of a message sender. If we believe that the sender has something to gain, we are less likely to believe the information in the message. If you are evaluating, you are not listening.

3. *Avoid distractions.* If you allow yourself to be distracted, you will miss some of the message. Concentrate upon the message.

4. *Listen to what is being said,* rather than how it is being said. Don't tune a speaker out simply because you don't like the style of delivery. Focus upon the message.

5. *Don't make any judgments until after the message has been sent.* If you become argumentative because of something said early in the conversation with which you do not happen to agree, you will miss the remainder of the message.

Employees may be reluctant to communicate with their supervisors for these reasons:

1. *They feel that supervisors don't listen.* If employees perceive that you are not really listening to them, they are not likely to continue to initiate communication with you. Some supervisors try to give the appearance that they are listening to their employees when, in fact, they are thinking about something else. Employees will become aware of these nonverbal cues and the message contained within that nonverbal communication will be clear to them. To those employees your lack of attention is saying, "I'm not really interested in what you have to say" or, "You're not important enough for me to listen to." For example, an employee once left a message that he wanted to speak to the boss. Near the end of the day, the supervisor stopped by the employee's desk to see what the message was about. The entire time the supervisor was there, he kept looking around the room and glancing at his watch. When the employee finished describing a problem he was having with a project, the supervisor immediately began talking about something else. It was clear to the employee that his supervisor hadn't been listening to what he had to say. The employee could only interpret this as a lack of interest on the part of the supervisor. Why would this employee continue to try to initiate communications with this supervisor?

2. *Employees don't see the results of their communications.* If employees offer suggestions and ideas about ways in which their work might be performed more effectively or efficiently, they will want to see some of these suggestions implemented. If there is a good reason why a suggestion cannot be used, the employee who made the suggestion should be informed. Employees are not likely to initiate communications if they do not receive feedback about their

earlier communications. Suppose an employee gives a great deal of thought to improving work methods and comes up with a slightly better way of doing things. She talks with her supervisor about her idea and is promised that her idea will be considered. Three months later she still hasn't heard anything further about it. Most people would rather find out their idea was rejected than hear nothing at all.

3. *Employees don't trust management.* Employees are not likely to communicate openly with supervisors if the climate is one of distrust and fear. If an employee makes a costly mistake, it is to your advantage to find out about it as quickly as possible so that it can be corrected. If employees believe that they will be punished or reprimanded for the mistake, they are likely to refrain from informing you about it immediately. Rather, they may try first to correct the problem on their own. If they are not successful, the problem has now had time to become more serious. It will be to your benefit to create a climate of trust and openness so that your employees will inform you immediately when problems arise.

4. *Employees perceive status differences.* Even if you create an open, trusting climate, there may still be some reluctance on the part of employees to initiate communication because you hold a position with more formal authority than do your employees. To some degree, you have the power to reward or punish these employees. You should work to minimize status differences between yourself and your employees so that they will feel more comfortable communicating openly with you.

The Grapevine System of Communication

The **grapevine** may be defined as a pattern of communications that does not follow any of the formal channels. Grapevine communication develops between informal groups within organizations. It is a system that typically arises because employees need more information than they are receiving by way of formal communication channels. If the organization does not provide certain information to employees, the grapevine will. A potential problem of the grapevine system is that it may not, in all instances, be able to supply information that is entirely accurate. One estimate suggests that grapevines are accurate 75 to 90 percent of the time. Still, the times when they are inaccurate can lead to serious problems.[14] For example, disgruntled employees often use the grapevine to spread rumors that create employee dissatisfaction.

Some authors suggest that supervisors should try to manage the grapevine. According to this plan, you would determine which employees seem to be most active in the grapevine and would develop personal relationships with them in an effort to encourage them to keep you informed of the information being sent within that system. Another suggestion is to plant information on the grapevine yourself. Most authors would agree, however, that the grapevine cannot be eliminated. It not only provides information needed by many employees, but it satisfies important personal needs for those employees who feel compelled to "be in the know."

Other authors have suggested that the best way to manage the grapevine is to improve upon formal communications. In effect, the organization and the supervisor should do a better job of keeping employees informed. If employees receive sufficient information from formal sources, they are less likely to rely upon the grapevine. In addition, the information they receive from formal sources is likely to be more accurate than information picked up through the grapevine.

Summary

Between 50 and 70 percent of a manager's or supervisor's time is spent involved in some form of communication. Yet, the tendency is to become complacent about our own ability to communicate effectively. The effectiveness of communications can be enhanced or hindered by our perceptions. Problems of communication can result from distortions of the perceptual process that may stem from external influences or internal influences. External influences relate to the physical properties of objects; internal influences involve selective perception, perceptual set, and closure.

Research has shown that only about 7 percent of a message is transmitted by words. The remainder is communicated through nonverbal cues. Categories of nonverbal cues include the environment, proxemics, postures, gestures, facial expressions, head/face/eye behaviors, and vocalics.

Feedback is one of the most important communication processes in which supervisors engage. Feedback is used to correct performance problems, and to encourage and motivate employees. For feedback to be constructive, it must be immediate, objective, specific, and corrective.

Much of the effectiveness of any communication depends upon the ability of the listener. Active listening involves concentrating upon the verbal and nonverbal message, and encouraging the sender by appearing to be interested in the message. It is also important in the active listening process to avoid distractions, learn to focus upon what is being said instead of how it is being said, and to refrain from evaluating the sender.

Employees may be reluctant to initiate upward communications with their supervisors if they perceive that the supervisor is not really interested in what they have to say, or if there is a lack of trust and openness between supervisor and employees. Supervisors must work to create a climate in which employees feel comfortable initiating upward communications.

The grapevine is a pattern of communications not sanctioned by the organization, and existing between informal work groups. Grapevines arise because employees are not receiving enough information through formal communication channels. While the grapevine can never be eliminated, it can be managed by improving formal communications.

Key Terms

active listening (p. 166)
closure (p. 160)
constructive feedback (p. 165)
decode (p. 160)
encode (p. 160)
environment (p. 162)
external influences (p. 159)
feedback (p. 165)
gestures (p. 164)
grapevine (p. 170)
head / face / eye behaviors (p. 164)

internal influences (p. 160)
listening (p. 166)
nonverbal cues (p. 161)
perception (p. 159)
perceptual set (p. 160)
postures (p. 163)
proxemics (p. 163)
restatement (p. 167)
selective perception (p. 159)
transmit (p. 160)
vocalics (p. 164)

Questions for Discussion

1. Explain how we can look directly at several objects and perceive only one or a few of them. What causes us to see some objects and not others?
2. How does the perceptual process influence the communication process?
3. What are the categories of nonverbal communication? Give examples of each.
4. Explain how the time element and color can affect communication.
5. What must supervisors do to ensure that the feedback they give employees is constructive?
6. Explain active listening. What are some of the ways listening effectiveness can be improved?
7. Why do grapevines develop in virtually every type of organization?
8. What can you, as a supervisor, do to manage the grapevine?

References

1. W. V. Haney, *Communication and Interpersonal Relations* (Homewood, Ill.: Richard D. Irwin, 1979).
2. A. Mehrabian, "Communication Without Words," *Psychology Today,* September 1968, 53–55.
3. M. Knapp, *Nonverbal Communication in Human Interaction,* 2nd ed. (New York: Holt, Rinehart, & Winston, 1978).
4. L. B. Wexner, "The Degree to Which Colors (Hues) Are Associated with Mood-Tones," *Journal of Applied Psychology* 38 (1954): 433–434.

5. J. E. Baird and G. K. Wieting, "Nonverbal Communication Can Be a Motivational Tool," *Personnel Journal* 58 (September 1979): 607–610, 625.

6. A. Mehrabian, "Significance of Posture and Position in the Communication of Attitude and Status Relationships," *Psychological Bulletin* 71 (1969): 359–372.

7. E. T. Hall, *The Hidden Dimension* (New York: Doubleday & Co., 1968).

8. Mehrabian, "Significance of Posture," 359–372.

9. J. H. Sheridan, "Are You a Victim of Nonverbal "Vibes"?" *Industry Week,* 10 July 1978, 36–42.

10. A. Mehrabian and M. Williams, "Nonverbal Concomitants of Perceived and Intended Persuasiveness," *Journal of Personality and Social Psychology* 13 (1969): 37–58.

11. H. Rosenfeld, "Instrumental Affiliative Functions of Facial and Gestural Expressions," *Journal of Personality and Social Psychology* 4 (1966): 65–72.

12. B. Weiss, "Constructing Your Criticism," *Supervisory Management* 26 (1981): 12–18.

13. S. W. Lundsteen, *Listening: Its Impact on Reading and the Other Language Arts* (Urbana, Ill. National Council of Teachers of English, 1971).

14. K. Davis, "Cut Those Rumors Down to Size," *Supervisory Management* 20 (June 1975): 2–7.

For each category of nonverbal cues, list at least five specific cues not discussed in the chapter. Interpret what message each cue conveys.

Compare your results with those of others. Did any of the interpretations differ?

Exercise

Nonverbal Cues

1. Environment
2. Proxemics
3. Postures
4. Gestures
5. Facial Expressions
6. Head/Face/Eye Behaviors
7. Vocalics

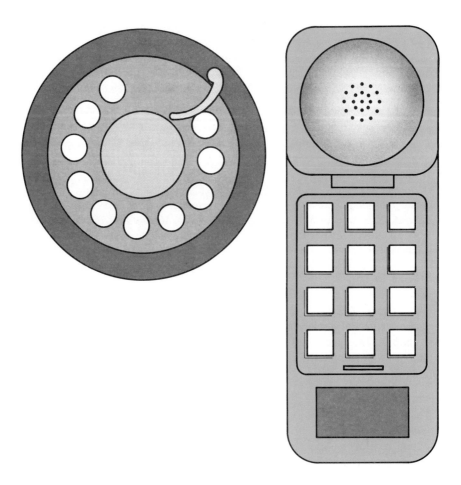

Exercise

How Perceptive Are You?

The purpose of this exercise is to demonstrate that we are not as perceptive as we might like to believe. This chapter has discussed many forms of perceptual selection and distortion that prevent us from really seeing the things that surround us every day.

You have been provided with the basic outline of the parts of a telephone. Your task is to supply the details to be found on this piece of equipment in making the sketch as complete as possible.

Kelly has been a supervisor in the mail room of JBS Manufacturing for ten months. Before that she had been one of the mail room clerks who sorted the company mail into the carts used by the messengers to deliver the mail to various departments within JBS. Kelly had worked in the mail room for five years before being promoted to supervisor.

During the time she was employed as a mail room clerk, Kelly had worked for two different supervisors. Both had been promoted to other divisions within JBS; however, Kelly felt that neither of these supervisors had seemed to care very much about their employees. The only communication that ever took place between these supervisors and the mail room employees, in Kelly's memory, was when they shouted orders about special packages or emergency deliveries. Kelly decided that she would not operate that way. She wanted her employees to feel comfortable communicating with her about any problems they were having, or making suggestions on ways to improve departmental work. She decided that the best way to accomplish this was to have an open door policy. Soon after she took over, Kelly typed the following intracompany memorandum and sent it to all her employees:

JBS MANUFACTURING COMPANY
Intracompany Memorandum

To: Mail Room Employees

From: Kelly West, Supervisor

Subject: Open door policy

In an effort to improve communication within the mail room, I'm instituting an open door policy. This means that my door is always open to you when you have a problem, question, or suggestion about work activities in the mail room. Please feel free to stop in and talk with me.

Soon after the memo was mailed, Earl Williams stopped in to see Kelly. "Kelly, I've got an idea how we can speed up mail sorting," he said. "It won't cost much and it should save us about two hours every day."

Case continues . . .

Case (cont.)

"Great, Earl," Kelly responded. "Send me a memorandum explaining what you think needs to be done. I'll review it and get back to you." Earl hesitated as if he had more to say, but then replied, "Okay, Kelly, I'll get it to you as soon as I can."

Several days later, Amy Anders knocked on Kelly's door, first thing one morning. "Kelly, I'm really tired of the way these departments treat us messengers," Amy complained. "You know they're supposed to separate their mail into first class, third class, air mail, and packages. Most of them don't bother to do that. To make matters worse, it seems that every department waits until I've sorted their mail, put it in my cart and gotten halfway down the hall before they call me back for some "important" mail they forgot to put in their mail bin. Can't we do something about this?" "You have to keep in mind, Amy, that we are a service department," Kelly explained. "Our mission is to provide mail service to departments within JBS so that they can proceed with their work uninterrupted. You just have to overlook some things."

"But Kelly," Amy argued, "it's not asking too much for these departments to separate their mail by class, is it?"

Kelly tried to explain her own position. "Look Amy," Kelly replied, "I don't have the kind of authority to go to these departments and order them to separate their mail. I wouldn't be in this job very long. Just do your job and don't worry about what other departments do." Kelly watched as Amy stormed out of the office and wondered if her open door policy was becoming more trouble than it was worth.

Questions

1. What do you think of Kelly's open door policy? Is it effective? Why or why not?
2. Analyze the communications that took place between Kelly and Earl. What do you think Kelly meant to say? What do you think Earl heard Kelly say?
3. How would you have handled the meeting with Earl?
4. Analyze the communications between Kelly and Amy. What did Kelly mean to say? What did Amy hear her say?
5. How would you have handled the meeting with Amy?
6. What does it take to have an effective open door policy?

Speaking in Front of a Group

From time to time you will be called upon to make a speech or presentation to a group. It may be an informal report given during the weekly supervisor's meeting about how your department is doing; or, it could be a more formal presentation. Unfortunately, many people are uncomfortable speaking in front of a group. In a recent survey, Americans ranked giving a speech as their greatest fear.[1] Fortunately, this fear can be overcome with some careful planning and preparation.

Preparation

If you are one of those people who get nervous when called upon to speak in front of a group, there is no substitute for preparation. Most people are nervous because they are unsure of themselves. Perhaps they have not had the opportunity to do much public speaking and, therefore, are unfamiliar with the activity entirely. It is not unusual to be uncomfortable doing something with which you are unfamiliar. For your first few speeches or presentations, you may actually want to overprepare. This preparation will include not only consideration of the topic and, perhaps, writing notes or a text; but it should also involve practice delivering the speech. As you become more comfortable with speaking in front of others, you will require less and less preparation.

Planning the Presentation

In planning your presentation, you need, first, to consider the specific purpose of your presentation in light of the characteristics of your audience. In other words, you will want to accomplish a specific purpose in making your presentation, such as informing or persuading your audience on some topic; but you must also consider how your audience is likely to respond to your presentation. This will involve trying to determine what your audience wants or expects to hear. You should consider such factors as how much detail to provide, how technical the presentation should be, and how much your audience already knows about your topic.

Few things will cause you to lose the attention of your audience more quickly than telling them something they already know or something they do not have the background to understand.

In preparing the content of your presentation, follow a basic outline that highlights the following:

1. *The purpose of the presentation.* Although your audience may be aware of the general purpose of your presentation, it is a good idea to restate the purpose as specifically as possible. This should be done in such a way as to catch the interest of the audience.[2] For example, you could say, "I'm going to talk to you for a few minutes about the new computer system the company is installing and how it is going to change our jobs." This introduction is much more attention getting than "My topic for today is the new computer system."

2. *The major points of discussion.* The discussion, or main body of the presentation, is made up of major points followed by facts, statistics, or research studies which support those points. Generally, it is inadvisable to try to cover too many major points in any one presentation. As you move from one point to the next during your presentation, you should alert the audience that you are doing so. For example, you might say, "Next, I'm going to explain our responsibilities for security once the new computer system is installed."

3. *The summary of key ideas.* Your presentation should conclude with a brief summary of what you have just said. You might also suggest some conclusions or implications that your audience might draw from your talk. For instance, "This is what the new computer system will mean for first-line supervisors."

An old saying observes this purpose–discussion–summary sequence of activities: "Tell the audience what you are going to tell them. Then tell them. Then tell them what you have told them."

During the Presentation

Under most circumstances it is not a good idea to read your presentation from a prepared text. Reading tends to make your presentation rather formal and dry, and you may sound rather monotonous to your audience, causing you to lose their attention. In addition, if you lose your place in the text, you may stumble for a few seconds (which will seem like hours to you), until you can relocate your spot.

It is probably best to practice your presentation until you can speak comfortably from a few notes. In general, the fewer notes the better and, ideally, those should refer only to the major points you want to be sure to cover. The disadvantages of having detailed notes are similar to those associated with reading from a prepared text.

After you gain some experience and confidence speaking in front of groups, you may be able to replace your notes with visual aids. Visual aids are materials that help the audience to focus upon a particular point. The overhead transparency is a good example of a visual aid. Usually, the visual aid makes a graphic display of some major point of the presentation. Or, it may be more of an outline of the major points to be addressed. Such a visual outline keeps the key elements of the presentation in front of the audience as you are discussing them. You can also use the visual aid as your own notes; this will make your presentation seem more relaxed and informal.

Another set of factors to consider during the presentation are the same non-verbal cues that were presented with the discussion of communication between two people. Some of the more common mistakes people make when speaking in front of a group are that they (a) talk too fast, (b) speak in a monotone, (c) talk too loudly or softly, and (d) fail to maintain eye contact.[3] When people are un-comfortable or nervous they very often begin to speak rapidly, and either too loudly or too softly. This is also a time they tend to develop a monotone and tend not to keep eye contact with the audience. All of these can cause the audience to focus more upon *how* the presentation is being made rather than *what* is in the presentation. You must appear relaxed and comfortable to your audience for your presentation to have its greatest impact. At least in part, this is accomplished by speaking in a normal voice (i.e., neither too fast nor too slow). You must vary your pitch, giving greater emphasis to more important words. The next time you are watching the evening news, listen carefully to the newsperson's delivery. Most of these trained speakers give a very wide fluctuation to their vocal pitch. In fact, if someone were to vary their pitch that much in an everyday conversation, you would probably wonder about them! What seems exaggerated in everyday conversation comes across as natural speech in a public speaking setting. Most people who have had little public speaking experience have difficulty with this; however, it only takes practice to become better. An excellent way to get this practice is to join a local Toastmasters or Toastmistresses club. These organizations offer the opportunity to practice public speaking and receive constructive criticism in a nonthreatening setting.

One way to make sure that you maintain eye contact with a large audience is to pick out several individuals in the audience and speak directly to them. These individuals should be at various locations in the audience—in the front-center of the room, the left-front, right-front, and left-rear. As you look from individual to individual, you will appear to be making eye contact with virtually everyone in the audience from time to time. This practice also seems to help reduce nervousness in speakers.

---

1. D. Wallechinsky and I. Wallace, *The Book of Lists* (New York: William Morrow Company, 1977).
2. A. D. Frank, *Communicating on the Job* (Glenview, Ill.: Scott, Foresman & Co., 1982).
3. W. S. Tracey, *Business and Professional Speaking,* 3rd ed. (Dubuque, Iowa: Wm. C. Brown Publishers, 1980).

References

Appendix

Written Communication

As a supervisor, you will have many occasions to write letters and memorandums. You will often want to record the results of a meeting in a memorandum to all participants summarizing what was decided. You may want to do something similar following certain informal discussions or agreements. Any time individuals have agreed orally to assume responsibility for activities or tasks, it is wise to put that agreement in writing, just in case any future disagreement or confusion should arise. Much of your written communication will take the form of an internal memorandum.

Memorandums have the advantage of being a quick and inexpensive form of communication. If you have a relatively simple message to communicate to others in the organization, this medium is probably the most appropriate. As is the case with any form of written communication, however, the disadvantage of the memorandum is that it is a one-way communication. The receiver has no opportunity to engage in active listening as part of the effort to ensure that the message received was the intended message. Because of this limitation, you must take extra care to make sure that your message is received and interpreted accurately.

Getting Started

Many people complain that when they have to write a letter, memorandum, or report, they just can't seem to get started. They may know what they want to say, but are unable to figure out how to say it. If you find yourself having difficulty getting started in this writing process, it may be a good idea to create an outline. Ask yourself what the primary idea is that you want to convey, and write it down. Then list several points in support of this idea. This procedure should organize and freshen the information in your mind so that you can begin writing.

Structuring the Letter or Memorandum

The most appropriate structure or format for most letters and memorandums is one which (a) begins with the main idea or message; (b) provides support to reinforce the main idea, and; (c) repeats or summarizes the main idea and describes what action, if any, you expect.

Tips for Writing Effectively   Table A. 1

Avoid big words when simple words will do.

Avoid technical jargon.

Use an active rather than passive voice. (''Ben completed the report on time'' instead of ''the report was completed on time.'')

Avoid cliches or popular sayings.

Use familiar words and phrases.

Be as brief as possible.

This format is appropriate for letters and memorandums being sent to people who are likely to be interested in the topic already or who will be pleased with the information in the memorandum.

For memorandums or letters likely to displease the recipient, a different format is suggested. In this case, it is not a good idea to start with the main idea or message. If you present the bad news right away, the reader is likely to become defensive or aggressive and miss the rest of the information contained in the letter or memorandum. For this type of written communication, the recommended format is to (a) begin with a neutral statement introducing the reason for the bad news. This statement should not give the reader any indication either that good news or bad news is to follow; (b) support the reasoning behind the bad news by presenting and analyzing the facts leading to this unpleasant decision or turn of events; (c) state the bad news, and; (d) close the letter or memorandum as positively as possible. Reemphasize the objective nature of the decision, suggest alternatives, and leave the door open to the possibility of future change. Your goal in writing letters or memorandums containing information likely to displease the reader is to persuade them to read your reasons and supporting information. In order to accomplish this, your reasons and supporting information must both be presented before the bad news, itself. Table A.1 gives some additional suggestions for writing effectively.

Writing Reports

Another form of written communication with which supervisors need to be familiar is that of the written report. You may not have to prepare written reports as frequently as you will write letters or memorandums, but when the occasion calls for a report, it is usually an important one. You may be called upon to collect and analyze information about an issue or problem, and then have to present that information, together with your conclusions and recommendations, to your superiors. Most effective business reports contain each of the following elements:

1. *A cover letter.* This letter is addressed to the person who asked that the report be prepared and states that the report is attached. It is common to thank anyone who helped in the preparation of the report in the cover letter, also.
2. *An executive summary or abstract.* This is a brief summary of the full report highlighting how the information was collected and analyzed and stating the report's major findings and conclusions.

3. *An introduction.* The introduction includes a discussion of the reasons why the study was undertaken. What problem or decision led to the study? It is appropriate to include background information and an assessment of current conditions. What led up to the problem? What exactly are we facing with this problem? What will happen if we do nothing?

4. *A statement of method.* The method section includes a discussion of what and how data were collected. For example, if you conducted interviews with a sample of employees, discuss what procedures you used to select these employees, and what questions they were asked.

5. *The findings.* Report what you have found. This should be an objective, factual reporting of the results of the study. This is not the place to draw conclusions or implications, or make suggestions. You will have an opportunity to do that in the next section. This section should present the findings, only, so that those who read the report can draw their own conclusions.

6. *Conclusions and recommendations.* This is the section in which you interpret your findings. In other words, your reader is told what the findings mean. Now it is appropriate for you to draw conclusions for the reader and suggest what implications the findings have for your organization or department. It is also appropriate to make recommendations based upon your conclusions and to offer your understanding of the findings.

Chapter 9

Evaluating Employee Performance

Learning Objectives

After reading this chapter, you should:

1. understand the multiple purposes of the performance evaluation process.
2. be aware of the different types of performance evaluation systems.
3. recognize the types of rater errors that commonly occur during performance evaluations.
4. understand the importance of the feedback process in performance evaluations.
5. be aware of ways to make the feedback interview more effective.

Introductory Incident

Ben was dreading the coming week. He had to conduct performance evaluations on two of his employees. He never really felt comfortable evaluating the performance of other people. "It's even worse now that JBS requires us to sit down face to face with each employee and discuss their evaluation with them," Ben had confided to a friend. "Some of these people just aren't performing up to par, yet if you give them a low rating on anything, you have to be prepared for an argument!" Since most organizations conduct formal performance evaluations of their employees, Ben wondered if most supervisors felt the way he did.

Unfortunately, this discomfort in conducting performance evaluations is something a great many supervisors and managers feel. Nevertheless, performance evaluations can be one of the most important activities that supervisors perform. This reluctance to evaluate the performance of other people often damages the accuracy of the evaluations. This chapter presents some ways of avoiding the common problems of performance evaluation and of making these evaluations more useful management tools.

The process of evaluating employee job performance is one critical to organizational operation since the results of this process impact upon organizational goal accomplishment, employee motivation, and employee performance. It is surprising, therefore, that a procedure so important should so often be conducted poorly.[1] This chapter examines some of the purposes of performance evaluation and discusses some of the types of evaluation currently in use. Special emphasis is placed upon the errors that evaluators typically make, and upon the ways that the performance evaluation process could be improved.

Performance Evaluation: Its Definition and Purposes

A number of phrases could be used to refer to the process of evaluating employee performance. Among the names so used have been performance appraisal, performance review, performance evaluation, and employee evaluation. Regardless of the name attached to the process, its importance to the organization, and the individual within the organization cannot be overemphasized. That importance is reflected in the following definition of **performance evaluation:**

> A performance evaluation is any personnel decision which affects the status of employees regarding their retention, termination, promotion, demotion, transfer, salary increase or decrease, or admission into a training program.[2]

As the definition suggests, performance evaluations have an impact upon many employment decisions. In doing so, they serve many organizational purposes. Ivancevich and Glueck have identified six purposes of performance evaluation.[3]

1. *Reward purposes.* Performance evaluations offer a rationale for deciding who receives salary increases, promotions, and other rewards.
2. *Personnel and employment planning purposes.* Performance evaluations can be usefully applied in skills inventories and human resource planning.

Primary Uses of Performance Evaluations

Table 9.1

Use	Small Organizations	Large Organizations	All Organizations
	Percent*	Percent	Percent
Compensation	80.6	62.2	71.3
Performance Improvement	49.7	60.6	55.2
Feedback	20.6	37.8	29.3
Promotion	29.1	21.1	25.1
Documentation	11.4	10.0	10.7
Training	8.0	9.4	8.7
Transfer	7.4	8.3	7.9
Manpower Planning	6.3	6.1	6.2
Discharge	2.3	2.2	2.3
Research	2.9	0.0	1.4
Layoff	0.6	0.0	0.3

*Columns do not add to 100% since organizations could identify as many primary uses as they chose.

From "Performance Appraisal—A Survey of Current Practices," by Alan H. Locher and Kenneth S. Teel, copyright May, 1977. Reprinted with the permission of *Personnel Journal*, Costa Mesa, California; all rights reserved.

3. *Developmental purposes.* Performance evaluations can help determine which employees need additional training, and what specific types of training are needed.
4. *Motivational purposes.* Performance evaluations are valuable tools to use for stimulating employees to higher effort in the performance of their jobs.
5. *Communications purposes.* Performance evaluations provide an opportunity for increased interaction and communication between supervisor and employee.
6. *Research purposes.* Performance evaluations can be used to validate selection techniques.

Table 9.1 displays the results of a study which examined how organizations actually use performance evaluations. The study found that both large and small organizations used performance evaluations primarily to make compensation decisions. Many organizations also used them quite frequently to provide feedback, to improve employee performance, and to make decisions about promotions. Unfortunately, few organizations seemed to use performance evaluations to the fullest advantage.[4] Only a small percentage of organizations considered training, manpower planning, and research, as primary uses of their performance evaluation systems. Performance evaluations like the selection techniques discussed in chapters 2 and 3, fall under the jurisdiction of the fair employment laws.[5] As was true for selection techniques, any instrument or form used in performance evaluation

Figure 9.1
Typical graphic rating
scale

GRAPHIC RATING SCALE

Name _____ Dept. _____ Position _____

Date _____ Date of Last Review _____

Instructions: Evaluate the employee on the job now being performed. Place a check
mark in the appropriate box next to each item to indicate the employee's level of
performance in that category.

	Excellent	Good	Satisfactory	Fair	Unsatisfactory
1. Quality of Work	☐	☐	☐	☐	☐
2. Quantity of Work	☐	☐	☐	☐	☐
3. Job Knowledge	☐	☐	☐	☐	☐
4. Dependability	☐	☐	☐	☐	☐
5. Effort	☐	☐	☐	☐	☐
6. Initiative	☐	☐	☐	☐	☐
7. Cooperation	☐	☐	☐	☐	☐
8. Ability to Learn	☐	☐	☐	☐	☐
9. Judgment	☐	☐	☐	☐	☐
10. Overall Performance	☐	☐	☐	☐	☐

Completed by _____ Date _____

Discussed with employee on _____

must be based upon a job analysis and the reliability and validity of that instrument must have been established. Performance evaluation instruments must be capable of accurately and objectively measuring important aspects of employees' performance.

Performance Evaluation Techniques

An integral part of any type of formal performance evaluation system used by an organization is the particular rating form or scale of that system. A wide variety of rating scales are currently in use; each has its own set of advantages and disadvantages. Most supervisors are not involved in the development of these forms, yet it is supervisors who will use them. Consequently, an understanding of the strengths and weaknesses of each type of form can help you, as a supervisor, make more effective performance evaluations.

Graphic Rating Scale

The most widely-used performance evaluation instrument, by far, is the **graphic rating scale.**[6] While slight variations exist in the form of these instruments, they all work in essentially the same way. Typically, a number of traits or characteristics is listed (e.g., quality of work, quantity of work, initiative). The supervisor gives the employee a rating for each of these traits on a simple scale that indicates the level of his or her performance (see fig. 9.1).

Graphic rating scales differ from each other in terms of the amount of information they include and in terms of the particular measurement scale they employ. The scale shown in the figure could be modified to include more information about each of the ten rated items. For example, the form could read:

> 1. Quality of Work: Consider the accuracy and dependability of the employee's work regardless of quantity.

Or, a different form of measurement scale could be used instead of the boxes shown in the figure. For example, the form could look like this:

Quality of Work

5	4	3	2	1
Excellent	Above Average	Average	Below Average	Poor

Figure 9.2 presents a different version of graphic rating scale; it defines points on the scale for the evaluator, as well as the items to be rated. In addition, the rating scale form includes an interview summary; it requires that the supervisor sit down with the employee and discuss the evaluation.

Essay Evaluation

The second most widely-used method of performance evaluation is the **essay evaluation.**[7] Under this method, the supervisor generates a written description of the strengths and weaknesses of the employee's performance. This is a method often used in combination with one of the other methods, such as the graphic rating scale. The advantage of this approach is that it gives the supervisor the freedom to explain or describe, in detail, any aspect of the employee's performance that requires such elaboration. The disadvantage of the method is that it does not yield a quantified rating of performance that can then be used for other purposes such as research or validating selection devices.

Critical Incident Method

A method closely related to the essay evaluation is the critical incident method. With the essay evaluation, supervisors simply describe an employee's job performance. This description is also given under the critical incident method, but instead of being totally open-ended, as is the case with the essay evaluation, supervisors know what behaviors are to be considered in this description; hence, the critical method has a greater degree of structure than the essay method. A set of behaviors, considered to be critical to the job, is developed by the personnel department and the immediate supervisors of the employees to be evaluated. These behaviors could be examples of very effective or very ineffective job-related behavior. Every time a supervisor observes an employee exhibiting one of the listed behaviors, it is recorded together with a short description of the behavior and why it was considered to be especially effective or ineffective. These are the **critical incidents.**

Figure 9.2
Employee performance
evaluation form

EMPLOYEE PERFORMANCE EVALUATION

NAME _____   EVALUATED BY _____

DEPARTMENT _____   DATE _____

GRADE LEVEL _____   POSITION _____

DAYS ABSENT THIS YEAR _____   MAJOR REASON _____

Circle level of performance most representative of this employee. Provide descriptive comments as needed. (Explanations of levels on attached sheet.)

INITIATIVE   1   2   3   4   5   6

Capacity for independent action. Degree that responsibility is assumed when directions are lacking.

_____

_____

CREATIVITY   1   2   3   4   5   6

Ability to think, develop and evaluate ideas, and offer constructive input to system.

_____

_____

QUANTITY OF WORK   1   2   3   4   5   6

Volume of useful output in light of opportunities offered and standards provided.

_____

_____

QUALITY OF WORK   1   2   3   4   5   6

Excellence of output, accuracy, dependability, and thoroughness achieved despite obstacles.

_____

_____

COOPERATION   1   2   3   4   5   6

Ability to use tact, courtesy, friendliness and an open-minded approach in working with and for others.

_____

_____

EFFICIENCY OF WORK   1   2   3   4   5   6

Relationship of quality of output and time consumed.

_____

_____

COMMITMENT/DEDICATION   1   2   3   4   5   6

Level of dedication to XYZ Corp. Commitment to current position and to attainment of goals.

_____

_____

JUDGMENT/DECISION MAKING   1   2   3   4   5   6

Ability to accumulate and analyze information required to arrive at sound decision in timely fashion.

_____

_____

OVERALL EVALUATION

Briefly compare employee to what you would consider to be the ideal person for this job classification, considering all qualities and characteristics of the individual.

_____

_____

_____

_____

_____

PROGRESS

Using the previous evaluation as the basis for comparison (when applicable), how has this employee changed?

_____

_____

_____

_____

Evaluation Level Explanations

1. One whose performance is unquestionably outstanding. Must regularly make exceptional personal contributions to company progress. When compared to others in same job classification, is consistently ranked in the top performance level on appraisal form.
2. Clearly above-average performance. Exceeds position requirements on all points. Obviously a potential candidate for advancement.
3. Meets all position requirements. Accomplishes assignments in a completely satisfactory manner. Can logically expect to advance at the same rate as the majority in the same job classification.

4. Meets requirements of job classification satisfactorily. Advancement not recommended based on this level of output.
5. Generally meets minimum requirements of job classification but performance may be below what is normally expected in some significant areas of the total position. Improvement can logically be expected.
6. Does not meet minimum requirements of job classification. An improvement plan and timetable must be included in this evaluation. Failure to improve could result in demotion or termination.

ALL RATINGS OF 5 OR 6 MUST BE EXPLAINED IN THE SPACE PROVIDED BELOW EACH SCALE.

**Figure 9.2
(cont.)**

Interview Summary

Complete the following during the performance evaluation interview with the employee so both may sign:

Major improvements suggested, to be analyzed by the supervisor

_____

_____

_____

_____

Employee reactions to the interview

_____

_____

_____

_____

State and explain the reasons why any portions of this evaluation were not completed.

_____

_____

_____

Additional Comments

_____

_____

_____

_____

_____

We hereby acknowledge we have completed our section(s) of this performance evaluation and have read it in its entirety.

Employee's signature _____ Date _____

Supervisor's signature _____ Date _____

Example of MBO Performance Appraisal			Table 9.2
Area of Performance	Objective	Achieved	Difference
Reduce Errors	6%	4%	−2%
Increase Output	4%	5%	+1%
Decrease Rejections	7%	10%	+3%

The advantage of this approach is that evaluation is focused upon behaviors critical to job performance. Just as with the essay method, however, these results cannot be used for all purposes since they are not quantified. Further, there is no way that all examples of extremely effective and ineffective behaviors can be included on the critical incident list; thus, some incidents will be missed that should have been included in the record.

Management by Objectives

The **management by objectives**(MBO) method of performance evaluation involves the mutual agreement of the supervisor and the employee upon certain objectives which the employee is to try to achieve by a specified date. These objectives are the gauge by which the employee's job performance is evaluated. The performance evaluation itself is a determination of the degree to which the employee has accomplished his or her objectives (see table 9.2).

Proponents of this approach claim that it results in a more objective assessment of performance because it emphasizes objectives rather than traits or characteristics.[8] Its critics, on the other hand, argue that MBO focuses too much upon individual objectives and not enough upon teamwork and that the method is extremely complex and difficult to implement effectively.[9] It is true that there are a number of areas of performance for which it is not easy to set quantified objectives. For example, it is quite difficult to quantify supervisory performance in such areas as development of employees, motivation of employees, and leadership.

Behaviorally Anchored Rating Scale

Sometimes called behavioral expectation scales (BES), a primary reason for choosing to use the behaviorally anchored rating scales (BARS) over other methods of evaluation is to reduce the amount of judgment required of the person doing the rating. The evaluator is cast more in the role of an observer and less in the role of a judge.[10] The evaluator simply observes employee job behavior and does not attach a subjective rating to it, as is done in the use of many of the other methods.

The **behaviorally anchored rating scales** approach uses critical incidents as anchor points on a scale. A set of critical incident statements is developed for each dimension of performance to be rated; each of these statements describes various

Table 9.3   Behaviorally Anchored Rating Scale

Organizational Ability in Checkstand Work		
Extremely good performance	7	This checker would organize the order when checking it out by placing all soft goods like bread, cake, etc. to one side of counter; all meats, produce, frozen foods, to the other side, thereby leaving the center of the counter for can foods, boxed goods, etc.
Good performance	6	When checking, this checker would separate strawberries, bananas, cookies, cakes, and breads, etc.
Slightly good performance	5	You can expect this checker to grab more than one item at a time from the cart to the counter.
Neither poor nor good performance	4	After bagging the order and customer is still writing a check, you can expect this checker to proceed to the next order if it is a small order.
Slightly poor performance	3	This checker may be expected to put wet merchandise on the top of the counter.
Poor performance	2	This checker can be expected to lay milk and by-product cartons on their sides on the counter top.
Extremely poor performance	1	This checker can be expected to damage fragile merchandise like soft goods, eggs, and light bulbs on the counter top.

From "Development of First-Level Behavioral Job Criteria," by Fogli, L., Hulin, C., and M. R. Blood, in *Journal of Applied Psychology,* 1971, 55, 7. Copyright © 1971 by the American Psychological Association. Reprinted by permission of the author.

degrees of employee performance that could be observed for that particular dimension. All the evaluator must do is observe the employee's job performance and choose the statement which best describes that level of performance behavior. In this way, the degree of subjective evaluation on the part of the evaluator is reduced. An example of a BARS developed for evaluating the performance of a supermarket checker appears in table 9.3. The figure shows the scale used to evaluate one dimension of checkstand job performance, in this case, that of organizational ability. Several scales measuring different aspects of checkstand work would be included in a complete BARS performance evaluation.

Behavioral Observation Scale

Latham and Wexley have suggested that **behavioral observation scales** (BOS) could be used as a means for giving greater focus to job behavior in performance evaluation.[11] Figure 9.3 illustrates the way in which the BOS measures the frequency of occurrence of particular behaviors in an employee. The values assigned to each of several statements relating to a single performance dimension are

Figure 9.3
Behavioral observation
scale for receptionist/
secretary

BEHAVIORAL OBSERVATION SCALE FOR RECEPTIONIST/SECRETARY

I. Secretarial Activities

1. Can type at least 70 words per minute.

1	2	3	4	5
Never	Seldom	Occasionally	Often	Frequently

2. Can type from a dictaphone recording.

1	2	3	4	5
Never	Seldom	Occasionally	Often	Frequently

3. Is never behind in filing correspondence.

1	2	3	4	5
Never	Seldom	Occasionally	Often	Frequently

4. Processes incoming mail promptly.

1	2	3	4	5
Never	Seldom	Occasionally	Often	Frequently

5. Can take at least 100 words per minute in shorthand.

1	2	3	4	5
Never	Seldom	Occasionally	Often	Frequently

Section I Total = _____

II. Receptionist Activities

6. Answers telephone courteously and promptly.

1	2	3	4	5
Never	Seldom	Occasionally	Often	Frequently

7. Greets visitors warmly.

1	2	3	4	5
Never	Seldom	Occasionally	Often	Frequently

8. Keeps visitors waiting for more than five minutes.

5	4	3	2	1
Never	Seldom	Occasionally	Often	Frequently

9. Screens incoming telephone calls accurately.

1	2	3	4	5
Never	Seldom	Occasionally	Often	Frequently

Section II Total = ____

Total Score = Section I + Section II = ____

Secretarial Activities: *
  Poor = 5–10   Average = 11–15   Good = 16–20   Excellent = 21–25

Receptionist Activities:
  Poor = 4–8   Average = 9–12   Good = 13–15   Excellent = 16–20

Overall Performance:
  Poor = 8–15   Average = 16–24   Good = 25–32   Excellent = 33–40

*NOTE: Categories and point ranges are determined by the organization.

Table 9.4

Comparison of Performance Evaluation Techniques

Criteria	Graphic rating scale	Forced Choice	MBO	Essay	Critical incidents	BOS/ BARS
Developmental Cost	Moderate	High	Moderate	Low	Moderate	High
Usage Costs	Low	Low	High	High supervisory costs	High	Low
Ease of Use by Evaluators	Easy	Moderately difficult	Moderate	Difficult	Difficult	Easy
Ease of Understanding by Those Evaluated	Easy	Difficult	Moderate	Easy	Easy	Moderate
Useful in Promotion Decisions	Yes	Yes	Yes	Not easily	Yes	Yes
Useful in Compensation and Reward Decisions	Yes	Moderate	Yes	Not easily	Yes	Yes
Useful in Counseling and Development of Employees	Moderate	Moderate	Yes	Yes	Yes	Yes

Adapted from Ivancevich, John J., and William F. Glueck, *Foundations of Personnel/Human Resource Management,* Revised Edition. Copyright © 1983 Business Publications, Inc. Reprinted by permission.

summed to derive the employee's rating on that dimension. Typically, these dimensional ratings are subsequently totaled to arrive at an overall performance score.

Which Technique Is Best?

Supervisors generally have very little to say about what performance evaluation techniques are used by the organization. Most of the time, personnel specialists develop the technique or scale, and supervisors are called upon to use it effectively. The remainder of the chapter will focus upon the types of rater errors to be avoided and upon recommendations for conducting effective performance evaluations. Table 9.4 will enable the reader to compare the advantages and disadvantages of different techniques quickly and in more detail.

A great deal of research has attempted to determine which of the rating scale formats is best. The conclusion to be drawn from this research is that scale format is not the critical issue. In other words, one scale format is not significantly better than any other in terms of increasing the accuracy of performance evaluations.[12] Supervisors do, however, need to be aware of the strengths and weaknesses of the particular scale employed by their organization if they are to use the scale in an effective manner.

Rater Errors

Even if the performance evaluation system is extremely well designed, serious problems can arise, particularly if supervisors are not well trained in the use of the system, or if they lack the motivation to use it as it was intended. The Introductory Incident suggested that many supervisors dread having to conduct performance evaluations. It is unlikely that these supervisors are highly motivated to conduct effective evaluations. Instead, they are more likely to be motivated to get the evaluation over with as quickly and as painlessly as possible. More than a few rater error problems stem from the fact that many supervisors do not like to evaluate the performance of another person.[13] It makes many supervisors uncomfortable to know that their evaluation of an employee's performance could have a significant impact upon an employee's eligibility to receive rewards, or even upon that employee's future with the organization. Reluctance to evaluate others may arise, at least in part, because supervisors lack confidence in the performance evaluation system or in their ability to use it.

All performance evaluation techniques involve an element of subjectivity on the part of the evaluator. Unless the evaluation can be based completely on some objective measure, like the number of objects produced in a day, some subjectivity in these assessments of performance is inevitable. Subjectivity can lead to a variety of rater errors; the effect of these errors is to decrease the accuracy of the entire evaluation. Figure 9.4 shows what subjectivity may do to ratings of employee job performance.

Halo Error

Halo error applies to the performance evaluation process just as it was shown in chapter 3 to apply to the interviewing process. **Halo error** in performance evaluation occurs when the supervisor or rater generalizes from one characteristic of an employee's job performance to all aspects of that performance. There may be one component of an individual's work that is so outstanding, or so bad, that the evaluator assumes the person functions at this level all the time and in every possible job context.

Figure 9.5 shows what a performance evaluation looks like when a high degree of halo error is present in the supervisor's ratings. All three employees have been rated by the same supervisor. Let's assume that this supervisor is very sensitive to the quality of work of the employees, believes that quality is extremely important, and watches it very closely. Halo error will occur if the supervisor lets

Figure 9.4
Subjectivity in
performance ratings

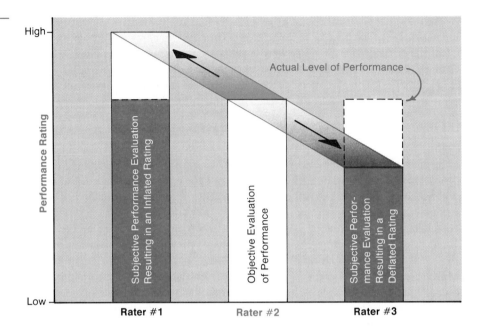

Figure 9.5
Halo error in performance
ratings

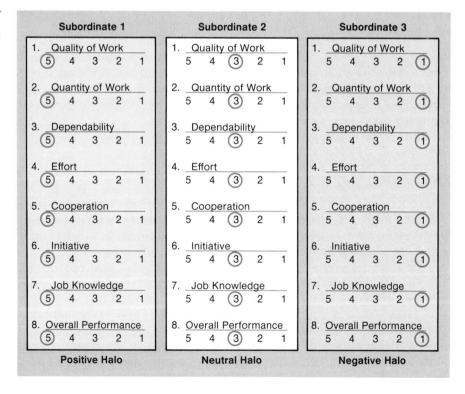

his or her evaluation of the quality of work of each employee affect the ratings of the other performance dimensions. This is what has happened in the cases of each employee rated in the figure. The ratings of items 2 through 8 are identical to the ratings given for quality of work. It is possible for a person to actually be excellent, poor, or average on every performance dimension, but it is highly unusual. If the aspects of performance being evaluated truly represent different dimensions of job performance, it is very unlikely that any employee will have performed at the same level on each of these dimensions; thus, there should be more variability in the ratings appearing in the figure. Accurate ratings for an employee are much more likely to range across the entire scale and so, reflect both the strong points and weak points of each individual. Halo error, therefore, biases one or more of the ratings given to these employees on dimensions of their job performances.

Unfortunately, halo error is difficult to control, primarily because supervisors are usually unaware that it is creeping into their evaluations of employees. In order to minimize the effects of the error, you must consider each aspect of performance separately and rate that dimension as objectively as possible. When deciding upon a rating for an employee's quantity of work, no thought should be given to the employee's quality of work. When rating the employee's dependability, no thought should be given to the employee's quality of work or quantity of work. Each dimension of job performance should be rated objectively and independently of all other dimensions.

Errors of Leniency, Harshness, and Central Tendency

An awareness of the subjectivity involved in many performance evaluation systems leads some supervisors to be either too hard or too easy in rating their employees' job performances. Some supervisors tend to give employees the benefit of the doubt and rate most of them relatively highly. Other supervisors may feel that because of the subjectivity involved in the rating process, they had better be strict so as to avoid rating anyone higher than they actually deserve. The latter group of supervisors is likely to rate all of their employees toward the low end of the scale. These predispositions constitute **leniency** and **harshness errors.** There is some evidence to suggest that employees are not happy with either type of supervisor. They do not like a supervisor whose evaluations are too harsh, and they do not respect a supervisor who is too lenient.[14] Figure 9.6 gives examples of job performance ratings influenced by leniency, harshness, and central tendency errors.

Central tendency error is committed by the supervisor who avoids using the high and low extremes of the scale for all employees' performance evaluations. All employees are given an average rating on all performance characteristics. Perhaps this supervisor is trying to play it safe, is unsure about his or her ability to accurately evaluate employee job performance, or is just uncomfortable giving any sort of rating. The easy way out is to rate everyone about the same. While

Figure 9.6

Harshness, leniency, and central tendency in performance ratings

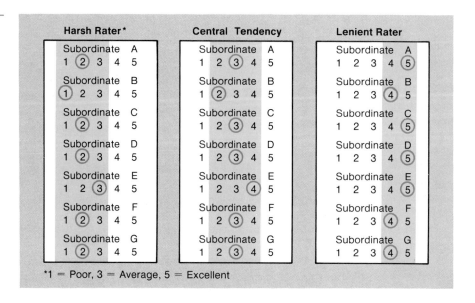

*1 = Poor, 3 = Average, 5 = Excellent

this type of error probably upsets the fewest number of employees, it totally destroys the value of the performance evaluation system. There is no way to differentiate among the best, average, or poorest performers, based on these ratings. Even if these distinctions could be made, the distance between these categories is lost. To accurately evaluate performance you need to know *how much* better one employee's performance is than another's.

As was pointed out in chapter 5 in the discussion of the effective use of money as a motivator, when salary decisions do not sufficiently discriminate among excellent, fair, and poor work performance, then money ceases to be an incentive. Such decisions contain central tendency error because the supervisor has overrewarded the worst performers and underrewarded the best performers! There is little reason for poor performers to try to increase their levels of performance and, in fact, there may be some incentive for the best performers to actually reduce the level of effort they put into their performances. Another alternative for good performers is to quit and find a job with an organization that pays them what they are worth.

In sum, the greatest penalty suffered from the presence of leniency or harshness error in performance evaluations, or even of central tendency error, is that the ratings of different supervisors cannot be compared. A rating of 2 on overall performance from a harsh supervisor may be comparable to a 4 from a lenient supervisor. The employee's actual performance level may be somewhere in between these two ratings.

Other Rater Errors

Several other interviewing errors discussed in chapter 3 can be errors of performance evaluation, also. Contrast error and the error of recency effects are two biases that can be found in both situations. It is difficult, perhaps, for many supervisors to avoid comparing employees, but it is a practice that can cause some employees to be rated lower or higher than they deserve, depending upon the performance level of the employee who is serving as the standard of comparison. To do this is to commit a **contrast error.** For example, assume that you supervise the work of five employees. One of these employees is an excellent performer. The other four are slightly above average. Because of the contrast between the excellent performer and the others, you give a lower rating to the four slightly above-average performers than they deserve. The fact that they do not compare favorably to the best performer has altered your perception of their performance and, though these individuals are slightly above-average performers, the unfavorable comparison directs your attention toward the negative end of the scale. Many of us make a similar error when watching our favorite athletes perform. On any given day, our favorite may not perform as well as the competitor. Our comments as we observe this disaster suggest that this athlete is about the poorest excuse for a competitor that we could possibly imagine! In fact, however, even on this "off day," the athlete is probably performing better than all but a handful of other athletes. We are rating the athlete's performance much lower than is deserved because we are drawing an unfavorable comparison with another performer. Error produced by the **recency effect** works in a similar fashion. There is a tendency for some supervisors to weigh the most recent performance of employees more heavily than performances which occurred in the more distant past. Supervisors should keep in mind that the performance evaluation should cover the entire period of time since the last evaluation.

Interpretation error is another that occurs with great frequency in performance evaluation situations. Interpretation causes problems with regard to (a) the terms used to rate employee performance, such as excellent, above average, and poor, and; (b) the trait or performance dimension being evaluated. What is average to one supervisor might be above average or excellent to another. Furthermore, words like dependability, initiative, and cooperation can be interpreted in many different ways. For example, Supervisor *A* might interpret dependability in terms of absenteeism or tardiness. Employees who do not miss work without reason and are on time are considered dependable by this supervisor. Supervisor *B* may interpret dependability in terms of the employee's willingness to take on additional assignments or work overtime with little advance notice. Employees who can be counted on when unexpected work or emergencies arise are considered dependable by Supervisor *B*. Discrepancies like this are likely to cause some unfavorable equity comparisons to be made among the employees of these two supervisors. Supervisor *A*'s employees see Supervisor *B*'s employees coming in late and missing work without reason, but still receiving high ratings on dependability. This seems inequitable to the employees who know they would receive very low ratings if they engaged in such behaviors.

Timing of Performance Evaluations

A supervisor does not generally control the frequency with which formal performance evaluations take place. Many organizations choose to conduct evaluations once a year, typically on the anniversary of the day the employee was hired.[15] It is widely acknowledged, however, that the less time between the actual performance behavior and the feedback, the more effective the feedback in changing behavior or in motivating an employee. If an employee is not performing at an acceptable level, it does not make sense to wait until the annual performance evaluation to discuss this with the employee. Unfortunately, however, this is often what happens.[16] Even if the organization conducts annual or semi-annual performance evaluations, supervisors should conduct informal evaluations on an ongoing basis.

The Feedback Interview

The extent to which the developmental and motivational purposes of the performance evaluation are achieved depends in large part on the effectiveness of the feedback interview. Many of the general principles of the interviewing process, as brought forth in chapter 3, are applicable to the performance evaluation feedback interview. Yet there are important differences. The primary purpose of the employment interview is to collect information. The primary purpose of the **feedback interview** is to provide information. At times, the information provided by the supervisor is not readily accepted by the employee; thus, supervisors must prepare themselves to deal with negative or defensive reactions on the part of the employee.

Preparation

Before calling the employee in for the interview, you must make sure that you are prepared. Adequate preparation might require a review of the performance evaluation rating form to refresh your memory of the exact ratings that were given and the reasons why those ratings were given. Supervisors must be able to justify the ratings to the employee. Without proper justification employees may not only question the fairness and accuracy of the performance evaluation process, but refuse to accept the results. Hence, when employees are told that they need to improve in certain areas, they may not see any point in trying since the evaluation has not been justified and so, in their eyes, is an inaccurate assessment.

Critical Incidents

If a rating scale has been used in the performance evaluation process, it may be difficult to justify your ratings to employees, no matter how accurate these ratings are. There is not a great deal of information in these forms. From the employee's perspective, the evaluation may appear to be highly subjective. One way supervisors may help justify their ratings to employees is through the use of an informal critical incident file. You may simply keep a record of exceptionally good and exceptionally bad performance during the year or evaluation period. These records are to be detailed descriptions of why the performance was exceptionally good or bad and are to include all pertinent facts of the situation. If an employee then questions a particular part of the evaluation, you have some specific examples of that employee's job performance to help justify the rating. It is imperative, however, that both good and bad examples be included in the critical incident file. Avoid developing the tendency of many supervisors and managers to take greater note of the poor than of positive performance examples.

Self-Ratings

It can be quite enlightening for both supervisors and employees when the employees are asked to rate themselves on the performance evaluation scale. During the feedback interview, the supervisor's ratings can be compared with the employee's and the differences between them discussed. This approach can be very useful in building open communication and trust between supervisors and their employees. Supervisors must be prepared to openly discuss the reasons why the ratings were given to the employees. If there is a wide discrepancy in the ratings on some area of performance, this difference must be reconciled. This will require honesty, objectivity, and trust from both parties.

Opening the Performance Evaluation Interview

Just as with the employment interview, a few minutes at the outset of the performance evaluation interview should be spent putting the employee at ease. These interviews are often emotionally charged, particularly if salary increases or other rewards are being given at the same time.[17] You should stress that this is not a disciplinary interview and that its purpose is to examine the employee's job performance in order to help that individual to improve, to grow, and to develop in the job. Your discussion should focus upon the future rather than upon the past.

Emphasize Behaviors

Once the employee has been put at ease, areas needing improvement should be discussed. It is important that you be as specific as possible and that only job behaviors be discussed. For example, telling an employee to be more cooperative may be good advice, but it does not give the employee any information about what must be done to achieve this. Telling an employee to respond more quickly to requests for information from other departments is a specific behavior that can be corrected.

Handling Negative Information

Keep in mind that handling negative information is difficult for many people; therefore, when discussing areas of the employee's job performance that need improvement, emphasize improving future performance rather than criticizing past performance. Focusing upon past behaviors may give the employee the impression that the primary purpose of the interview is disciplinary. This impression can cause the employee to become defensive and less receptive to feedback of any kind. To emphasize future performance is to let the employee know that the primary purpose of the evaluation is to help improve performance.

Jointly Agree upon Objectives

Once performance strengths and weaknesses have been brought into the open it is an excellent time to jointly agree upon objectives for the next year or new time period. These objectives should be the product of input and discussion from both supervisor and employee. The objectives should be aimed at performance improvement, in general, but be geared more specifically toward correcting the performance problems identified during the evaluation.

End on a Positive Note

Once the areas in need of improvement have been adequately considered, the positive aspects of the employee's performance should again be emphasized. In other words, begin and end the interview on a positive note.

Allow Employee to Ask Questions

Before closing the interview, the employee should be given the opportunity to ask questions. No interview should be ended until you are sure that the employee fully understands and accepts the performance ratings, as well as the reasons for those ratings.

Though accurate evaluation of job performance is difficult and complex, its potential for affecting employee motivation and for influencing the allocation of rewards makes this activity one that is central to the role of supervisors and to the smooth operation of many other organizational activities.

Summary

Performance evaluation is defined as any personnel decision affecting the status of employees regarding their retention, termination, promotion, demotion, transfer, salary increase or decrease, or admission into a training program. This definition suggests that performance evaluations may serve many purposes within the organization. Those discussed in the chapter were reward purposes, personnel and employment planning purposes, developmental purposes, motivational purposes, communication purposes, and research purposes.

While a variety of performance evaluation techniques are currently in use supervisors typically have little input into the decision of which technique will be put into operation. A knowledge of the strengths and weaknesses of different rating scales will enable supervisors to be more effective in the use of the one chosen by their organizations. This chapter examined the graphic rating scale, the essay evaluation, critical incidents, MBO evaluations, and behaviorally anchored rating scales, and behavioral observation scales.

Several rater errors are common to the performance evaluation process just as they occur during interviewing. These include halo, leniency, harshness, central tendency, contrast, primacy, recency, and interpretation errors. A knowledge of what causes these errors to occur and what effect they have upon ratings will enable supervisors to minimize their occurrence. In turn, more accurate and, therefore, more useful performance evaluations will take place.

The extent to which the performance evaluation process is successful in developing and motivating employees depends, in large part, upon the feedback interview. The development and motivation of the employee can be greatly affected by the way in which this information is fed back during the evaluation. The emphasis of the feedback interview should be upon encouraging future performance; it should not be used as the occasion to reprimand for past performance. Discussion should center upon specific job behaviors which the employee will be able to correct or to improve upon.

Key Terms

behavioral observation scales (p. 192)
behaviorally anchored rating scales
   (p. 191)
central tendency error (p. 197)
contrast error (p. 199)
critical incidents (p. 187)
essay evaluation (p. 187)
feedback interview (p. 200)

graphic rating scale (p. 186)
halo error (p. 195)
harshness error (p. 197)
interpretation error (p. 199)
leniency error (p. 197)
management by objectives (p. 191)
performance evaluation (p. 184)
recency effect (p. 199)

Questions for Discussion

1. What are the purposes of formal performance evaluations?
2. Compare the different performance evaluation techniques presented in this chapter. Which do you think is best? Which do you think is least valuable? Why?
3. What is meant by the term "rater error"?
4. Define each of the following rater errors:
    a. halo
    b. leniency and harshness
    c. central tendency
    d. contrast
    e. recency effects
    f. interpretation
5. What can be done to minimize rater error?

6. How often should performance evaluations be conducted? Why not more frequently or less frequently?
7. What should supervisors do to prepare for the performance evaluation feedback interview?
8. How can critical incidents be useful to supervisors in conducting a feedback interview?
9. Which performance evaluation scale or technique do you prefer? Why?

References

1. M. J. Kavanagh, "Evaluating Performance," in *Personnel Management,* ed. K. M. Rowland and G. R. Ferris (Boston: Allyn and Bacon, 1982), 187–226.
2. G. P. Latham and K. N. Wexley, *Increasing Productivity through Performance Appraisal* (Reading, Mass.: Addison-Wesley Publishing Co., 1982).
3. J. M. Ivancevich and W. F. Glueck, *Foundations of Personnel/Human Resource Management,* Rev. ed. (Plano, Texas: Business Publications, Inc., 1983).
4. M. E. Schnake, "The Performance Evaluation as a Motivating Tool," *Supervisory Management* 23 (1978): 29–32.
5. G. B. Giglioni, J. B. Giglioni and J. A. Bryant, "Performance Appraisal: Here Comes the Judge," *California Management Review* 24 (1981): 14–23.
6. A. H. Locher and K. S. Teel, "Performance Appraisal: A Survey of Current Practices," *Personnel Journal* 56 (1977): 245–247, 254.
7. K. S. Teel, "Performance Appraisal: Current Trends, Persistent Progress," *Personnel Journal* 59 (1980): 296–298, 316.
8. G. S. Odiorne, *Management by Objectives* (New York: Pitman Publishing Corporation, 1956).
9. H. Levinson, "Management by Whose Objectives?" *Harvard Business Review* 48 (1970): 128–129; M. E. Schnake, "Management by Objectives: Review and Evaluation," *Managerial Planning* 27 (1979): 19, 22–23.
10. D. P. Schwab, H. G. Heneman, III, and T. A. DeCotiis, "Behaviorally Anchored Rating Scales: A Review of the Literature," *Personnel Psychology* 28 (1975): 549–562.
11. G. P. Latham and K. N. Wexley, *Increasing Productivity through Performance Appraisal* (Reading, Mass.: Addison-Wesley Publishing Co., 1981).
12. W. C. Borman and M. D. Dunnette, "Behavior-based versus Trait-oriented Performance Ratings: An Empirical Study," *Journal of Applied Psychology* 60 (1975): 561–565; T.A. DeCotiis, "An Analysis of the External Validity and Applied Relevance of Three Rating Formats," *Organizational Behavior and Human Performance* 19 (1977): 247–266.
13. D. McGregor, "An Uneasy Look at Performance Appraisal," *Harvard Business Review* 35 (1957): 90–94.
14. G. P. Latham and K. N. Wexley, *Increasing Productivity through Performance Appraisal* (Reading, Mass.: Addison-Wesley Publishing Co., 1982).
15. U.S. Bureau of National Affairs, "Employee Performance: Evaluation and Control," *Personnel Policies Forum,* survey no. 108 (Washington, D.C.: Government Printing Office, 1975).
16. Schnake, "The Performance Evaluation," 29–32.
17. M. E. Schnake, "Apples and Oranges: Salary Review and Performance Review," *Supervisory Management* 25 (1980): 32–36.

For each of the performance dimensions listed below, write a paragraph describing how you would define or interpret that dimension. Your instructor will give you further instructions.

1. Dependability
2. Initiative
3. Cooperation
4. Effort
5. Quality of Work
6. Promotability

1. How similar were the definitions generated by the students of the class?
2. What are the implications of this exercise for the manager or supervisor who must conduct performance evaluations in an organization?
3. What can be done to minimize the problem of supervisors making different interpretations of performance dimensions?

You must evaluate the performances of your employees. Their salary increases will be determined based upon your evaluation. For each of the following employees, indicate the size of the raise that you would give by writing a percentage in the space next to their names.

_____ % **John Wilson:** John has been with the organization for fifteen years and in his current job for eight years. He seems to be quite satisfied with this job and shows no interest in increased responsibility or in promotion. In fact, John has refused overtime work on several occasions when you really needed him and seems unwilling to break his daily routine. Even when there is a crisis, it is difficult to get John to do something outside of his ordinary daily routine. Aside from this characteristic, however, John's job performance is quite good. He turns out an acceptable amount of work with very few errors and is never late or absent from work without good reason. In addition, he seems to get along very well with all of his fellow workers.

_____ % **Susie Burton:** Susie has been with the organization for five years and has been in her current job for the entire time. She is extremely easy to get along with and all of her fellow workers think very highly of her. While Susie does good quality work, she tends to be rather slow. Quite frequently, in fact, her coworkers have had to help her catch up so that the departmental quotas could be met. She is so well liked that none of her coworkers have complained. Susie had not worked before she accepted this job five years ago. She had to begin working because she was recently widowed and had three small children to support. You assume she is having trouble financially, since she keeps asking for any overtime work that is available.

____ % **Joe Brandt:** Joe has just finished his first year in the job. His performance has been quite a surprise to you. Joe's qualifications appeared to be only average when he applied for the job; however, you needed to fill the position quickly, so you took a chance and hired him. He has turned out to be one of the top performers in the department. It is obvious to you that Joe takes his job quite seriously and is putting forth a great deal of effort. The result has been that Joe frequently ends the week with the highest output, often with the fewest rejects, as well. You would certainly like to see Joe keep this up. Unfortunately, his coworkers do not seem to have accepted Joe yet. You have observed Joe on many occasions eating lunch alone while the others ate together.

____ % **Ann Bethel:** Ann has worked for you for three years. During this time she has been consistently above average in her performance, in terms of output. She also tends to have a slightly above-average rejection rate, however. You have suggested to her several times that she slow down a little and try to reduce the number of rejections, but she does not seem to have taken your advice. After observing her work for a couple of days, you decide that she is more concerned with talking to her fellow workers and socializing than she is about her job. The reason that she consistently turns out an above-average quantity of work is that it has become a game in her work department to see who can produce the most. The other workers gave up the game after it became clear that no one could beat Ann. Ann, however, continues to make sure that she has the biggest numbers at the end of the day. Ann's husband has a very good executive level job with a large company nearby, so you know she does not have to work, and she demonstrates no apparent need for money.

____ % **James Towers:** Jim has been with the organization for eight years and has been in his present job for the last three. He is well liked by his coworkers and, in fact, seems to have become their informal leader. Jim is always the one who speaks for the group or brings complaints or suggestions to your attention. His quality and quantity of work are excellent. The only problem with Jim's performance is tardiness. Several times a month Jim is a few minutes late getting to work in the morning or getting back from lunch. You do not want Jim's output or quality of work to decline, but you are afraid other employees may begin to be late if they see Jim getting away with it. You have mentioned this problem to Jim a couple of times and his tardiness would decline for a while, but would then slowly increase once again.

1. How similar were the salary increase recommendations of the class? What would explain this?
2. What factors did you (or your group) consider when making your recommendations? Would you eliminate any of these from your consideration if you had to make the recommendations over again?
3. Which factors do you think should be considered, and which do you think should not be considered in salary increase decisions?

Case

The Annual Performance Review

Ben started to fill out the performance evaluation form for Susan Murphy, one of his employees. While Susan's performance had been more than satisfactory during the past year, Ben was bothered by a phone call he had received last week from Ted Danvers, the manager of General Accounting for JBS. Ted had called to complain that Susan had been giving some of his people a bad time. It seems that Susan felt Accounting was not forwarding some reports that she needed so, on several occasions, Susan had called Accounting to complain that the reports were incomplete and that someone in the accounting department was failing to do the job. Finally, Susan called Ted to complain and they had gotten into an argument that ended when Ted hung up on Susan. Ben certainly didn't want any friction between his department and General Accounting. These two departments had to work too closely together on too many projects during the year. On the other hand, Ben was certain that Susan was having trouble getting those reports from Accounting. The person who was in that position before Susan had complained of the same problem. Ben completed Susan's evaluation form as follows:

Performance Evaluation Form

Employee: Susan Murphy

Supervisor: Ben Jamison

Scale: 1 = Poor 2 = Below Average 3 = Average

4 = Above Average 5 = Excellent

Quantity of Work: 4

Quality of Work: 3

Dependability: 3

Ability to Work with Others: 2

Initiative: 3

Effort: 4

Overall Performance Rating: 3.25

Meanwhile, Susan Murphy was excited about her annual performance evaluation interview, scheduled for tomorrow. She was expecting a very high performance rating and a good raise to go with it. She knew that her supervisor, Ben Jamison, was not in the habit of giving high evaluations to his employees unless they did something exceptional. Nevertheless, Susan felt that she had performed extremely well all year and deserved such a rating. She had kept after the accounting department to do a better job of forwarding those monthly reports to her and they finally seemed to be getting the message. In addition, she had uncovered a pricing error in the computerized billing system that had saved the company a great deal of money. She had filled out her own self-evaluation form in this manner:

Self-Rating Performance Evaluation Form

Employee: Susan Murphy

Supervisor: Ben Jamison

Scale: 1 = Poor 2 = Below Average 3 = Average

4 = Above Average 5 = Excellent

Quantity of Work: 4

Quality of Work: 4

Dependability: 5

Ability to Work with Others: 4

Initiative: 5

Effort: 5

Overall Performance Rating: 4.5

At the scheduled time for the performance evaluation interview, Susan walked into Ben's office. They exchanged evaluation forms. Susan was shocked to see how Ben had evaluated her performance. As Ben read over Susan's evaluation of herself, he knew that this was not going to be an easy feedback session. "Well Susan, I can see we disagree on a couple of things. At least we'll have something to talk about." Susan didn't say anything.

Questions

1. What can cause a situation like this to develop? What factors can lead up to this type of situation?
2. What could be done to prevent such a situation from developing in the future?
3. Should Ben revise his ratings so that they are more similar to Susan's?
4. If you were Ben, what would you do now so that the performance improvement and motivational purposes of the performance evaluation are accomplished?

Chapter 10

Discipline, Grievances, and Problem Employees

Learning Objectives

After reading this chapter, you should:

1. be able to describe the four primary categories of problem employees.
2. be aware of specific steps that supervisors may take to deal with each type of problem employee.
3. understand why a formal discipline process is necessary.
4. know how to use punishment effectively.
5. be able to describe how to discharge an employee.
6. be aware of the common reasons underlying employee grievances.
7. understand how to deal with grievances.

Terry leaned back in his chair and began to consider his possible courses of action. He had two employees whose performances were falling to unacceptable levels. In addition, Terry was afraid that their behavior might begin to affect the other employees. He knew he needed to correct these problems before they progressed any further, but he didn't know exactly how those corrections could be made.

Jane had been an above-average performer until about four months ago. At that time, her performance began to deteriorate and she began coming to work late a couple of times a week. Recently, she seemed to be calling in sick several days out of each month. Jane has been in Terry's department for three years, and until four months ago, Terry had been very satisfied with her performance. He hated to fire her since she had been an excellent employee for such a long period; however, he wasn't sure what other alternatives were available.

Terry's problem with Stan was more straightforward. Stan has been with JBS for seventeen years. Until recently, he worked in the shipping department. Three weeks ago, that part of the company was reorganized and Stan's job was eliminated. Terry happened to have an opening at that time, so Personnel requested that he place Stan in that position. Not long after Stan came to work in Terry's department, Terry began to suspect that Stan was drinking during his lunch hour. He was fine in the mornings, but for a period of time after lunch there was a noticeable deterioration in his performance. This behavior was clearly unacceptable, but still Terry was unsure how he should proceed. Should he just walk up and fire Stan, or were there other steps he should take first?

Regardless of your effectiveness as a supervisor, you will be faced, from time to time, with the responsibility of handling grievances and disciplining problem employees. While such duties are never pleasant, discipline must be recognized as an important element of the operations of many modern organizations. Discipline may be viewed, in a sense, as the organization's way of making its complaints heard and of taking some action. Grievances, on the other hand, are the employees' way of making their complaints heard by the organization.

Problem Employees

A supervisor may exert a great deal of effort trying to provide a motivating, safe, and satisfying work environment; unfortunately, there are employees who will not respond to those efforts. Occasional problems with employees are bound to occur, regardless of your effectiveness as a supervisor. There are some employees who will be difficult, no matter how enriched their jobs are, how many rewards they receive, or how they are treated. These employees, called **problem employees,** can typically be classified into one of four categories, based on the kind of problem the individual creates in the work situation. These are performance problems, personal problems, illegal acts, and rule violations.[1]

Performance Problems

Some employees are simply ineffective performers. **Performance problems** may result from a lack of motivation (the willingness to perform); a lack of ability (the capacity to perform), or situational constraints (the opportunity to perform).[2] Miner has developed a list of possible causes of performance problems designed to be used for diagnosing ineffective performance.[3] That list appears in table 10.1.

Causes of Performance Problems   Table 10.1

Problems of intelligence and job knowledge. These include insufficient job knowledge, insufficient verbal ability, and insufficient special ability related to the specific job.

Emotional problems. These include frequent anxiety, depression, and anger as well as more serious psychological problems (neurosis and psychosis). Drug and alcohol abuse also fall within this category.

Motivational problems. These problems arise when employees are frustrated in satisfying important needs at work (e.g., success, self-actualization, attention, recognition, interaction).

Physical problems. This category includes physical illness or handicap, inappropriate physical characteristics, and insufficient muscular or sensory ability or skill.

Family problems. This category consists of any type of family crises (e.g., divorce, death, severe illness, separation from the family).

Problems caused by the work group. Work group problems may arise because the work group has an informal norm which limits performance levels or output.

Problems originating in company policies. These include placing employees in positions for which they are not qualified, supervisors having too many subordinates to effectively supervise them, and maintaining inappropriate performance standards.

Problems stemming from society and its values. The primary cause of these problems is conflict between job demands and cultural values (e.g., equity, freedom, moral and religious values).

Problems arising from the work context and the work itself. This category includes unsatisfactory working conditions, excessive danger, undesirable geographic location, and unpleasant tasks.

From People Problems: The Executive Answer Book, *by John Miner. Copyright © 1985 by John Miner. Reprinted by permission of Random House, Inc.*

It is clear from this list that any performance problem may stem from a variety of possible causes. A careful diagnosis of each problem must precede any attempt at their solution. The problem could stem from the employee, the organization, other employees, or even the supervisor. The specific cause of the performance problem must be identified before it can be successfully resolved. Specific causes of the performance problem suggest specific corrective strategies. These strategies may take the form of additional job training, redesigning the job, moving the employee to a different job, changing the motivational strategy used, or removing the obstacles to good performance. In the Introductory Incident, Jane's performance began to deteriorate only recently. Before deciding what action to take, Terry must first determine the specific cause of Jane's performance deterioration. It may be a temporary problem over which Jane has little control (e.g., divorce, death in the family, illness).

Personal Problems

The category of **personal problems** includes drug and alcohol abuse, and family problems. Many employees will face these sorts of problems at some point in their careers, and it is part of the responsibility of the supervisor to become involved when they begin to affect job performance. In the Introductory Incident, Stan has an obvious alcohol problem that is affecting his job performance. Terry must take steps to make Stan recognize that he has an alcohol problem and agree to participate in a rehabilitation program.

It has been estimated that about 10 percent of the labor force are alcoholics and another 10 percent are borderline alcoholics.[4] The direct cost to industry, in terms of lost productivity and the related expenses of alcoholism, is estimated to be around $20 million per year.[5]

It is relatively easy to spot employees with alcohol problems if you are aware of the symptoms. Those symptoms include increased absenteeism and tardiness, frequent reports of minor illnesses, hangover (headache, shaking, thirst), decreased job performance and, in some instances, family and financial problems.

When alcohol problems on the job are discovered, the employee should be confronted immediately. You should document the effects that the alcohol problem is having on the employee's performance. For example, you might document the problem by presenting the employee with a comparison of the records of previous output and current output, or of previous and current rejection rates. Having concrete evidence in hand makes it more difficult for the employee to simply deny that a problem exists. Some organizations require suspected alcoholics to obtain a medical report if they deny that they have a problem.[6] You should offer to help the employee, but make it a condition of continued employment that a rehabilitation program, such as Alcoholics Anonymous, be joined. If the employee refuses to enter a rehabilitation program or stops attending sessions, the employee should be terminated. It must be made clear to the employee, from the outset, that termination is the consequence of not participating in rehabilitation. You should also document each step you have taken in attempting to help the problem employee. Should termination be necessary a record of your efforts could prove very serviceable.

Many organizations handle drug abuse in the same way alcohol problems are handled. Both problems lead to similar job-related consequences, namely, absenteeism and tardiness, decreased job performance, and increased accidents. If employees are found to be addicted to an illegal drug, they are typically given the same alternatives as those with alcohol problems. They must enter a rehabilitation program or be terminated. If an employee is found to be selling illegal drugs while at work, however, termination is usually immediate.

Ways of Preventing Employee Theft	Table 10.2

1. The employee should be made to feel that the job is worth keeping and that it would not be easy to earn more money elsewhere.

2. Maintain normal good housekeeping practices. Leave no piles of rubbish, rejects, or boxes lying around; no disused machines with tarpaulins on them; no unlocked, empty drawers. This will help to limit the number of places where stolen goods can be hidden. The first act of the thief is to divert merchandise from the normal traffic flow

3. Paperwork must be carefully examined and checked at all stages so that invoices cannot be stolen or altered.

4. Employees' cars should not be parked close to their places of work. There should be no usable cover between the plant doors and the cars.

5. Women employees must not be allowed to keep their handbags next to them at work. Lockers that lock must be provided for handbags. Merchandise has a way of disappearing into a handbag; once the bag is closed a search warrant is needed to get it open again.

6. Whether the plant is open or closed at night, bright lights should blaze all around its perimeter so that no one can enter or leave without being seen.

7. There should be adequate measures to control the issuance of keys.

8. As far as possible, everyone entering or leaving the plant should have an identification card.

9. Doors not used in the regular flow of traffic should be kept locked.

10. Safeguard everything of value, not just obvious items, that could possibly be removed by thieves.

From Ivancevich, John J., and William F. Glueck, *Foundations of Personnel/Human Resource Management,* Revised Edition. Copyright © 1983 Business Publications, Inc. Reprinted by permission.

Illegal Acts

This category of **illegal acts** comprises a variety of activities including employee theft, misuse of organizational facilities or property, embezzlement, and sabotage. Statistics show that these and other forms of white collar crime have increased in recent years. The U.S. Chamber of Commerce estimated that the total cost of white collar crime in 1980 was $200 billion!

Many companies feel that prevention is the most effective solution to the problem. Ivancevich and Glueck identify ten ways to prevent employee theft.[7] These appear in Table 10.2.

While many items in this list would have to be established as organization-wide policy in order to be effective, others can (and should) be performed informally by supervisors. Locking doors, checking paperwork and housekeeping are examples of these informal safeguards.

Rule Violations

Most organizations have established some rules for employee behavior on the job. Insubordination (i.e., refusal to follow a supervisor's instructions), fighting, gambling, tardiness, safety, and verbal or physical abuse of supervisors would be considered **rule violations** in most organizations.

In order for rules to be effective in guiding the behavior of employees, they need to be placed in writing and clearly communicated to employees at the time they join the organization. From time to time there should be other communications designed to remind employees of these rules. It can be easy for employees to forget that a rule exists if they do not see it enforced for some time.

Besides communicating the rules of the organization, it is a good idea to communicate the probable consequences of breaking each rule. In general, rules are more effective if the consequences of their violation are spelled out in advance and if those consequences are severe enough to make employees want to avoid them.

The Discipline Process

The objective of the discipline process should be to correct employee behavior. In administering discipline, supervisors should be future oriented as opposed to past oriented. When you focus upon the past, the tendency is to view discipline as retribution for previous incorrect or illegal activities. This approach to discipline creates somewhat of a "get even" mentality in both supervisor and employees. While it is difficult to divorce the past entirely, since the discipline is being administered for a previous act, the focus should be upon correcting behavior for the future.

Many organizations, both union and nonunion, follow the progressive discipline process discussed in chapter 2. Many labor contracts spell out precisely what supervisors can and cannot do in disciplining employees. You'll recall that the progressive discipline process calls for successively severe punishments for each repeated offense (see table 10.3). Such a method stands in conflict with research findings which suggest that for punishment to be most effective, it should be relatively severe at the outset.[8] Under a progressive discipline program, the first several punishments may not be strong enough to stop the behavior. If the undesirable behavior is rewarding to the employee, that individual might be willing to accept several steps in the progressive discipline process before deciding to stop engaging in the behavior. Progressive discipline is so widely accepted among organizations and the courts that it is not likely to be soon discarded in favor of some other method.

JBS Corporation Rules and Penalties

Table 10.3

Rule	1st Offense	2nd Offense	3rd Offense
1. **Refusal to obey order of supervisor**	3-day suspension	discharge	
2. **Theft of company property**	discharge		
3. **Possession of weapon on company property**	discharge		
4. **Performing personal work on company time**	written warning	3-day suspension	discharge
5. **Stopping work before break, lunch, or quitting time**	written warning	3-day suspension	discharge
6. **Inadequate performance**	written warning	3-day suspension	discharge
7. **Refusal to obey safety rules**	written warning	5-day suspension	discharge
8. **Alcohol or illegal drug use on company property**	discharge		
9. **Physical violence**	discharge		
10. **Unexcused absence or tardiness**	written warning	2-day suspension	5-day suspension

Punishment

Recently, researchers have begun to question the long-held beliefs that punishment is not an effective modifier of behavior in organizations. For years, people have argued that: (a) the effects of punishment are only temporary and that once the punishment is removed, the undesirable behavior returns; (b) punishment often results in undesirable emotional side effects, such as withdrawal, aggression, or anxiety, and; (c) punishment is unethical or inhumane.

Variables Influencing Punishment Effectiveness

Arvey and Ivancevich argue that there is little research evidence to support any of these criticisms.[9] Further, they have identified several variables that influence the effectiveness of punishment. These are:

1. *Timing.* Punishment should be given as soon after an undesirable behavior as possible. The employee must associate the punishment with the specific behavior that you are trying to eliminate.

2. *Intensity.* Punishment should be relatively intense from the outset. The first administration of punishment should be strong enough to make the employee want to avoid it in the future. Many progressive discipline programs contain weak forms of punishment in the early stages. Some employees may not perceive these as punishing; others may simply choose to accept the punishment until it becomes more harsh.

3. *Schedule.* Punishment should be administered on a continuous schedule. Every time a punishable behavior occurs, it should be punished. Remember, what is an undesirable behavior from the organization's perspective is often rewarding, in some way, to the person engaging in that behavior. If such behavior occurs but goes unpunished, the person is given positive reinforcement for exhibiting that behavior. This is another reason why punishment should be relatively intense from the outset. Since many undesirable behaviors result in some reward for the individual, the punishment for that behavior has to be strong enough to offset the rewards.

4. *Consistency.* Supervisors must be consistent in the administration of punishment; that is, it should not matter who engages in an undesirable behavior or when it occurs. It is punished just the same. It is helpful if the organization has a written set of rules with the punishments for infractions of those rules clearly spelled out. Not only should supervisors be consistent in the administration of punishment across employees and over time, but supervisors throughout the organization should be consistent with each other in the administration of punishment. It is difficult to explain to employees why they are being punished for an activity that others are not.

5. *Method of administration.* The administration of punishment must be impersonal and objective; that is, punishment should be aimed at specific behaviors as opposed to specific individuals. Employees must believe that no matter who engages in the undesirable behavior, they will be punished for it. When personalities are allowed to enter into the administration of punishment, defensive behavior on the part of employees is likely to be the response.

6. *Rationale.* Supervisors should take the time to explain clearly and specifically why the punishment is being administered. Do not simply assume that the employee knows why he or she is receiving a punishment. Take time to discuss the reasons with the employee.

7. *Relationship with punishing agent.* Research has shown that punishment is more effective when it is administered by an agent, or supervisor, who has a good working relationship with the employee receiving the punishment.[10] There must be a substantial degree of trust and openness between supervisor and employee.

8. *Knowledge of alternative responses.* Once punishment has been administered, you should make the employee aware of alternative responses. Inform the employee of other, more desirable behaviors that the individual could engage in to receive positive reinforcement. If the employee is not aware of any alternative behaviors, or does not know which behaviors result in desired rewards, the only way to get any reinforcement is to continue to exhibit the undesirable behavior.

Using Punishment in the Work Setting

The use of punishment in organizational settings typically receives unfavorable press; however, if you have worked in any organizational setting for very long, you have no doubt witnessed its use. It is not really a question of whether or not to use punishment. Punishment is, and will continue to be, used quite frequently. The question is how to use it effectively.[11]

Such a statement is not to imply that punishment is as effective as positive reinforcement. Sims has pointed out that in comparative tests of situations in which punishment and positive reinforcement were used, positive reinforcement consistently emerges as the more effective alternative.[12] It seems that there are, however, at least three sets of circumstances under which punishment may prove effective. One is when the undesirable behavior is rewarding to the employee, but the supervisor has no control over this reward. (The example used in chapter 4 was a student who misbehaves in class. The reward comes from the attention received from other students.) If the supervisor had control over the reward, then extinction could be used. When the reward is not under the control of the supervisor and the behavior must be eliminated, punishment seems the likely alternative.

The second situation is when supervisors do not have the authority to give many positive rewards. When you are being held responsible for results but do not have the flexibility to give raises or other rewards for good performance, there is little alternative but to use some form of punishment to deter unacceptable behavior.

Finally, time constraints may require that punishment be used. If employees are engaging in a behavior that is potentially dangerous, it is important to eliminate this behavior as quickly as possible. The situation may not allow the time it takes to establish an alternative desirable behavior through positive reinforcement.

Discharge

The ultimate form of punishment is **discharge** or termination. Typically, discharge is the final step in the progressive discipline process for those who continue to break rules even after counseling. Many organizations have established guidelines for supervisors and managers to follow when discharging an employee. Common among these guidelines are progressive discipline or warning discussions with the employee, careful documentation, a final warning discussion, and written confirmation of the final warning. The final warning makes it clear to employees that they are in danger of losing their jobs if they continue with their present behavior. It usually details the problem and suggests what the employee can do to correct it, as well. The final warning also includes a time limit within which the employee must make the correction.

Suggestions to Supervisors

Whether or not your organization has a formal discharge procedure, there are several things to keep in mind with respect to the termination of employees.

1. *Don't put it off.* A common mistake of many supervisors is to wait too long to discharge an employee. It is understandable that people feel uncomfortable discharging other individuals from their jobs; but if it has been determined that discharge is the answer, nothing can be gained by waiting. If discharge is appropriate, it is likely that other employees are aware of the problem and wondering why you have not done something about it. Delaying the discharge could create the impression among other employees that you are willing to tolerate this problem behavior.
2. *Never discharge an employee on the spot or out of anger.* Make sure that you have collected all of the facts of the case before firing an employee. Organizing your information and checking your facts gives you time to make sure that discharge is appropriate and gives you time to cool off, also. Firing an employee on the spot while angry may be perceived as an attack upon the employee. Termination should be administered impersonally and objectively, just as any form of punishment should be given. It is unlikely that you can be impersonal and objective if you are angry with the employee.
3. *Make sure that you have detailed documentation.* More and more employees are challenging discharges in court under the Civil Rights Act or the Age Discrimination in Employment Act. Many have been successful in regaining employment because the employing organization lacked proper documentation of the problem. **Documentation** should include the names of all persons involved in any incident, the date and time of the incident, the location of the incident, and a description of the incident itself. The documentation should demonstrate that the problem is one of some duration and that the organization has made every reasonable effort to help the employee to correct it. In other words, you should document the progressive discipline process.

The Discharge Interview

It is not until the discharge interview that the employee is actually told that he or she has been discharged. Naturally, this will be a traumatic event for many employees. In order to minimize the emotionality of this interview, you should:

1. Emphasize job-related behaviors. Focus on the behavior and not the person. Do not appear to be attacking or criticizing the employee.
2. Let the employee ask questions or make statements. This is an excellent time to put active listening into practice. The opportunity to talk will help keep the employee dealing with facts and not emotions.
3. Avoid arguments. There is nothing to be gained by getting into an argument with the employee. At this point, the decision has been made and there is no further reason for dispute.
4. Do not leave room for uncertainty and do not leave the door open. Do not promise the employee that you will check with someone else about the case at hand. The discharge should be final when the employee leaves your office.
5. Make sure the employee understands the reasons for the discharge. It is unlikely that the employee will be very receptive during this interview. Nevertheless, you should try to ensure that, before the interview is over, the employee understands specifically why he or she has been discharged.
6. Keep the interview short. As already mentioned, this is not the time for discussion or argument. There is nothing to be gained by either party in prolonging the interview. In general, the discharge interview should last no more than ten to fifteen minutes.
7. Try to end the interview on a positive note. If there is a next step, such as personnel department or outplacement counseling, describe this to the employee. Wish the employee well and express confidence that he or she will find suitable employment shortly.

Discharging an employee is a serious step for both employee and organization. It should take place only after every effort has been made to help the employee correct the existing problem.

Grievance procedures are a mechanism by which organizations may hear employee complaints and settle disputes between employees and supervisors. Most labor agreements contain a grievance procedure clause, but even many nonunionized organizations have such procedures. Since unionized organizations have grievance procedures spelled out in writing in the labor agreement, these procedures tend to be more detailed than those for nonunionized organizations.

The number of steps included in the grievance procedures depends, to some extent, upon the size of the organization; the procedures of larger organizations typically include more steps. A typical grievance procedure in a unionized organization follows a pattern of development.

Grievance Procedures

Step 1: The grievance is submitted to the employee's immediate supervisor. This may be done orally or in writing using a grievance statement like the one shown in figure 10.1. If the supervisor does not resolve the matter to the employee's satisfaction, the grievance can be appealed, thus taking the process to step 2.

Step 2: The grievance is discussed by a union representative, such as the chief plant steward or business agent, and a high-level manager representing the organization. Usually, this high-level manager is some member of the personnel or industrial relations department. If the grievance cannot be resolved, step 3 follows.

Step 3: At this point, the highest ranking officers of both the union and the organization meet to try to resolve the grievance. Typically, it is the plant grievance committee and the plant manager who now become involved. If the grievance remains unresolved, the process advances to the final step.

Step 4: The final step in the grievance procedure is **binding arbitration.** A third party (the arbitrator) is agreed upon by both union and management, to be brought in to hear the case and make a decision. The two parties agree in advance to abide by whatever decision the arbitrator makes.

The primary goal of a nonunion organization's grievance procedure is to encourage open communication and show employees that the organization is concerned with their welfare.[13] The most widely-used grievance procedure in nonunionized organizations is the **open door policy.**[14] This policy means that all employees of the organization have the right to discuss a complaint with some top-level manager. When the organization designates one individual to hear and investigate complaints, that person is typically referred to as a **corporate ombudsman.** Often, however, the open door policy is more informal in nature. Some managers may stress the fact that they have an open door policy. Others do not.

The open door policy presents two major problems. First, complaints that should be resolved at lower levels, may be brought to the attention of top-level managers. These managers can easily get overloaded with relatively insignificant problems. Second, some employees may be reluctant to talk with an upper-level manager about more serious problems. Unless there is a climate of trust and openness in the organization, employees could fear some form of retribution for complaining to higher levels of management.

Most grievances can be resolved successfully by the immediate supervisor, if that supervisor is willing to listen to employee complaints and treat employees fairly. In 1980, General Motors reported that approximately 75 percent of their formal grievances were solved at step 1.[15] Table 10.4 offers a few suggestions to supervisors for preventing the appeal of grievances beyond step 1.[16]

Supervisors can do several things to prevent grievances from ever being filed. Collectively, these amount to having an open door policy at the supervisory level. Grievances that arise do so most often because employees perceive that they have been treated unfairly. In 1978, the issues which most often reached arbitration

Figure 10.1
Grievance statement

Grievance Statement

Employee: _John Meyer_   ID # _42354071_

Dept.: _Maintenance_   Supv: _Don Evans_

Statement of Grievance: _I have had a good work record in this department for the past seven years. When the Maintenance Engineer Level I job opened up two weeks ago, I was sure that I would get it. Instead, Don Evans promoted Mike Donaldson who has been with JBS for only three years. I believe that I am more qualified for the Level I job than Mike. I feel that this decision should be reversed or that I should receive a comparable promotion into another Level I job._

Employee Signature: _John Meyer_

Received by: _Tim Wilson, Personnel Mgr._

Date: _August 1, 1978_   Time: _1:20 P.M._

Table 10.4	Preventing Grievance Appeals

1. Treat all grievances seriously. While it may not appear to be anything significant to you, it may be a serious enough problem in the employee's eyes to appeal all the way to binding arbitration.

2. Investigate the complaint immediately. Talk with the employee as soon as possible and actively listen to his or her story.

3. Examine the labor agreement carefully. Obtain help from the personnel department if you are unsure how to interpret any portion of the agreement.

4. If you can determine the cause of the grievance and if you have authority to do so, correct the problem immediately. Avoid long delays in handling grievances.

5. Always remain calm. Do not respond to the employee if you are angry. Postpone the meeting until you can proceed calmly and objectively.

6. Make sure that you have all available evidence before making a decision.

were discharge and disciplinary issues, or had to do with seniority, work assignments, or overtime.[17] It is impossible to prevent misunderstandings and misperceptions from occurring. It is not impossible to show employees that you are willing and eager to listen to them when they have a problem or complaint. Company policies must be enforced for all employees. When discipline or punishment becomes necessary, it must be administered impersonally and with an eye toward improving future performance. Generally, the better the working conditions and the more freedom and participation employees are allowed, the less likely employees will be to initiate grievances. Grievances may still be filed; but if employees know that their supervisor is open and responsive to their problems, the grievances are likely to be resolved at the supervisory level.

Summary

Problem employees typically fall into one of four categories: performance problems, personal problems, illegal acts, and rule violations. In order to deal with problem employees, organizations must follow some established discipline process. Both unionized and nonunionized organizations typically follow some type of progressive discipline procedure. Recent research has shown that, contrary to long-held beliefs, punishment may be used effectively in work settings.

Punishment should occur as soon as possible after the undesirable behavior is exhibited and be relatively intense at the outset. Punishment should be administered on a continuous schedule to minimize any reward that the individual may be receiving from the undesirable behavior. A continuous schedule of punishment also strengthens employees' perceptions of consistency. Punishment should be administered impersonally and should be accompanied by a discussion of the reasons for the punishment. This discussion would include a specification of more appropriate behaviors. Punishment is a likely alternative for supervisors when they do not control many positive rewards and when the extinction of the undesirable behavior is not possible. Discharge, the ultimate punishment, should be used only after serious attempts to help the employee correct problem behaviors have failed.

Grievance procedures provide a mechanism by which organizations can hear employee complaints and settle disputes between employees and supervisors. Unionized organizations typically have their grievance procedures spelled out in their labor agreements. These procedures usually call for the grievance to be heard by successive levels of labor and management until the problem is resolved. If the problem cannot be handled at any of these levels, an outside arbitrator is called in for binding arbitration.

Most grievances can be resolved at the supervisory level if supervisors listen carefully to employee problems and act quickly to reach some understanding. Supervisors can also do a great deal to keep grievances from being filed in the first place. Employees who feel that their supervisors are interested in their welfare and are willing to listen to employee problems are less likely to file formal grievances.

Key Terms

binding arbitration (p. 222)
corporate ombudsman (p. 222)
discharge (p. 220)
documentation (p. 220)
grievance procedures (p. 221)
illegal acts (p. 215)

open door policy (p. 222)
performance problems (p. 212)
personal problems (p. 214)
problem employees (p. 212)
rule violations (p. 216)

Questions for Discussion

1. What are the four primary categories of problem employees?
2. What are the causes of performance problems? Suggest a strategy that supervisors might use to correct each type of performance problem.
3. What are the causes of personal problems?
4. What should supervisors do when they believe that one of their employees has an alcohol or drug abuse problem?
5. What can supervisors do to prevent employee theft?
6. What should supervisors do to enforce organizational rules?
7. Describe the discipline process currently used by most organizations.
8. Can punishment be used effectively in work settings? How?
9. Is punishment unethical or inhumane? Why or why not?
10. What guidelines should supervisors follow in discharging an employee?
11. Describe the grievance process in unionized organizations.
12. Describe the grievance process in nonunionized organizations.
13. How should supervisors treat a grievance so that it is not appealed to higher levels?
14. What can supervisors do to prevent grievances from being filed in the first place?

References

1. J. M. Ivancevich and W. F. Glueck, *Foundations of Personnel/Human Resource Management,* rev. ed. (Plano, Texas: Business Publications, 1983), 496–506; D. J. Cherrington, *Personnel Management: The Management of Human Resources* (Dubuque, Iowa: Wm. C. Brown Publishers, 1983), 593–598.

2. M. Blumberg and C. D. Pringle, "The Missing Opportunity in Organizational Research: Some Implications for a Theory of Work Performance," *Academy of Management Review* 7 (1982): 560–569.

3. J. M. Minor, *The Challenge of Managing* (Philadelphia: W. B. Saunders, 1975).

4. National Industrial Conference Board, "Company Controls of Alcoholism," *Studies in Personnel Policy,* no. 167. (New York: Conference Board, 1969).

5. G. Perkins, "Alcoholism in the Workforce," *Management World* 7 (1978): 7–10.

6. S. G. Wagner, "Assisting Employees with Personal Problems," *Personnel Administrator* 27 (1982): 59–64.

7. Ivancevich and Glueck, *Foundations of Personnel/Human Resource Management,* 504.

8. R. D. Arvey and J. M. Ivancevich, "Punishment in Organizations: A Review, Propositions, and Research Suggestions," *Academy of Management Review* 5 (1980): 123–132.

9. Ibid.

10. R. D. Arvey, G. A. Davis, and S. M. Nelson, "Use of Discipline in an Organization: A Field Study," *Journal of Applied Psychology* 69 (1984): 448–460.

11. M. E. Schnake, "Vicarious Punishment in a Work Setting: An Empirical Test," *Journal of Applied Psychology,* in press.

12. H. P. Sims, "Further Thoughts on Punishment in Organizations," *Academy of Management Review* 5 (1980):133–138.

13. Cited in H. J. Chruden and A. W. Sherman, *Managing Human Resources,* 7th ed. (Cincinnati: South-Western Publishing Co., 1984), 389.

14. W. E. Baer, *Grievance Handling* (New York: American Management Association, 1970).

15. J. P. Swan, "Formal Grievance Procedures in Nonunion Plants," *Personnel Administrator* 26 (1981): 66–70.

16. D. W. Ewing, "What Business Thinks about Employee Rights," *Harvard Business Review* 55 (September-October, 1977), 81–94.

17. Federal Mediation and Conciliation Service, *31st Annual Report* (1978), 46–48.

Exercise

The Termination Decision

Bob Wells, a longtime supervisor for JBS, walked out of a meeting with his boss, John Wilson. John had informed Bob that, due to cutbacks, Bob's department would most likely be losing one or two positions within three months. This meant that Bob would have to decide which of his employees to lay off in the event economic conditions did not improve. "Besides," John had reminded him, "just last week we discussed what to do about some of your problem employees. Maybe this will be the solution. Give me a ranking of your employees, in the order that you would like them to be laid off, by the end of next week."

Bob went back to his office and wrote the following descriptions of the employees in his department. Using the information below, give each of these employees a ranking from 1 to 5 where 1 = the first employee to be laid off, 2 = the second to be laid off, and so on. The company is not unionized and has never faced layoffs before; therefore, there is no precedent or labor agreement to guide you in making your decisions.

_____ **Harry:** Harry transferred into my department six months ago from Shipping. He has been with JBS for four years. It is too early to be certain, but Harry seems to be one of my better performers. He is highly motivated, always does more than is expected of him, and is very friendly and cooperative.

_____ **Alecia:** Alecia has been with JBS for fifteen years and in my department for six years. Her performance is marginal. She barely does enough to get by and her quality of work is below average. It seems like I have to keep after her to do anything at all. I rated her as "below average" on her last performance evaluation.

_____ **Steve:** Steve has been in my department for nearly two years. He has average abilities and could be a good performer. He does not seem to take his job seriously, however. He constantly stretches lunch and break times. I sent him across town last week to pick up some reports and it took him one hour and forty-five minutes. It should have taken forty-five minutes at most. I gave him an "average" rating on his last performance evaluation.

_____ **Rick:** Rick has been an above-average performer ever since he joined my department five years ago. He is highly talented and motivated, but has been going to night school for the past four years working on his bachelor's degree in business administration. I have heard him say to coworkers that when he finally gets that degree, he will be looking for an interesting job. I estimate that he will be finished with his degree in two more years.

_____ **Mary:** Mary is an average performer. She has received an "average" rating on her performance evaluation every year since she joined the department eight years ago. I have suspected for the past three years that she has a drinking problem. While it does not seem to affect her job performance, it is really difficult to be certain, since she has always been a marginal performer. I am sure that I have smelled alcohol on her breath nearly every day after lunch and several times when she arrived for work in the morning.

Case

One Month on the Job

Will had accepted a job as computer programming department supervisor upon his graduation from Eastern College one month ago. He has a solid background in computer programming and systems analysis, as well as in supervision and management. He was excited about this opportunity to put his education and training to work.

The first few weeks on any new job are likely to be anxiety-producing and uncertain to some degree, but Will was beginning to feel comfortable in his new position. The six programmers he supervised seemed to have accepted him and he felt that a good working relationship was developing in the department. The six programmers all have similar backgrounds; all are graduates of the computer programming degree program of the local community college, and all are male. Four of the six employees were hired six months ago and were placed in a training program after the decision was made to expand the computer programming department. The other two employees have been with JBS and in the programming department for the past four years. In fact, until the expansion, they were the programming department, in its entirety.

Since these programmers did not have to interact with customers or other employees in order to do their work, Will asked for, and received, permission to begin a flextime working hours program. Programmers were free to schedule their own hours of work with two restrictions: (1) everyone had to be in the office between the hours of 11:00 A.M. and 2:00 P.M. to be available for departmental meetings and job assignments and (2) everyone had to work forty hours per week. If a programmer was working on a tough project he might put in twelve hours one day and only four hours the next. This schedule allowed employees flexibility in scheduling both personal appointments and their own work activities. All of the programmers seemed pleased with the implementation of the flextime program.

Will was sitting in his office at 5:30 P.M. reflecting on how well things had gone during his first month on the job. All of his employees seemed very happy and most projects were being completed on time, or even ahead of schedule. As he walked through the office on his way to the car, he noticed that one of his programmers was still working. He saw that it was one of the newer programmers, Jim Ferris.

"Got a problem, Jim?" Will inquired. "You're working on that new accounting summary program with Bill, aren't you? You know that Accounting wants to be able to use that program by the middle of the month. Will it be ready?"

"Why don't you ask Bill?" Jim snapped angrily.

Will was surprised at the response. "I don't understand, Jim. Is there a problem that I should know about?"

"If you would spend a little more time supervising this department, you would know what's going on," Jim retorted. "I shouldn't have to be the one to tell you. But I'm so angry that I will anyway. I'm not the only one who's mad. All four of the new programmers have been talking about looking for new jobs. Ever since you started that flextime program, we've been doing all the work. Bill and Henry don't put in anywhere near forty hours a week. They work long enough to be seen and then disappear. Don't you keep some kind of record of how many hours we work every week? If you did, you'd see that Bill and Henry only put in about thirty hours. They know that no one is checking on them and they're taking advantage of it. They also know that you're new and easygoing, and that you're not likely to call them on the carpet about it. They're really taking advantage of you, too, you know."

Will replied, "I'm sorry, Jim. I had no idea. I've been so busy looking for ways to improve things that I hadn't noticed this problem. I can promise you that I will do something about it immediately."

Instead of going home, Will walked back to his office and closed the door. He decided that he should make some plans about how to handle this problem and he should do it before Monday. He pulled out the company's Standard Operating Procedures (SOP) manual and began to look through it. He quickly discovered that JBS had no formal discipline procedure.

I guess that means I can handle this anyway I want, he thought. The best thing will be to call in each of the new programmers, individually, first thing Monday morning. If they corroborate Jim's story, I'll have no choice but to fire Bill and Henry on the spot.

Questions

1. What do you think of Will's strategy for handling the problem in his department?
2. If you were Will, how would you handle it?
3. Assume that Will goes in to talk to his boss before doing anything. The boss decides that JBS really needs a formal discipline procedure to guide supervisors and assigns the development of such a procedure to Will. Since Will does not know very much about discipline, he comes to you for advice. What recommendations would you make to Will? What should be included in a formal discipline procedure?

Part 2
Supervising Groups

Chapter 11

Group Dynamics

Learning Objectives

After reading this chapter, you should:

1. recognize the differences between formal and informal groups.
2. be aware of the reasons why groups form.
3. be able to describe the stages of group development.
4. know what effect roles, norms, and status have upon group behavior.
5. understand the causes and results of group cohesiveness.
6. be able to discuss the effect of groups upon individual behavior.
7. know how to deal with groups.
8. know how to conduct effective meetings.

Kris was beginning to wonder if she had made the right decision in hiring Paul last month. It was not so much that Paul was a poor performer. He was bright enough and seemed to catch on to the work quickly. The problem was with coworkers.

Paul had just finished an associate degree in business from the local community college when he applied for the job in Kris' department. While the job didn't require any formal education, Paul had seemed very eager and willing to work, so Kris hired him.

From the very begining, the other employees in the department did not have very much to do with Paul. In the past, they had always helped new employees to learn the ropes. But, with Paul they would not volunteer help of any kind unless Kris specifically asked that they do so. Kris had noticed, also, that Paul usually ate lunch alone. She could never remember hearing any of the others invite Paul to any of the social functions, activities which seemed to be very popular among the rest of the employees.

Kris could not be sure why the work group was rejecting Paul. The only explanation she could think of was that Paul was younger, single, and better educated than the others. In her estimation however, this didn't seem to be reason enough to cause the others to exclude him. She wondered whether there was anything she could do to help Paul gain the acceptance of the work group.

While we may not always be aware of it, groups significantly influence our behavior on a daily basis. All of us belong to many different types of groups, each of which exerts some demand upon our behavior. Family, friends, athletic clubs, and coworkers form the basis for some of the groups to which we belong. While these groups are not likely to change our basic beliefs, values, and needs, they exert strong pressures upon us to behave in certain ways. This chapter provides a definition of the term group and examines a variety of types of groups. The more specific reasons why groups form and the stages through which most groups pass in the course of their development are also discussed. Finally, the examination of a number of properties, or common characteristics, of groups and group members will provide the framework within which to talk about methods supervisors may use to deal effectively with groups.

Groups Defined

Not all gatherings of people are "groups" as the term is defined and used for purposes of this text. A crowd at a football game is not considered a group; neither are several people waiting for a bus or a mob rioting in the streets. Several characteristics distinguish groups from other gatherings of individuals. The definition of the term group will help make this distinction clear:

> A **group** is a collection of two or more people sharing a common goal
> or interest, who interact with one another, have differentiated roles,
> and perceive themselves to be a group.

This particular definition suggests that, for a group to exist, its members must (a) have a common goal, (b) interact with one another or be interdependent, (c) think of themselves as being a group, and (d) occupy specific roles within a group structure.[1]

Types of Groups in Organizations
Table 11.1

Group Type	Characteristics	Example
Command	Formal group Involves manager-employee relationships Formed by the organization	Head coach of a college football team Supervisor and employees
Task	Formal group Formed by the organization Formed to accomplish a specific task or to solve a particular problem	Team of six supervisors from a department assigned to solve a quality control problem Committee on determining training needs
Informal	Not formed by the organization Members drawn together because of common interests or similarities Group goals may differ from organizational goals	Group of employees who meet at neighborhood bar after work each Friday Group of employees who have joined together to try to prevent threatened layoffs

Groups may be classified in a number of ways. One of the most useful is to distinguish between formal groups and informal groups.

Classification of Groups

Formal Groups

Formal groups are those whose formation is initiated by the organization for the purpose of accomplishing specified tasks. Two types of formal groups are command groups and task groups. **Command groups** are groups made up of a supervisor or manager and that individual's employees. These groups are relatively permanent and appear on the organizational chart. **Task groups,** on the other hand, are temporary formal groups. These groups are put together by the organization to deal with a specific problem or project. When the problem or project is solved or completed, the group is disbanded. Task groups may not appear on the organizational chart if they are not expected to be in existence for any great length of time.

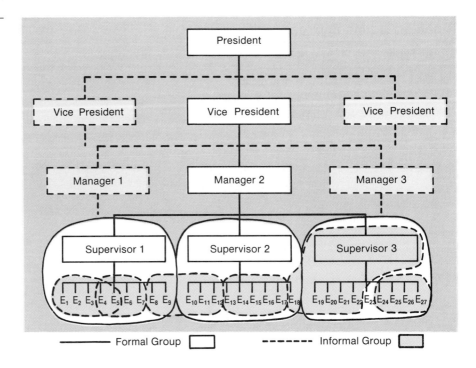

Informal Groups

Informal groups are not initiated by the formal organization. They arise when
individuals come together by choice because of common interests, beliefs, or personal attraction. Individuals join informal groups primarily to satisfy individual
needs that cannot be satisfied outside of group membership. Though these groups
are not sanctioned by the organization, informal groups exert a powerful influence upon the performance of individuals, of formal work groups, and, therefore,
of the organization.

The Formation of Groups

Formal groups are a product of the organizing process. Recall from chapter 1
that organizations follow operational procedures that enable organizational objectives to be reached. These procedures or activities cannot be established as the
ones necessary for attaining organizational goals until a great deal of planning
is first done and those objectives have been named. Typically, organizational operation entails a great diversity of activity. These activities must be grouped together in some logical fashion, during the planning process, to ensure that needed
activities are performed correctly and that these activities do not conflict with
one another. Most often this is accomplished by grouping similar activities together in departments or divisions, and by then placing supervisors and managers
in charge of the various groupings.

Informal groups, on the other hand, arise because individuals have perceived that some need can be satisfied through membership in such a group. Needs relating to affiliation, self-esteem, security, interpersonal attraction, and goal attainment are a few of the types of needs that could be satisfied through informal group membership.

Affiliation

Perhaps you have heard the story of the janitor who won several million dollars in the state lottery. When asked about his plans for the future, he replied that he would buy a new house, a new car, pay some bills, and take a couple of weeks off from work. It was surprising to many people that a multimillionaire would keep his job as a janitor at all. These people failed to consider the importance of social needs, or the need for affiliation, that many people satisfy through group membership. In all probability some of the janitor's closest friends were his fellow employees. Quitting his job, even though he no longer needed the money, could have jeopardized or even ended these relationships.

Identity, Self-Esteem, and Status

Group membership can contribute to the satisfaction of esteem and status needs if individuals feel proud to be members of the group, or if being a member is perceived as prestigious to some extent. Membership in an important or prestigious group allows individuals to feel that they are important.

Groups can contribute to individual feelings of identity. The need to interact with others often stems from the need to reassure ourselves that our perceptions of ourselves are correct.[2] Group membership allows us to compare our ideas, beliefs, and perceptions with others.

Security

There is safety in numbers, as the saying goes. Many people feel more secure in the context of a group. It is difficult to pinpoint individual responsibility for group decisions; thus, some individuals feel more secure about making suggestions and offering ideas in group situations. If the organizational decision turns out to be a bad one, management can point the finger at the group, but cannot fix blame on any individual. Furthermore, individuals often receive reassurance and support from other group members, reducing feelings of insecurity and vulnerability. Individuals know that if they have a problem, they can go to the group for help.

Interpersonal Attraction

Interpersonal attraction is another common reason that people join groups. Most of us feel more comfortable when we are around people similar to ourselves. Similarity of basic values and beliefs seems to be more important than many other characteristics, such as age, income, or place of birth.

Several factors tend to influence decisions of group membership based upon interpersonal attraction, three of the most important of which are proximity, similarity, and opportunity for interaction.

1. *Proximity.* **Proximity** refers to the physical distance between individuals. Individuals located closer together have greater opportunities for interaction; individuals who work together or in the same general location tend to form informal groups.
2. *Similarity.* Interpersonal attraction, to a large degree, is based upon similarity of needs, values, and beliefs. Interaction is more likely to be a rewarding experience when it takes place between individuals similar in characteristics. One of the primary rewards people gain from interaction is mutual support for, and agreement with, their ideas. Such support and agreement is likely to arise when the individuals are similar in terms of values, beliefs, and needs.
3. *Opportunity for interaction.* Sometimes constraints are placed upon individuals' opportunities to interact even though their locations are in close proximity to one another. It is not unusual for the work, itself, or for organizational rules to prevent employee interaction in work settings. In such situations it is unlikely that an informal group will form, even if all other factors conducive to group formation are present.

Assistance in Meeting Goals

Group effort can many times accomplish goals that individuals, acting alone, could not achieve. For example, many people hold the belief that it is important to help the needy and set this as a personal goal. There are few of us, however, who can do much about this problem on our own. But by joining one of the volunteer groups (e.g., the Red Cross), we can accomplish our personal goal by combining our efforts with those of others who have the same objective.

In work settings, employees are often reluctant to ask their supervisors to repeat instructions if they are still unsure what to do after the supervisor has finished explaining the assignment. These employees are usually not as reluctant to ask the work group for assistance. The supervisor controls, to some extent, the rewards that employees desire; hence, employees do not want to appear ineffective to the supervisor. The work group is perceived as more supportive and generally, not as threatening as the supervisor.

Stages of Group Development

The process of formation is similar for most groups, development following a general pattern that can be broken down into stages. The amount of time spent at any stage may vary among groups but the sequence remains the same.[3] Four distinct stages of development make up that sequence; those stages are forming, storming, norming, and performing.[4]

Stage 1: Forming

In the **forming** stage, group members try to learn what behaviors the group finds acceptable. Employees begin to discover what is expected of them in terms of output; they learn the particulars associated with appropriate dress, lunch and break times, and quitting time. These times followed by the group are not necessarily those set more officially at the organizational level. For example, organizational policy might determine that fifteen-minute breaks be taken in the morning and afternoon. The informal group could establish twenty-minute breaks as the norm. Or, the informal group might tolerate leaving work a few minutes early at the end of the day, but look quite negatively upon being a few minutes late in the morning.

Stage 2: Storming

During what is called the **storming** stage, members are beginning to learn which behaviors are acceptable and unacceptable, but are still reluctant to give up their individuality to become just another group member. A great deal of conflict among group members can occur at this stage.

Stage 3: Norming

Members who remain in the group through the first two stages begin to form close interpersonal relationships with other members at the **norming** stage. Members also begin to take on the various roles necessary to getting the group's goals accomplished.

Stage 4: Performing

Not until the **performing** stage is group effort channeled toward task accomplishment. During the first three stages effort is concentrated toward becoming a group and forming a group structure. But by stage 4, members have adopted roles within the group and have begun performing them. Attention now becomes focused upon accomplishing the goals that the group has set for itself.

As the group progresses through these four stages of development, individuals learn, first to trust each other, then to fulfill a particular role within the group, and finally to work together to accomplish the group's goals. During the course of this development, a group structure is formed.

Most groups, formal or informal, have structural characteristics just as organizations do. This structure is necessary to enable the group to accomplish its goals. Elements of **group structure** include norms, roles, status and cohesiveness.

Group Structure

Norms

Norms are the acceptable standards of behavior that come to be shared by the group's members. Norms serve as the criteria by which behaviors are defined as acceptable or unacceptable for the group. Most norms are informal or unwritten, and are learned through a process of trial and error, and by observing other members. When group members accept a norm, that standard exerts a substantial influence upon their behavior.

The group can put considerable pressure on its members to conform to the group norms. One form of pressure is the punishment of isolation or of the threat of expulsion from the group. If group membership has been rewarding for these members, either strategy will be a powerful inflence upon behavior.

The group may also exert more subtle pressure to conform. A classic experiment by Asch revealed the impact that group pressure can have on individual judgment.[5] In the experiment Asch seated people in groups of seven or eight and asked them to compare two cards held up by the experimenter. On one of the cards was a single line; on the other were three lines of varying length (see fig. 11.2). As the figure indicates, the lines on the second card were of quite different lengths. Each subject had to announce aloud which of the lines from the second card matched the length of the line on the first card.

Asch set up his conformity experiment by arranging it so that only one naive subject at a time was in the room. The other six or seven "subjects" (called confederates) knew what the experiment was all about and were instructed to give incorrect answers. The confederates were always allowed to announce their answer before the naive subject. For example, all of the confederates might say that line *c* matched the line on card 1. Asch's results showed that subjects gave answers they knew were wrong about 35 percent of the time. These individuals knew they were giving incorrect answers, but they wanted to be consistent with the others in the group. This experiment illustrates the strength of the need of many people to fit in with the group or to avoid appearing to be different.

Roles

Every group member occupies at least one role within the structure of the group. A **role** is the set of expected behavior patterns associated with a particular task or position within the group. The roles of formal groups (i.e., departmental or work group roles) are activities that must be performed by individuals in specified positions. For instance, the chairperson of the management department at State University is expected to organize and control the Department of Management. The supervisor of Accounts Payable/Receivable is expected to see to it that bills are paid and that amounts due are collected.

The informal group also has roles that need to be performed if the group is to be successful. Informal group roles may be divided into three categories: task roles, building and maintenance roles, and individual roles.[6] Task roles relate to the goals of the group. Problem solving, decision making, information gathering, and idea evaluation are examples of task roles. Building and maintenance roles

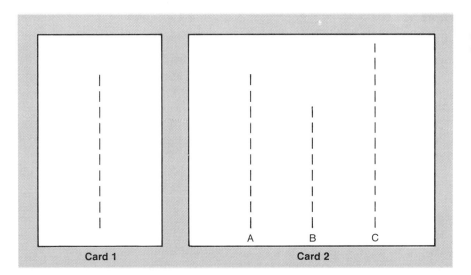

Figure 11.2
Examples of cards used
in Asch experiment

Card 1   Card 2

A   B   C

are directed at keeping the group together and functioning as a unit. Members occupying these roles are supportive of others; they try to reduce conflict when it develops, encourage communication between all members, and are willing to compromise for the sake of the group. Both task roles and building and maintenance roles are necessary for group effectiveness in accomplishing its goals.

The third category of roles is individual roles. These roles quite often prove to be dysfunctional to the group. Individual roles are directed at satisfying individual needs and incorporate little concern for the group. If you have ever been a member of a group, you have probably noticed members who interfered with group progress by diverting discussion from the task at hand; who seemed to argue or disagree more than necessary; who tried to get attention for themselves or attempted to dominate group discussion; or who chose to fool around rather than participate in group discussions.

Problems are likely to arise unless individual roles are minimized. Problems can arise from task and building and maintenance roles, as well. Employees are members of both formal and informal groups, and often, more than one informal group. Each of these groups has its own set of norms and roles. When the roles of one group are inconsistent with the roles of another group, **role conflict** is said to exist. If you are unsure what behaviors are expected of you, you will experience **role ambiguity. Role overload** occurs when an individual receives too much information about their role in the group. Individuals may perceive that other group members' expectations of them are too high. **Role underload** takes place when the expectations of group members are too low. Each of these situations can cause stress for the individual until the problem is resolved.

Status

Another characteristic of group structure that emerges during the group development process is that of status relationships. **Status** differentiates members from one another, and is generally considered to be a relative ranking of prestige within the group. Individuals attain status in a variety of ways. Sometimes status accompanies position within the formal organization; supervisors generally have higher status than employees. Informal group leaders often have higher status than other group members. Organizations sometimes provide employees with symbols of status. For example, supervisors typically have larger desks than their employees. Higher-level managers may have even larger desks with carpeting in their offices and a larger nameplate than supervisors.

Status can affect the way in which employees view themselves and the way in which they believe that the organization views them. The distinctions in status may appear at different levels in different organizations. Differentiations may be made between supervisors and employees in some companies. Others may make no separation at that level, but make very visible distinctions between the status symbols accorded to supervisors and those given to their managers. In this situation, the supervisor would be found sitting at the same type of desk, in the same physical location as their employees, while the manager would have a private office with an expensive desk, large nameplate, and plush carpeting. Supervisors working within such a context could easily feel that the organization was sending them a message that they were not particularly important which, in turn, would be detrimental to morale at the level of the supervisors.

Status can also be acquired because of personal characteristics, such as education, age, sex, expertise, and high job performance. No matter what its particular source, status has a strong affect upon the behavior of group members.

Cohesiveness

Group cohesiveness may be defined as the degree to which members want the group to continue and want to remain members of the group. There is substantial evidence suggesting that members of cohesive groups communicate more frequently and openly with one another.[7] Further, it has been found that members of cohesive groups are more likely to be more energetic in group activities and less likely to be absent from group meetings than members of less cohesive groups.[8] Group cohesiveness, therefore, can function as an important influence upon group and individual behavior. An awareness of some of the variables influencing the level of cohesiveness in groups will broaden the understanding of the likely consequences of cohesiveness for the work situation.

Group cohesiveness is the product of individuals' satisfaction with their group membership and their desire to continue this membership. Several factors influence the degree to which cohesiveness develops in a group:

Variables Affecting Levels of Group Cohesiveness

Group size. Smaller groups are more likely to develop high levels of cohesiveness than larger groups. Members of larger groups have more difficulty interacting with all other members. The larger the group becomes, the more likely it is that some members will become reluctant to participate freely. Any reluctance to participate is likely to lead to a decline in the satisfaction some members feel. As a group continues to grow, it is likely to begin to break down into smaller groups at some point as members attempt to increase the amount of interaction they have with other members.

Homogeneity of members. People tend to join groups whose members are similar to themselves, particularly with respect to beliefs and values. Groups whose members are **homogeneous,** or quite alike in their characteristics, are likely to become more cohesive than groups whose members are **heterogeneous,** or mixed in terms of those characteristics. It is difficult to imagine a highly cohesive group whose members' basic beliefs and values are very different.

Isolation. The more a group is physically isolated from other groups or individuals, the more cohesive it is likely to become. Isolation makes it difficult for members to interact with anyone outside the group; thus, almost all interaction is within the group and any close relationships that develop will most likely develop with other group members. This physical isolation sometimes generates in group members a suspicious view of anyone not belonging to the group. A clear distinction between "insiders" and "outsiders," is a perception which further contributes to the cohesiveness of the group.

Success of the group. Almost by definition, groups that succeed in accomplishing important group goals are apt to be cohesive. Similarly, members are more likely to be satisfied with their membership if the group is successful.

Competition with other groups. Competition produces results similar to those brought about by physical isolation. When two groups are in competition with one another, members tend to identify even more strongly with their own groups. Members begin thinking in terms of "we" versus "they" (i.e., insiders versus outsiders).

External threats to the group. When groups perceive that they are being threatened by other individuals or groups, they tend to band together and become even more cohesive. There is perhaps no stronger influence upon group cohesiveness than a commonly shared threat. Threats to a work group can come from a number of sources, including individuals outside the group, other work groups, or even the supervisor.

In general, the more satisfied group members are with their memberships, the more highly cohesive the group will be. Besides the factors mentioned, members may derive membership satisfaction from the status, prestige, or feelings of security associated with belonging to the group.

Deterents to Cohesiveness

Just as success, competitive situations, isolation, small size, homogeneity, and external threats can stimulate group cohesiveness, so the relative absence of these elements can cause group cohesiveness to decline. For example, failure to accomplish important goals, a large group size, and heterogeneity of members would all produce negative influences upon group cohesiveness. Each of the following also act as restraints on the development of cohesiveness:

1. *Attraction to external groups.* Members who become attracted to external groups are likely to experience a decline in the degree to which they wish to remain members of the focal group.
2. *Competition or conflict among group members.* If two or more group members begin competing with one another for such things as control of the group, resources, or status, group cohesiveness is likely to decline. This is especially true if the competition escalates into conflict. Other group members are likely to begin to take sides and the conflict may spread throughout the group.
3. *Turnover among group leaders.* One unifying force in any group is the group leader. The leader is often viewed by other members as having the highest prestige and status within the group. Some members may initially have been drawn to the group because they identified with, or admired, the leader. If such a leader leaves the group cohesiveness is likely to decline unless some other member emerges as a strong leader. Without such a leader group members are likely to start being attracted to external groups and leave the group, themselves.
4. *Rewards based upon individual performance.* If rewards are administered in such a way that group members perceive themselves to be in a win-or-lose situation, cohesiveness is likely to decline. A win-or-lose situation is one in which members believe that if they are to get greater rewards, someone else must get fewer rewards. An individual's rewards are, therefore, believed to be earned at the expense of some other group member. Such a perception is likely to lead to competition and, perhaps, conflict within the group.

Consequences of Group Cohesiveness

It is impossible to make the unqualified statement either that group cohesiveness is always desirable or that it is always undesirable. To a large degree, the desirability of group cohesiveness depends upon the extent to which the goals of the group are consistent with the goals of the organization. Group cohesiveness creates a willingness in members to exert greater amounts of effort in attempting to accomplish group goals. From the organization's perspective, this cohesiveness is undesirable if the group goals are inconsistent with organizational goals. The key is to bring about goal integration. **Goal integration** is achieved when group members believe that accomplishing organizational goals enables them to accomplish group and individual goals.

Factors Affecting Group Cohesiveness   Table 11.2

Factors Increasing Cohesiveness	Factors Decreasing Cohesiveness
Agreement on group goals	Disagreement on group goals
Frequent interaction among members	Infrequent interaction among members
Personal attractiveness of members	Attraction to external groups
Competition with other groups	Competition among group members
Success in accomplishing important group goals	Failure to accomplish important group goals
Small size	Large size
Presence of external threat	Heterogeneous members
Physical isolation of group	Turnover of group members
Homogeneous members	

Sometimes, high group cohesiveness causes members to identify very strongly with the goals of the group, but not necessarily with the goals of the organization. This result is called suboptimization. **Suboptimization** is a problem because, where it occurs, group members have lost sight of the more general organizational goals and have become totally concerned with the achievement of the group's goals. Maintaining and building the group becomes more important than contributing to the organization.

The more cohesive the group, the more likely the members will resist change. By definition, group cohesiveness implies that members are satisfied with the group as it is and so they are reluctant to support change for fear that it might negatively affect the group. Members are, quite simply, happy with the status quo.

Group cohesiveness gives the group a great deal of power over individuals. As has already been pointed out, groups frequently use isolation or the threat of expulsion to get members to conform to group norms. In a highly cohesive group, where members are very satisfied with their memberships, it is not surprising that this technique works.

Group cohesiveness may have a positive or negative effect upon performance or productivity, depending upon the circumstances. If the group accepts the organizational goals, then cohesiveness is likely to have a positive effect upon performance. Members will be committed to accomplishing organizational goals because to do so is consistent with the goals of the group. On the other hand, if the group does not accept organizational goals, then the effect of cohesiveness upon performance will be negative to the extent that the group will sanction the withholding of effort on the job or even, perhaps, the sabotage of any attempts to accomplish organizational goals.

Supervising Groups

According to Bradford, formal leaders, including supervisors, perform three primary roles through which they are able to manage informal groups within organizations.[9] First, there are some activities that informal group members do not have the authority to perform. It is the formal leader who must perform the role involving such management activities as hiring, termination, and performance appraisal. In their second role, formal leaders help group members to grow and develop. Often this involves sharing some of the leadership activities with the group; delegation and participation can be used to develop employees to their potential. Finally, the formal leader must interface with external groups and individuals. Groups exist within a very complex environment of other formal and informal groups and individuals, both within and outside the organization. Formal leaders must interact with these parts of the environment in order to acquire resources for the group, negotiate cooperation with other groups, and gather information needed by the group.

Supervisors must be aware of the structural characteristics of groups in order to understand what effects those characteristics could be having upon the behavior of individuals. The behavior of individuals is often affected and changed by group membership; and individuals often behave in groups in ways they would not behave independently of the group.

Since the informal group leader typically exercises some degree of influence upon the norms and goals of the group, supervisors should try to identify and work closely with those informal group leaders. It is critical that the informal group accept the formal organization's goals to the greatest extent possible. Otherwise, the informal group may exert effort in directions other than those which lead to the accomplishment of those goals. If supervisors are able to convince informal group leaders of the importance of the formal organization's goals, these leaders are likely to be able, in turn, to influence other group members. Where goal integration is achieved, supervisors may want to take steps to help increase the cohesiveness of the informal group. Where sufficient goal integration is not possible, supervisors may wish to take steps to reduce cohesiveness.

Holding Effective Meetings

One group setting in which many supervisors spend a great deal of time is that of meetings. Meetings can be effective and can serve many useful purposes, but unless they are managed effectively, they can become virtual wastes of time.

The primary advantage of meetings is that they enable people to get together face-to-face to share ideas, problems, and information. If a complex decision must be made, a meeting on the subject affords the opportunity to gather input from a variety of individuals, each of whom has the potential to make a unique contribution to the decision-making process. If a decision is likely to have any bearing upon different departments or divisions within the organization, the decision, once made, may be better accepted if representatives from each of these areas are present at the meeting. Unless the meeting is carefully planned and managed, however, it can fail to accomplish anything.

Preparing for the Meeting

As a supervisor, if you have called the meeting or are responsible for its planning, the first thing you should do is develop an agenda. An **agenda** is a list of items or topics that need to be discussed; these items should relate directly to the objectives you hope to accomplish by holding the meeting.[10] A copy of the agenda should be sent to all participants in advance of the meeting so that everyone planning to attend will have time to consider the items to be discussed, gather information related to a topic, or otherwise prepare for the meeting. This advance preparation should reduce the amount of time taken up at the start of the meeting for the answering of general questions about the purpose of the meeting.

Give careful consideration to who should attend the meeting. This will be determined, at least in part, by the purpose of the meeting. If the purpose of the meeting is to make a decision that will have impact upon more than one department within the organization, then each of these departments should be represented. Each department should have the opportunity to provide input, voice objections, and suggest alternatives in advance of the decision. These departments are much more likely to be committed to implementing the decision once it is made if they feel they have been given ample opportunity to offer input. As a general rule, only those who have a strong interest in at least one item on the agenda should be invited to the meeting. A great deal of time can be wasted by involving uninterested participants who will try to discuss items not on the agenda.

Finally, don't call a meeting unless you have a good reason.[11] If you can accomplish your objectives by sending memos or making telephone calls, do so. Many employees resent being called away from their work to discuss relatively simple or trivial matters.

During the Meeting

You have prepared an agenda and have mailed it to participants in advance of the meeting. Once the meeting begins, you must stick to that agenda. Do not let the discussion get sidetracked to issues not on the agenda. You may have to regain the proper course of the meeting by saying something like, "That's an interesting idea, but it's not on the agenda for this meeting. Perhaps we can add it to the agenda of the next meeting."

Start and stop the meeting on time. The agenda should include a timetable for discussion and this timetable is something you should follow very closely. If you are new to the organization or work group, you may not get everything covered during your first few meetings. It may take employees a couple of meetings to learn that when you set times for a meeting, you will adhere to them. Never delay the start of a meeting waiting for participants who are late. Such a delay only punishes those who are on time and it rewards those who are late. This is especially important if you are relatively new to the organization. Employees learn what types of behaviors are acceptable during their first few contacts with you. One of the things they should learn is that you begin and end meetings on time.

As you begin the meeting, you should first clarify the purpose of the meeting and then state what you hope to accomplish by the end of it. Too often, meetings are called to discuss a particular issue, but no action is taken. In these meetings the entire time allotted is spent discussing the issue, and stating and restating points of view. This makes it necessary to call another meeting before any decision can be made.

Encouraging Participation

One of the biggest advantages of meetings is that a variety of individuals, each with different backgrounds, education, and experience, have an opportunity to provide input on a common subject. Some individuals may be reluctant, however, to participate in the presence of these other people. They may very well have important information that should be brought to the attention of the others but many people lack the self-confidence to speak in front of a group. As the meeting leader, you should be sensitive to the hesitancy of some individuals and actively encourage everyone to participate.

One method that has been found to be successful in encouraging participation is called nominal grouping.[12] **Nominal grouping** is a process requiring the execution of the following steps:

1. State the problem or question to the group very precisely. Make the group aware of any underlying assumptions, limitations, or constraints of the issue.
2. Ask the group to respond in writing with any questions, solutions, or requests for additional information. The anonymous written response gives individuals lacking the self-confidence to speak in public the chance to participate in a way that makes them more comfortable but is still productive to the group.
3. Summarize the written responses and provide the group with this information.
4. Allow for some discussion of the responses. Even though some criticism of an individual's suggestion could arise, it is unlikely that such criticism will discourage that person from further participation since the provider of the suggestion cannot be identified.
5. After some discussion, ask once again for written responses, suggestions, ideas, requests, or solutions.
6. Repeat steps 2 through 5 until a majority of group members agree upon a solution.

After the Meeting

Immediately after the meeting, you should summarize the major points in writing and distribute copies to all participants. You may want to designate a secretary or participant to record the **minutes** as a permanent record of what transpired at the meeting. In the event of any uncertainty or disagreement about what was decided, the minutes can be used as a reference and source of clarification. If

Holding Effective Meetings	Table 11.3

Steps to Take

Preparing for the Meeting

1. Do you have a good reason for calling the meeting?
2. Prepare an agenda and distribute it to participants in advance.
3. Carefully consider who should attend the meeting.

During the Meeting

1. Start and end the meeting on time.
2. Do not wait for latecomers.
3. Stick to the agenda.
4. Don't let discussion stray from agenda items.
5. Encourage all members to participate.
6. Make sure meeting objectives are accomplished.

After the Meeting

1. Provide a written record of the meeting and distribute it to all participants.

more than one meeting is required to reach a decision, minutes will alleviate the necessity of repeating the discussion of items covered in previous meetings.

Summary

Groups were defined as a collection of two or more people who share some common goal or interest, interact with one another, have differentiated roles, and perceive themselves to be a group. Groups may be categorized as either formal or informal groups. Two types of formal groups are command groups and task groups.

Groups form for a variety of reasons. Formal groups arise as output from the organizing process. Informal groups become established because individuals perceive that group membership can satisfy some need that will otherwise go unsatisfied. Such needs may include security, affiliation, esteem, identity, and status. Informal groups cannot form, unless individuals have opportunities to interact with one another.

Most groups go through similar stages in the course of their development. The chapter discussed four stages of group development: forming, storming, norming, and performing. As a group progresses through these four stages, members learn, first, to trust each other; second, they determine what roles members will occupy; and, finally, the attention of the group becomes focused upon goal accomplishment.

Groups begin to take on certain characteristics as they develop; these characteristics form a group structure. Norms are the acceptable standards of behavior established by the group and shared by its members. Roles are sets of expected behavior patterns. Three categories of group roles were identified: task roles, building and maintenance roles, and individual roles.

Group cohesiveness was defined as the degree to which members want the group to continue and want to remain members of the group. Members of cohesive groups tend to communicate more frequently and more openly with one another, are willing to exert a considerable amount of effort on behalf of the group, and are less likely to be absent from group meetings than members of noncohesive groups.

On the negative side, members of cohesive groups tend to resist change, lose sight of overall organizational goals, and may withhold effort if the group is not one that accepts organizational goals.

Cohesiveness is likely to be higher in small groups whose members are homogeneous. Other factors affecting cohesiveness include the physical isolation of the group, the group's success in accomplishing important group goals, competition with other groups, the presence of external threats to the group, attraction to external groups, competition or conflict among group members, turnover of group leaders, and the existence of individual reward systems.

When interacting with a group in the context of a meeting, it is important to create an agenda and stick to it. Meetings can be great time wasters unless they are planned in advance and carefully managed. One of the advantages of meetings is that they bring together individuals possessing different experience, training, and education. To capitalize on this advantage, however, supervisors must encourage participation from members who lack self-confidence in group situations. Nominal grouping is one technique that may be used to encourage all members to participate in discussions and decision making.

Key Terms

agenda (p. 247)	norming (p. 239)
command groups (p. 234)	norms (p. 240)
formal groups (p. 235)	performing (p. 239)
forming (p. 239)	proximity (p. 238)
goal integration (p. 244)	role (p. 240)
group (p. 234)	role ambiguity (p. 241)
group cohesiveness (p. 242)	role conflict (p. 241)
group structure (p. 239)	role overload (p. 241)
heterogeneous (p. 243)	role underload (p. 241)
homogeneous (p. 243)	status (p. 242)
informal groups (p. 236)	storming (p. 239)
minutes (p. 248)	suboptimization (p. 245)
nominal grouping (p. 248)	task groups (p. 234)

1. Define the term *group* as it was used in the chapter.
2. Explain the difference between formal and informal groups.
3. Why do formal groups arise? Why do informal groups arise?
4. What are the factors which influence whether individuals will join a group for reasons of interpersonal attraction?
5. Describe each of the stages of group development. What changes occur during each stage?
6. Describe the characteristics of a group that is likely to progress very quickly through the stages of group development.
7. Describe the characteristics of a group that is likely to progress very slowly through the stages of group development.
8. What are norms? How do they influence the behavior of group members?
9. What are roles? How do they influence the behavior of group members?
10. How do groups get members to conform?
11. Explain role conflict, role ambiguity, role overload, and role underload. What effect does the presence of each have upon individual behavior?
12. How do individuals acquire status within groups?
13. What is group cohesiveness?
14. How do some groups become highly cohesive?
15. When might a supervisor want to decrease the cohesiveness of a group that he or she supervises?
16. When might a supervisor want to increase the cohesiveness of a group that he or she supervises?
17. What factors cause cohesiveness to increase?
18. What factors cause cohesiveness to decrease?
19. What does it take to conduct an effective meeting?

References

1. M. E. Shaw, *Group Dynamics* (New York: McGraw-Hill, 1976).
2. L. Festinger, "A Theory of Social Comparison," *Human Relations* 7 (1954): 114–140.
3. J. M. Ivancevich and J. T. McMahon, "Group Development, Trainer-style and Carry-over Job Satisfaction and Performance," *Academy of Management Journal* 19 (1976): 395–412.
4. B. W. Tuckman, "Developmental Sequence in Small Groups," *Psychological Bulletin* 63 (1965): 384–399.
5. S. E. Asch, "Effects of Group Pressure upon the Modification and Distortion of Judgments," in *Groups, Leadership, and Men,* ed. H. Guetzkow (Pittsburgh: Carnegie Press, 1951), 177–190.

6. K. D. Benne and P. Sheats, "Functional Roles of Group Members," *Journal of Social Issues* 4 (1948): 41–49.
7. B. E. Lott and A. J. Lott, "The Formation of Positive Attitudes toward Group Members," *Journal of Abnormal and Social Psychology* 61 (1960): 297–300.
8. M. E. Shaw, *Group Dynamics* (New York: McGraw-Hill, 1976).
9. D. L. Bradford, *Group Dynamics* (Chicago: Science Research Associates, 1984).
10. E. F. Konczai, "Making the Most of Meetings," *Supervisory Management* 27 (March 1982): 2–6.
11. P. R. Timm, "Let's Not Have a Meeting!" *Supervisory Management* 27 (August 1982): 2–7.
12. A. L. Delbecq, A. H. Van de Ven, and D. H. Gustafson, *Group Techniques for Program Planning: A Guide to Nominal Group and Delphi Processes* (Glenview, Ill.: Scott, Foresman, & Co., 1975).

Exercise

Analyzing Your Group Roles

List all of the formal groups of which you are a member and the primary role(s) you occupy. Then list all of the informal groups of which you are a member and the primary role(s) you occupy. How do you think you came to occupy each of these roles? Do you occupy the same type of role in each group? Why or why not?

"The employees in my department appear to be interested in getting by and doing nothing more," Dennis complained. "I've tried everything I know of to motivate them to perform at higher levels, but nothing seems to work."

"It's not your fault," Ted reassured him. "You inherited a real mess when you replaced Wes last month. Wes was too easy going with his employees. He seemed to be more interested in getting his employees to like him than he was concerned with their productivity. And then there's Jeff. Wes and Jeff were close friends. Anything Jeff wanted to do was okay with Wes. Obviously, that gave Jeff a great deal of power and status with the other employees. When they wanted something, they would go to Jeff. He'd go to Wes, who never refused them anything."

"Now you've got a situation where whatever Jeff says, goes with the other employees in the department," Ted continued. "If he told them to stop working and go home at one o'clock in the afternoon, I really think they'd do it! The only way you're going to get control of your department is to get rid of Jeff somehow."

Dennis thought about Ted's remarks as he walked back to his office after lunch. He really had to do something. As things stood now, he was afraid to ask anyone to do anything out of the ordinary for fear Jeff would tell them they didn't have to do it. He was sure they would listen to Jeff before they would listen to him. If he gave Jeff that opportunity it would soon be clear to everyone who was running the department, and his authority as a supervisor would be totally destroyed.

On the other hand, Dennis thought to himself, what would happen if he fired Jeff or had him transferred to another department? How would the other employees respond to that? I can't think of any other alternatives, Dennis concluded as he sat down at his desk.

Just then the phone rang. It was Fred, another supervisor with JBS. "Dennis, you'd better get that crew of yours in line," Fred warned. "I've got things stacked up in my department because your employees refuse to put in any overtime. Some guy named Jeff said they had never worked any overtime in the past and they had no intention of starting now. It's the busy season right now. Everyone has to work some overtime to keep up. Who is this Jeff anyway? He said that JBS can't expect its employees to give it more than eight hours every day."

"Thanks for letting me know about this, Fred," Dennis said. "I'll take care of Jeff." Well, that's it, Dennis thought as he left his office. He concluded then that the only thing left for him to do was to walk up to Jeff and fire him so that the other employees would know who was the boss of the department.

Questions

1. What is the real problem in this situation?
2. Do you agree with Dennis' assessment of the situation? Do you agree with his proposed solution?
3. What would you do if you were in Dennis' position?
4. What could you do, as Wes' replacement, to avoid the kinds of problems illustrated in this case?

Chapter 12

Managing Conflict

Learning Objectives

After reading this chapter, you should:

1. be able to define conflict.
2. understand the various types of conflict.
3. know the primary causes of conflict.
4. be able to discuss both positive and negative results of conflict.
5. be aware of some common responses to conflict.
6. know several techniques that supervisors can use to manage conflict.

Pete slammed the phone down and headed for his boss' office. I've got to put a stop to this before the company starts getting complaints from customers, he thought as he stepped into the elevator.

Pete supervises five accounting clerks in the order processing department at JBS Manufacturing. Accounting clerks' responsibilities include processing supplier invoices for payment and billing customers for shipments. Pete's employees have been having trouble lately getting their work done on time.

The efficiency of the order processing department depends quite a lot on the efficiency of the shipping department. Order Processing cannot bill any customer until Shipping sends the bills of lading, which are the records of each customer's name, address, and the types and amounts of products that were sent. Pete's department uses these documents to bill the customers for the shipment. Obviously, if Pete's employees do not receive these documents, they have no way of knowing which customers to bill for what products.

Pete first became aware that a problem existed when he received the computer printout on the finished goods inventory levels for JBS products. He noticed that the inventory levels were much lower than he expected. He called the warehouse and found out that there had been a number of shipments for which his department had not received any bills of lading.

Pete's next move was to call Don Baker, the manager of the shipping department, to ask why Order Processing had received no bills of lading on these shipments. Don's reply was "I don't have time to worry about your job and mine too. Billing customers is your job. I've got enough to do to deal with shipments to customers. If you've got a problem handling your job, I suggest you have a talk with your boss."

Pete decided to do just that. He knew that JBS was losing money because billing to customers was a month or two late. JBS could have been earning interest on the customer payments. The company was also losing money unnecessarily on their insurance payments. Pete's department was responsible for informing the accounting department of weekly inventory levels for insurance purposes. For the last two months, JBS had been paying for insurance on these products that had already been shipped. If Pete didn't get things straightened out in a hurry, the whole situation was liable to turn into a very serious and costly problem.

Sometimes it seems like we're not working for the same company, Pete thought. I don't understand why our departments can't work together instead of against each other.

Until recently, management and organization textbooks approached the subject of conflict in organizations as though it was a completely undesirable element of corporate life, causing damage to the proper functioning of the organization. This point of view has altered somewhat with the realization that certain types of conflict can be beneficial to most organizations. Organization efforts today place less emphasis on eliminating conflict and more on finding ways to manage conflict in order to take advantage of its potential to produce positive results. As a supervisor, you will face many opportunities to become involved in conflict management. Because of your position in the organizational hierarchy, you may be called upon to resolve conflict between individual employees, between your work group and another supervisor's work group, between your employees and yourself, between your employees and middle management, and between yourself and another supervisor.

Conflict is a process involving two or more individuals or groups that are opposed on some idea or point of interest; it is a process that may manifest itself in only a brief occurrence, or it may take place over a relatively long time period. Thomas more specifically refers to conflict as a process which begins when one party perceives that the other has frustrated, or is about to frustrate some concern of his.[1] According to this definition, conflict begins the moment an individual or group perceives that another party is about to prevent the satisfaction of an important need or the accomplishment of an important goal. It is at this moment that the individual or group being regarded as the adversary or threat will start to be affected by this perception. They may feel additional pressure, stress, or anger, or may begin engaging in behaviors to retaliate against the source of the conflict.

What Is Conflict

Conflict may arise between any individuals or groups within an organization; it may also occur within individuals or groups. As a supervisor, you are likely to have to deal with each of these types of conflict.

Types of Conflict

Intrapersonal Conflict

Intrapersonal conflict is conflict within an individual. For example, a supervisor might give an order to an employee to do something that the employee considers to be morally wrong. The employee now faces conflict between wanting to do as the supervisor says, and doing something he or she believes to be wrong. Similarly, an employee might be told to perform a task in a particular way when the employee knows there is a much better way to do it. This employee must then choose between doing the task as the supervisor wants it done, and performing the task in the way the individual personally feels is best. Basically, conflict within an individual occurs because of goal conflict. **Goal conflict** results when an individual wants to accomplish two or more mutually exclusive goals, meaning that the nature of these goals is such that to achieve one of them is to preclude the achievement of the others. Similarly, goal conflict arises in the opposite situation. An individual could be faced with two undesirable goals or alternatives and be forced to choose one of them. For example, a supervisor must terminate an employee or continue to put up with extremely low performance levels. Both alternatives are unpleasant, but a choice must be made.

Three basic types of intrapersonal conflict can be identified:

1. *Approach–approach conflict.* When an individual is faced with a choice between two or more mutually exclusive alternatives, all of which are desirable, that person experiences **approach–approach conflict.** Upon graduating from college, you may be faced with a decision between two very attractive jobs. One has a higher salary, while the other promises to be more challenging and interesting. You may be attracted to both jobs but you cannot, obviously, accept both.

2. *Avoidance–avoidance conflict.* When an individual must choose between two or more undesirable alternatives **avoidance–avoidance conflict** is the likely result. Employees quite often must either perform an undesirable activity or face some form of punishment. Neither alternative is desirable, yet one must be chosen.

3. *Approach–avoidance conflict.* When an individual is faced with a single alternative but this alternative has both desirable and undesirable characteristics, the person must deal with **approach–avoidance conflict.** For example, you might be offered a promotion with a much higher salary at a time when money is extremely important to you. The new job also requires a great deal of travel, however, an aspect of the job that you will not enjoy.

The importance of these forms of conflict, from the point of view of a supervisor, is clear. Intrapersonal conflict can have positive or negative effects. A person experiencing approach–approach conflict could become more highly motivated because of the development of this conflict. On the other hand, if the conflict persists for a long period of time, the person could begin to experience such a level of stress that it could be damaging to the person's job performance and physical health.[2] Supervisors must be prepared to advise and counsel employees so that levels of intrapersonal conflict do not become so high that the employee's job performance suffers.

Interpersonal Conflict

Interpersonal conflict occurs between individuals. It may arise because of personality differences, competition over resources differences in basic beliefs and values, or incompatible goals. Situations involving interpersonal conflict are common to the supervisor's experience. They encounter frequent and substantial differences in values, beliefs, and goals among even small groups of employees. Age, for example, is a recurrent contributor to interpersonal conflict. Employees who differ widely in age very often entertain equally dissimilar beliefs and values. Such differences are what tend to create suspicion or lack of trust among younger and older employees.

As was pointed out, the differences in the goals that individuals want to accomplish sometimes create a source of conflict. When individuals have incompatible personal goals, conflict is likely to result. Perhaps a new employee perceives a need for change and pushes strongly to initiate it. An employee who has been in the department for a longer period of time may resist any attempts at change and may work just as hard to keep things the way they are. Of course, conflict of this type could occur between a supervisor and employee, as well.

Reward systems that pit employees against one another are quite likely to stimulate conflict while it is possible for competition to produce high levels of motivation among employees, reward systems that foster a "win-lose" mentality may allow conflict to replace competition, unless something is done to prevent it. The win-lose mentality is a perception of available rewards as fixed and relatively limited. In these situations it is up to the supervisor to maintain the situation as one of competition rather than conflict. If employees believe that the supervisor administers rewards equitably, basing those allocations upon objective and performance-related criteria, then competition is more likely to result than is conflict. If the system by which rewards are administered is viewed as subjective or arbitrary, and not closely related to performance, competition is likely to give way to conflict. Employees may perceive that the only way they can get more rewards is to prevent someone else from receiving as many rewards as they are now getting. Since, within the scope of their understanding, rewards are not closely related to job performance, the only way to get more is to engage in conflict-oriented behaviors aimed at furthering one's own position at the expense of someone else. For example, an employee might withhold information that another employee needs in order to prevent that person from performing well.

Intragroup Conflict

Intragroup conflict is conflict that occurs within groups. Most of the group members are likely to be affected. While interpersonal conflict may be similar to, and could even develop into intragroup conflict, there are explicit differences between these two types of conflict. Interpersonal conflict may occur between two individuals who are not members of the same work group; or may occur between individuals who hold positions at different levels within the organizational system (e.g., the supervisor and employee). Intragroup conflict, however, must take place among members of a single work group. This type of conflict is the one most likely to affect the performance of the group and the degree to which members cooperate with one another.

Two forms of intragroup conflict have been identified.[3] **Substantive conflict** refers to conflict over the content of objectives or the tasks. Disagreement about what should be set as the group's goals or about the way the task is to be performed would be considered substantive conflict. **Affective conflict** refers to conflict that results primarily from personality clashes or issues unrelated to the group's tasks.

Both types of conflict can lead to serious consequences if left to resolve itself. Substantive conflict is sometimes easier to clear up since it is concerned with more objective issues. Affective conflict often creates a more difficult set of circumstances for the supervisor since it centers upon more subjective and emotional issues.

Intergroup Conflict

Intergroup conflict is conflict that occurs between two or more groups. While supervisors are not likely to provide the final resolution of intergroup conflict, they are very likely to be involved in the process of finding an answer to the problem. If intergroup conflict produces a feeling of competition between groups, it could have positive effects because competing groups very often perform at levels higher than they otherwise would. If, however, the competition escalates

Table 12.1	Sources of Conflict
	1. Incompatible goals
	2. Limited resources
	3. Role ambiguity
	4. Communications obstacles
	5. Status and power differences
	6. Task interdependence

to the level where one group wins and the other loses, the outcomes are generally negative, at least in the long run. The winning group tends to relax and become complacent. The losing group often becomes more cohesive, learns from its mistakes, and performs better in future competitions. In such cases, the winning groups, over time, always become the losing groups. Eventually, a great deal of hostility, mistrust, and lack of communication between the groups is generated.[4] Supervisors are wise to work together to minimize the amount of conflict between their work groups or departments.

Sources of Conflict

Just as intrapersonal conflict is different than the other types of conflict because it takes place within the individual rather than between or among individuals or groups, so the causes of intrapersonal conflict are generally different from the causes of the other forms of conflict. Some sort of goal conflict is typically at the heart of intrapersonal conflict. In order to help an employee resolve this type of conflict, a supervisor generally engages in some coaching or counseling of the employee, or assists by clarifying the associated roles and expectations.

The causes of conflict between individuals and groups are numerous. Some of the more predominant instigators of conflict include limited resources, role ambiguity, communication obstacles, status and power differences, and task interdependence.

Limited Resources

One of the major reasons that conflict develops between individuals and groups is because of competition for limited resources. When resources such as office equipment or furnishings are limited, individuals and groups have little choice but to compete for them. Reward systems often encourage competition. If rewards are based upon the performance level of individuals, and if employees know that the amount of money available for raises is limited, the opportunity for conflict is greatly heightened. As has been pointed out, limited resources create **win-lose situations.** Employees perceive that the only way to get more of any limited resource is to make sure that the other party gets less. Such a perception sets the stage for conflict.

Role Ambiguity

Role ambiguity is a term which refers to the extent to which individuals and groups within an organization understand what is expected of them. Groups and individuals feeling high degrees of role ambiguity may not have a clear understanding of their responsibilities or of the constraints upon them. The result could be that two parties would try to assume responsibility for the same thing. For example, if the organization does not make it clear that a task is the responsibility of a particular group, two groups could begin to compete for it. If neither group has been given the formal authority and responsibility to perform the task, conflict is likely to develop. It is also possible for conflict to result because neither of the groups wants to assume responsibility for a task not clearly assigned by the organization. Hence, role ambiguity can produce conflict between groups or individuals because both want to assume responsibility for the same thing, or because they both want to avoid it.

In the Introductory Incident, Pete believed that Don Baker's department was responsible for providing certain information, while Baker obviously did not believe that it was his department's responsibility to provide that information. At this level, there is clearly role ambiguity about responsibility. Given Don's rather terse reply to Pete's inquiry, however, some more deep-seated conflict is indicated. It is difficult, from the information given, to precisely determine whether the conflict is between Don and Pete's departments, or between Don and Pete. On the surface it appears to be interdepartmental conflict over an area of responsibility. Any effort to resolve the conflict by uncovering the more particular causes of the conflict would require more extensive analysis of the situation.

Communication Obstacles

Communication obstacles, are likely to be present in any conflict episode. Several such obstructions to understanding are more apt then others to produce conflict in the work place. Most prominent among these is the absence of frequent communication between groups or individuals representing different structural levels of the organization or different informal groups. When individuals or groups lack information about other individuals or groups, misperceptions and distrust can develop. Misperception and distrust are typical precursors of conflict. Conflicting groups tend to develop a "we-they" mentality; they regard the actions and motives of other groups as suspicious and tend to ignore or distort communications from these groups in order to perpetuate that point of view. Once communication channels are opened, groups often discover that the differences between them are minimal—that the problems they face are highly similar and that the goals to which they aspire are shared.

Status and Power Differences

Status and power differences between groups or individuals often contribute to conflict. In a classic study of the relationship between waitresses and countermen, Whyte observed conflict based upon differing perceptions of status and power.[5] In the situation, the countermen filled the orders that the waitresses called in. Waitresses were perceived by countermen to occupy a status in the restaurant lower than their own since countermen were older, had more seniority, and were typically higher paid. The countermen seemed to resent having their work initiated by workers of lower status. Since the work of the countermen could not begin until a waitress called in an order, the countermen felt controlled by the waitresses to a certain extent. This feeling caused psychological discomfort because it conflicted with the status differences that countermen perceived between themselves and the waitresses. Waitresses had the power to initiate the work of the countermen, yet they did not have as much status.

A second restaurant did not have this problem. There, waitresses placed their written orders on a spindle and the countermen picked them off to read and fill them. This eliminated a great deal of face-to-face interaction between the two and, therefore, reduced most of the conflict. Apparently, countermen did not feel they were being given work to perform by employees with less status than themselves when the orders were indirectly given.

Task Interdependence

When two or more individuals or groups are dependent upon one another for successful job performance, the opportunity for conflict increases. **Task interdependence** means that one party cannot do its work unless the other party does its work, too. In the Introductory Incident, Pete's department was dependent upon the shipping department for billing information. The shipping department, however, was not dependent upon Pete's department for anything and felt little pressure to comply with Pete's requests. It is likely that this conflict will have to be resolved by a higher authority.

Task interdependence results in conflict for two primary reasons. First, as exemplified in the Introductory Incident, when only one department is dependent the independent department may not feel the need to comply with requests. This department may see these requests as unreasonable or unnecessary since fulfilling these requests is not seen as vital to their own operation. Second, task interdependence can result in conflict when the individuals or groups have different goals, priorities, or disagree upon the way the tasks should be performed. A classic example of different goals and priorities involves the production and sales departments of a manufacturing firm. The sales department wants a wide variety of products in order to appeal to as many customers as possible. The production department, on the other hand, wants to limit the number of different products in order to keep production costs down.

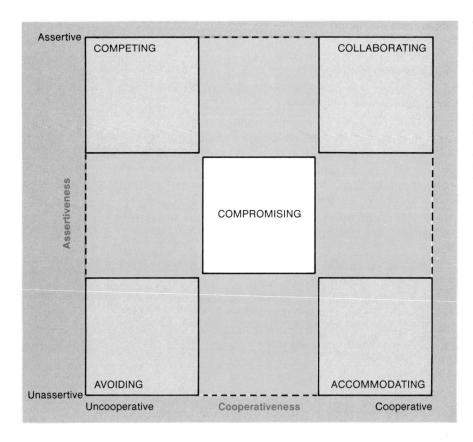

Figure 12.1
Reactions to conflict

*From "Support of the Two-Di-
mensional Model of Conflict
Handling Behavior," by Ruble,
T. and K. Thomas, in* Organizational Behavior and Human
Performance, *1976, 16, 145.
Copyright © 1976 by Aca-
demic Press. Reprinted by
permission of Academic Press
and the author.*

Reactions to Conflict

The parties involved in conflict may react to it in a number of ways. Ruble and Thomas have proposed a useful two-dimensional model for understanding conflict strategies.[6] According to this model, people deal with conflict based upon the dimensions of cooperativeness and assertiveness. Cooperativeness is the degree to which you attempt to satisfy the other party's concerns. Assertiveness is the degree to which you try to satisfy your own concerns. The relative strength of these two tendencies within individuals determines the way in which they tend to react to conflict situations (see fig. 12.1). At one extreme, where an individual is highly assertive but not at all cooperative, the reaction to conflict is to use a **competing** strategy. These individuals attempt to resolve the conflict by overcoming the opponent. A competing strategy involves very little consideration of the other person's position. At the other extreme, where the individual is very cooperative but not assertive, the **accommodating** strategy is the reaction to conflict. Individuals who adopt this strategy tend to surrender to their opponents.

Between these two extremes are three other strategies for reacting to conflict. **Compromising** occurs when both parties try to satisfy some of their concerns; each side is willing to give in to the other, somewhat, so that both gain something from the resolution of the conflict. A compromising strategy often prevents the conflict from escalating to more dangerous levels. **Collaborating** is the attempt to fully satisfy the concerns of both parties and is, perhaps, the most difficult to employ of the five strategies shown in the figure. It may also, however, produce the most permanent resolutions of conflict in situations where that strategy is successful. Since collaboration involves the attempt to identify the reasons for the conflict and the willingness to discuss those reasons openly and objectively, this method of dealing with conflict tends to result in more long-term solutions than the strategies which do not practice this type of cooperation. Finally, the most ineffective technique for dealing with conflict is that of **avoiding.** Individuals who use this strategy simply withdraw from the conflict and attempt to ignore it. Since nothing is done to eliminate the reasons for the conflict, it is likely to surface again, and soon. Unfortunately, this strategy is fairly common to organizations. It is uncomfortable for many supervisors and employees to bring conflict into the open for discussion; therefore, avoidance is the strategy frequently chosen.

Thomas has suggested that the identifiable characteristics of a particular situation determine which conflict resolution strategy is most appropriate.[7] These characteristics are enumerated in table 12.2. According to Thomas, each conflict resolution strategy is appropriate for certain contexts but is inappropriate for others. Avoidance, for example, while recognized as least effective of the strategies, might still be appropriate if the issue is trivial, if you perceive little chance of winning, or if you need time to gather additional information.

Outcomes of Conflict

It has already been pointed out that conflict can produce both positive and negative results. The specific nature of those results depends to a great extent upon the way conflict has been managed. Table 12.3 lists some of the potential outcomes of conflict, both positive and negative.

Negative Outcomes

Extremely high levels of conflict, especially affective conflict, are likely to yield negative oucomes. Increased distrust, decreased communication, falsification of information, increased anxiety and stress, and damage of the emotional and physical health of the conflicting parties are possible results. Time and energy spent attempting to deal with the conflict are wasted, constituting another negative outcome. If the conflict is allowed to persist, it is probable that the performance of the organization will eventually be affected.

Positive Outcomes

It is from moderate levels of conflict, and particularly substantive conflict, that positive results can come if that conflict is managed effectively. Conflict arising over substantive issues, such as finding a better way to perform a task, may energize individuals and groups to come up with a solution before the other party does. It also may stimulate creative thinking about the issue.

Situational Appropriateness of Conflict Resolution Strategies   Table 12.2

Conflict Mode	Situation	Conflict Mode	Situation

Competing

1. When quick, decisive action is vital—e.g., emergencies.
2. On important issues where unpopular actions need implementing—e.g., cost cutting, enforcing unpopular rules, discipline.
3. On issues vital to company welfare when you know you're right.
4. Against people who take advantage of noncompetitive behavior.

Collaborating

1. To find an integrative solution when both sets of concerns are too important to be compromised.
2. When your objective is to learn.
3. To merge insights from people with different perspectives.
4. To gain commitment by incorporating concerns into a consensus.
5. To work through feelings which have interferred with a relationship.

Compromising

1. When goals are important, but not worth the effort or potential disruption of more assertive modes.
2. When opponents with equal power are committed to mutually exclusive goals.
3. To achieve temporary settlements to complex issues.
4. To arrive at expedient solutions under time pressure.
5. As a backup when collaboration or competition is unsuccessful.

Avoiding

1. When an issue is trivial or more important issues are pressing.
2. When you perceive no chance of satisfying your concerns.
3. When potential disruption outweighs the benefits of resolution.
4. To let people cool down and regain perspective.
5. When gathering information supercedes immediate decision.
6. When others can resolve the conflict more effectively.
7. When issues seem tangential or symptomatic of other issues.

Accommodating

1. When you find you are wrong—to allow a better position to be heard, to learn, and to show your reasonableness.
2. When issues are more important to others than yourself—to satisfy others and maintain cooperation.
3. To build social credits for later issues.
4. To minimize loss when you are outmatched and losing.
5. When harmony and stability are especially important.
6. To allow subordinates to develop by learning from mistakes.

From Thomas, K. W., "Toward Multi-Dimensional Values in Teaching: The Example of Conflict Behaviors," *Academy of Management Review*, 2, 487. Copyright © 1977 Academy of Management. Reprinted by permission of the publisher and the author.

Table 12.3	Outcomes of Conflict	
	Positive Outcomes	**Negative Outcomes**
	Acts as motivator or stimulus	Increases distrust
	Stimulates creative thinking	Decreases communication
	Signals need for change	Falsifies information
	Provides source of feedback to supervisors or managers	Increases anxiety and stress
	Brings problems into the open	Wastes time and energy
	Clarifies areas of responsibility	Decreases performance

In many cases conflict signals the need for change within an organization. For example, when departments begin to disagree over who has the authority to perform particular tasks, the need for structural change clarifying authority and responsibility relationships is indicated. Conflict over goals might suggest that the organization's environment has changed; this, in turn, would call for more fundamental changes to be made in the goals and objectives of departments or of the entire organization. When conflict points the way to needed change within the organization, it functions to increase the organization's ability to adapt to its environment. The same conflict also increases innovative activity within the organization. As its members search for solutions to the conflict, they may discover new ways of doing things, or new opportunities that, if pursued by the organization, could improve the whole system.

Finally, organizational conflict is a major source of feedback. Conflict makes supervisors and managers aware of problems that need their attention. For example, if two of your employees frequently disagree over whose responsibility it is to perform a certain task, the disagreement should serve as feedback for you, suggesting that you need to clarify the roles of those employees.

Supervising the Conflict Situation

In general, it is accurate to say that the presence of conflict makes supervising more difficult. This is so because when individuals or groups engage in conflict, they divert energy and effort away from their tasks and objectives, and direct it instead toward the conflict situation. Supervisors need to be aware of conflict management techniques that can be employed in resolving conflict quickly.

Managing Intrapersonal Conflict

In principle, the managment of intrapersonal conflict is a matter of determining the cause of the conflict and of counseling the employee. In practice, intrapersonal conflict may be difficult even to recognize, let alone manage, unless the employee is willing to take you into his or her confidence. Since intrapersonal conflict can have a serious impact upon an employee's ability to perform, it is important that you develop a sensitivity to employees who might be experiencing this type of conflict. Make sure that employees understand that you are available and willing to help them resolve any personal conflict they may encounter. In addition, make sure that you do not become the source of any employee's intrapersonal conflict. This can happen if, for example, you assign tasks incompatible with the individual's value system, if you give ambiguous task assignments, or if you place too much or too little challenge, autonomy, and responsibility upon subordinates.

Managing Interindividual, Intragroup and Intergroup Conflict

Several ways of dealing with conflict between individuals and groups have already been suggested. These range from temporary, short-term solutions to permanent conflict resolution. Sometimes the cause of the conflict suggests the solution. For example, conflict over responsibility suggests modification of the organizational structure. Conflict that stems from a competitive reward system suggests that change in the way rewards are administered is needed. The adoption of more general conflict management techniques may also be appropriate, regardless of the type of conflict causing the immediate problem.

Establish Rules and Procedures

If conflict seems to occur frequently over the same issue, future conflict might best and most easily be avoided by establishing a few rules and procedures. For example, if conflict among employees regularly arises over the priority of items typed by a common secretary, you might prevent that disagreement in the future by establishing an order of priority for various types of documents, or by requiring all documents to be typed on a first-come, first-served basis. If the conflict is, in fact, over the priorities of the typist and is not a personality conflict, this method should produce a relatively permanent solution to the problem.

Appeal to a Higher Authority

When the parties to the conflict are unable to resolve it themselves, an appeal for help to a supervisor or manager is often made. If the conflict is largely affective or personal, each party can be counseled by the higher authority to be more tolerant of personal differences and to concentrate more heavily upon the objective aspects of the work situation. If the conflict is substantive, on the other hand, the supervisor or manager may be called upon to make a decision resolving the issue. Great care must be taken to gather all available information before making such a decision. You, in the capacity of a higher authority, must try to determine if any of the information has been distorted by one party in order to damage the position of the other. It could be very damaging to your relationship with employees to make a decision favoring one party, only to find out later that this party had distorted some of the information you used in reaching your decision.

If the conflict is intergroup, and it cannot be resolved by negotiating with the supervisor of the other group involved, you may need to appeal to an even higher authority. Before you approach your boss with the problem, however, make sure that you have your facts straight. Then be prepared to discuss the matter in a very objective, behavior-based manner. Deal only with the facts of the case as you understand them. Inform your boss of the behaviors that seem to be causing the problem and never evaluate or degrade the other party.

Limit Interaction

If the individuals or groups involved in the conflict are not interdependent, it may be possible to solve the problem simply by restricting the interaction between them. For example, if the conflict between two individuals is of a personal nature and they do not need to deal with each other in order to get their work accomplished, then prohibiting them from interacting may provide a temporary solution, at least. It may prevent open hostilities from erupting on the job, even though it is not likely to resolve the conflict. Nothing has been done to alleviate the reasons for the conflict and so it is likely to resurface as soon as the two parties begin to interact again. Regardless, reducing the amount of contact can be a useful short-term measure to implement while searching for a more permanent resolution to the conflict.

Set Superordinate Goals

It has been demonstrated that one of the major causes of conflict is goal incompatibility. Reverse this notion and it suggests that if two parties have goals that are very compatible or similar, there is little likelihood of conflict between them. What actually tends to occur is that the two parties begin to work together to accomplish their similar goals. This introduces the idea of the superordinate goal. A **superordinate goal** is one that is shared by all parties involved. As a supervisor trying to find a solution to conflict between individuals, it could be very beneficial to emphasize the idea of a superordinate goal. Focus upon the areas of agreement shared by the conflicting parties and emphasize, also, all issues related to task performance. Stress particularly the importance of completing the assigned tasks and of making a contribution to the goals of the organization.

The advantage of using superordinate goals to reduce conflict was shown in a classic experiment which took place in a boys' camp.[8] The boys were separated and placed in a number of different cabins. The researchers worked actively to stimulate competition between these cabin groups. Within each cabin, the boys became highly cohesive groups; however, between the cabins, conflict soon became relatively severe. The boys engaged in frequent name calling, raids on other cabins and, on occasion, physical conflict. At this point, the researchers created two superordinate goals. They created the problem of a water shortage that could only be solved if everyone worked together. In addition, the boys had to cooperate to repair the only means of transportation that could be used to get to a place to buy food. The superordinate goals of acquiring water and food drastically reduced the amount of conflict between the cabins. Of course, you will not be able to "create a water shortage" every time you have to negotiate a conflict. You can, however, focus upon objective, work-related issues that are important to all parties involved.

Negotiate

Most of the conflict episodes with which you will deal as a supervisor will require some amount of negotiation.[9] **Negotiation** is a process in which two or more parties attempt to resolve conflicting interests by exchanging information. You will have to determine the real source of the conflict and the perceptions of the conflicting parties. If the conflict is over a substantive issue, a solution can be negotiated between the two parties based upon the facts of the case. It will still be up to you to determine what those facts are since the parties involved in the conflict may not be able to see the issues clearly.[10] It will also be your responsibility to make all parties to the conflict aware of the complete set of facts. Conflict is often the result of misperceptions. If you can make the objective nature of the problem known to all involved, the conflict will be much more smoothly resolved.

Summary

Organizational conflict is a fact of organizational life. Until recently, it was assumed that organizational conflict of any type was undesirable and should be eliminated. Now, however, the potential positive outcomes of conflict are being recognized. Some of these positive outcomes include the potential for increasing motivation, providing feedback, indicating the need for change, and making supervisors aware of problems.

Conflict exists at the moment that one party believes that another party is about to block the satisfaction of an important need or the accomplishment of an important goal. It is at this point that the first party is likely to react to the second party in some way, based upon how cooperative and assertive the first party tends to be. Individuals who are cooperative and nonassertive are more likely to react to the conflict in an accommodating manner. Individuals who are assertive and uncooperative tend to react to conflict aggressively and competitively.

It is important that supervisors be able to recognize different types of conflict if they want to correctly diagnose the situation. Conflict within an individual is intrapersonal conflict and occurs between two or more individuals. These individuals may or may not be members of the same work group. Intragroup conflict occurs within a work group and affects most of the members of that group. Intergroup conflict occurs between two or more work groups.

Conflict may arise for a variety of reasons, the most important of which are limited resources, role ambiguity, communication obstacles, status and power differences, and task interdependence. The source of the conflict often suggests its solution. When the specific source of the conflict is not obvious, however, several other conflict management strategies are available. These strategies include making use of rules and procedures, appealing to a higher authority for a decision, limiting interaction between the conflicting parties, emphasizing superordinate goals, and negotiating.

Key Terms

accommodating (p. 263)
affective conflict (p. 259)
approach-approach conflict (p. 257)
approach-avoidance conflict (p. 258)
avoidance-avoidance conflict (p. 258)
avoiding (p. 264)
collaborating (p. 264)
competing (p. 263)
compromising (p. 263)
conflict (p. 257)
goal conflict (p. 257)

intergroup conflict (p. 259)
interpersonal conflict (p. 258)
intragroup conflict (p. 259)
intrapersonal conflict (p. 257)
negotiation (p. 269)
role ambiguity (p. 261)
substantive conflict (p. 259)
superordinate goal (p. 268)
task interdependence (p. 262)
win-lose situation (p. 260)

Questions for Discussion

1. Define conflict. When is it most likely to arise?
2. What is likely to happen to each party involved in a win-lose conflict resolution?
3. Define the following terms:
   a. intrapersonal conflict
   b. interpersonal conflict
   c. intragroup conflict
   d. intergroup conflict
   e. approach-approach conflict
   f. approach-avoidance conflict
   g. avoidance-avoidance conflict
4. How does intrapersonal conflict differ from the other types of conflict discussed in this chapter?
5. Explain the difference between substantive and affective conflict.
6. How can role ambiguity cause conflict? Which types of conflict are likely to result from role ambiguity?
7. Explain the two-dimensional model of reactions to conflict. Is this model a useful one for supervisors in analyzing conflict situations? Why or why not?
8. What are some possible negative and positive outcomes of conflict?

9. What determines whether conflict results in positive or negative outcomes? Explain.
10. Why is it considered a short-term or temporary solution of conflict to simply limit or prohibit interaction between conflicting parties? What would be considered a long-term or permanent conflict solution?
11. Discuss several conflict management techniques available to supervisors for alleviating each of the four major types of conflict.

References

1. K. W. Thomas, "Conflict and Conflict Management," in *Handbook of Industrial and Organizational Psychology* ed. G. D. Dunnette (Chicago: Rand McNally & Co. 1976).
2. A. P. Brief, R. S. Schuler, and M. Van Sell, *Managing Stress* (Boston: Little, Brown & Co., 1980); A. B. Shostak, *Blue Collar Stress* (Reading, Mass.: Addison-Wesley Publishing Co., 1980).
3. H. Guetzkow and J. Gyr, "An Analysis of Conflict in Decision-making Groups," *Human Relations* 7 (1954): 367–381.
4. R. R. Blake and J. S. Mouton, "Reactions to Intergroup Competition under Win-Lose Conditions," *Management Science* 4 (1961): 420-425.
5. W. F. Whyte, "The Social Structure of the Restaurant," *American Journal of Sociology* 54 (1949): 302–310.
6. T. Ruble and K. Thomas, "Support for a Two-dimensional Model of Conflict Behavior," *Organizational Behavior and Human Performance* 16 (1976): 143–155.
7. K. W. Thomas, "Toward Multidimensional Values in Teaching: The Example of Conflict Behaviors," *Academy of Management Review* 2 (1977): 484–490.
8. M. Sherif, "Superordinate Goals in the Reduction of Intergroup Conflict," *American Journal of Sociology* 63 (1958): 349–456.
9. R. H. Hermone, "Resolving Differences," *Supervisory Management* 28 (May 1983): 30–35.
10. L. Weiss, "Revisiting the Basics of Conflict Resolution," *Training and Development Journal* 37 (November 1983): 68–70.

The purpose of this exercise is to give students the chance to practice conflict resolution using objective information presented by two conflicting groups. Your instructor will divide the class into two groups on the basis of such factors as male/female, Greek/Independent, conservative/liberal, younger/older, or rural/city.

Exercise

Resolving Intergroup Conflict

Step 1 of this exercise involves each group making three lists of characteristics. Assuming the class was divided into Greek and Independent groups, the first list to be prepared by the Greek group would be: how Greeks see Greeks. Their second list: how Independents see Greeks. The third list: how Greeks see Independents. At the same time, Independents will be preparing similar lists: how Independents see Independents, how Greeks see Independents, and how Independents see Greeks. When both groups have completed their lists, tape them to the wall or chalkboard so that each group can read the other group's lists. There should be no discussion during this time.

In step 2 of the exercise each group is given the opportunity to ask questions of the other group. No one is to make comments on the items listed by the other group. Do not criticize, evaluate, or disagree with the other group's lists. You may only ask questions of the other group. You must get the floor from the instructor before you may ask a question. For example, a Greek group member might ask, "Why do Independents see Greeks as uninterested in all non-Greek campus activities?"

When the instructor calls a halt to the question-and-answer period, compare your positions. How similar were the perceptions of groups before the question-and answer-period? Did you modify your perception of the other group after the questioning? How could this process be used in organizations to resolve conflict between individuals or groups?

From Frantzve, J. L., "Conflict Resolution," *Behaving in Organizations: Tales From the Trenches,* p. 147. Copyright © 1983 Allyn and Bacon, Inc. Reprinted by permission.

Erica accepted the job of supervisor of the finishing department at JBS Manufacturing just two months ago. Through discussions with her boss, she learned that the supervisor she replaced had been more concerned with being liked by his employees than with the productivity of the department. Consequently, current productivity in the finishing department was relatively low. One of the primary goals Erica's boss had set for her as departmental supervisor was to increase discipline and improve productivity. Erica knew that in her new position she was going to have to be less concerned with friendship than with output, and promised to do her best.

Throughout her first two months on the job Erica made it a point to learn as much as she could about her employees and their relationships with one another, at the same time that she learned about work processes. After studying the work process, she concluded that it could not be improved without substantial investment in new equipment.

It was during her second week on the job that Erica noticed that two of her employees, Art and Randy, seemed to be very quiet when in each other's presence. When she spoke to either of these employees individually, they were always friendly; but whenever they were together, neither had much to say. Erica suspected at the time that the two did not get along very well. As long as it did not appear to affect their work, however, she felt it was none of her business.

As more time passed, Erica began to learn more about both Art and Randy and their relationships with other employees. Both had joined JBS at the same time, five years ago. As the senior employees in the department, they were both looked up to by the younger employees. Several years ago, Art had applied for a job opening in the finishing department that would have meant a promotion and a raise. He openly discussed his plans with Randy. Randy also applied for the position without telling Art and subsequently received the promotion. The friendship ended abruptly. A year ago, Art was finally promoted to the finishing department and tension began to build to its present level.

Case continues . . .

Case (cont.)   It seemed to Erica that the other employees in the department had recently begun to choose sides. Some looked to Art as their informal leader, while others chose Randy. Erica feared that this could turn into a major problem since the success of the finishing department depended upon teamwork among the employees. As an item came into the department, a team of employees had to sand, trim, apply a primer, and then paint it. As the two most senior employees, Art and Randy served as team leaders. Because these teams were made up of employees from both sides, however, Art and Randy both tended to give the employees from the "other side" the job of sanding since it was the least desirable. When employees were assigned to sand by "the opposition," they would not take great care with their work. If the sanding was not done well the final coat of paint would not stick to the surface of the item and it would have to be reworked. Consequently, employees possessed the power to make the team leader look bad and, in so doing, took revenge for being assigned to the distasteful job of sanding. This had happened to Randy only two days ago. Randy had immediately stomped over to where Art was working and accused him of telling the employee to do a poor job of sanding even though he was assigned to Randy's team. Art just laughed and walked away saying that Randy was paranoid. The incident ended with that comment, but Erica sensed, nevertheless, that the tension between the two was greater than ever.

Questions

1. What is the source of the conflict in this situation?
2. Does the source of the conflict suggest a solution?
3. If you were in Erica's position, how would you handle the situation?
4. Analyze your suggestion. Does it provide a permanent resolution to the conflict, or is it temporary?

Chapter 13
Labor Relations

Learning Objectives

After reading this chapter, you should:

1. be aware of the major labor laws affecting labor-management relations.
2. understand why employees join labor unions.
3. be able to describe a typical organizing campaign.
4. know what labor and management can and cannot do during an organizing campaign.
5. understand what supervisors' responsibilities are in administering a labor agreement.
6. be able to describe the decertification process and what supervisors can and cannot do during this process.
7. know what supervisors can do to help the organization remain nonunion.

Al looked up from the papers on his desk to see Mike and Jerry walking rapidly toward him. As they neared his desk, Mike said, "Al, we're asking all of the supervisors to meet at Jerry's desk after work tonight. We've got a real problem on our hands."

Al said that he would be there as soon as he could and hurried to finish his paperwork. He wondered what kind of problem had Mike and Jerry so upset. As far as Al knew, things had been going well enough in his department.

As Al arrived at Jerry's desk, he heard Mike telling the other supervisors of information he had received to the effect that a number of employees had contacted a union for purposes of organizing JBS. "If we allow a union to get in here, we'll lose control over our employees," Mike was saying. "We won't have any flexibility in dealing with our people. Everything will get written into the labor contract—how rewards are administered, when and how we can administer discipline. I don't want to be told how to supervise my employees. Now, what can we do to fight this organizing attempt?"

Al didn't know much about unions, since he had never worked in a unionized organization before. He was aware, however, that there were legal constraints on what an organization and its representatives could do during an organizing attempt. Al felt the need to caution the other supervisors before they unknowingly broke some law. "Wait a minute Mike. Aren't there some laws on the books that limit what supervisors and managers can do during an organizing attempt? Our first step had better be to contact Personnel and find out what kinds of things we can and cannot do. I'll call the personnel director and arrange a meeting for first thing in the morning. Let's just meet in the personnel department at 8:15 tomorrow morning."

Some might argue that unions are on the decline and, consequently, that supervisors no longer need to know that much about them. While the first part of that statement is correct, the second part is not.

It is true that unions today represent fewer employees than they have in years past. Currently, only about 20 percent of the nonfarm labor force are union members compared to the 25.5 percent that were members in 1953.[1] Part of this decline may be attributed to the corresponding decline in the number of manufacturing jobs in our economy. Unions have historically been strong in manufacturing industries. As our economy shifts to include more and more service-related jobs, unions have had to move into unfamiliar territory. According to National Labor Relations Board information, unions have not won a majority of their elections since 1973.[2] An additional force operating against unions has been that employees are increasingly voting unions out of their organizations. This process, known as **decertification,** has increased 22.8 percent over the past few years.[3]

Nevertheless, it is important that supervisors make themselves aware of labor law, the organizing process, and how to work under a labor agreement. While less than 20 percent of the nonfarm labor force is unionized, this figure represents approximately 20 million people. Even supervisors who are working in nonunionized organizations need to have some knowledge of unions so that they can effectively represent their organization during an organizing campaign.[4]

While unions have existed in the United States since about 1792, the first of the three most significant labor laws was not passed until the 1930s. Before this time there was little legislation of any kind to cover labor-management relations. It was not until the 1920s that public sentiment started to become more pro-union. This was largely due to the increased abuse of employees by employers during this period. Employers were virtually free to set wages, working conditions, and hours as they wished. Neither was there any requirement that employers meet with employees to discuss any of these conditions. In an attempt to protect employees by limiting management activities the National Labor Relations Act of 1935 was passed.

Labor Law

National Labor Relations Act of 1935; the Wagner Act

The basic purpose of the **National Labor Relations Act of 1935,** or Wagner Act was to restore the balance of power between labor and management. Prior to its passage, management had no incentive to bargain in good faith with employee representatives. As a result, these representatives were often ignored by management. The Wagner Act affirmed the right of employees to form or to join unions, and required management to bargain in good faith with employee representatives. The act also identified five unfair labor practices on the part of employers. With the passage of this act it became unlawful to:

1. interfere with employees' attempts to form or join a union.
2. support or create a union for employees which would be more favorable to management.
3. discriminate against employees or applicants for employment on the basis of union activities in the attempt to discourage union membership.
4. discriminate against employees who file charges or testify before the National Labor Relations Board.
5. refuse to bargain collectively with an employee representative.

The Wagner Act also created the **National Labor Relations Board** (NLRB), the purpose of which is to administer and enforce the provisions of the act. The NLRB is a five-person agency with two primary functions:(1) To hold elections to determine the bargaining agent for employees of a particular organization; and (2) To investigate charges of unfair labor practices against either management or labor, and to prosecute violators in federal court.

The Wagner Act was clearly pro-union. While it identified unfair labor practices on the part of management, it said nothing about unfair labor practices of unions. As a result, some unions began trying to force employees to join unions. In practice, many unions required employees to join the union before they could be hired, a practice known as a **closed shop.**

Labor-Management Relations Act of 1947

The **Labor-Management Relations Act of 1947,** also known as the Taft-Hartley Act, was passed in response to the unfair practices of unions. Its purpose was to restore balance to the relationship between unions and management. The act instituted a number of important changes.

1. While the act prohibited closed shops, it did allow union shops and agency shops. Under a **union shop,** employees are required to join the union within a specified time period, usually thirty days. Under an **agency shop,** all employees are required to pay the union dues even if they do not join the union. The act further allows states to pass laws prohibiting union shops. Figure 13.1 shows the twenty states which currently operate under such legislation. These states have **"right-to-work" laws.**
2. Employees were given the right to refrain from union activity as well as engage in it.
3. Unfair labor practices on the part of unions were identified. These practices include coercing workers to join the union, refusing to bargain in good faith, and charging excessive initiation or membership fees to employees operating in a union shop.
4. The act provided that certification elections can be held only once in a twelve-month period.
5. Employees were given the right to hold decertification elections.

Labor-Management Reporting and Disclosure Act of 1959

Also called the Landrum-Griffin Act, the **Labor-Management Reporting and Disclosure Act of 1959** was designed to prevent the corruption and abuse of employees by union leaders. The act initiated the control of increases in dues, as well as of the suspension and firing of union members. This legislation also made it mandatory that union officials file yearly reports with the secretary of labor.

These three laws are directed at private employers. In fact, the Wagner Act specifically excludes federal, state, and municipal employers from its coverage. At present, federal government employees are covered by Title VII of the **Civil Service Reform Act of 1978.** This act established the Federal Labor Relations Authority (FLRA), an administrative body modeled after the NLRB and established for the purpose of enforcing the provisions of the act. Many states now have legislation governing state employees. Although these public-sector employees typically have fewer rights than their counterparts in the private sector (e.g., many public employees are prohibited from striking), unionization in the public sector has grown dramatically in recent years. This trend is likely to continue.

Figure 13.1
States with "right-to-work" laws

☐ States with "right-to-work" laws
☐ States without "right-to-work" laws

The primary reason most employees decide to join unions is that of dissatisfaction. Dissatisfaction may arise for a variety of reasons related to one or more of the following variables:

Economics. A primary source of dissatisfaction stems from economic aspects of employment, such as pay and fringe benefits.

Quality of working conditions. Working conditions include hours of work and the physical characteristics of the job situation (e.g., temperature, cleanliness, and ventilation).

Job security. Job security is a category that the unions emphasize in an organizing campaign. Employees want the security of knowing that they will have their jobs in the future.

Treatment by supervisors. Recall from the discussion of equity theory in chapter 4 that perceptions of equitable treatment can be powerful motivators. If employees perceive that they are being treated unfairly, it is not unlikely that they would consider contacting a union as a possible way of restoring equity. Employees, acting as individuals, typically have little power to change an organizational situation. They may perceive that their chances of improving the situation will be much improved if they band together.

The nature of the work. Employees who are unsuited or unprepared for their particular jobs, or who receive little enjoyment from their work are more likely to be interested in joining a union.

Why Do Employees Join Unions?

You and a Union Contract

****

What does it mean to join a union and work under a contract?

1.   A union contract clearly spells out the wages that employees will receive. One of the basic foundations of unionism is that employees who do the same work should get the same pay. And this rate of pay should allow you and your family to live comfortably. Unfortunately, the wages of many workers without the protection of a union contract have not kept pace with the cost of living.

2.   A union contract provides for seniority. Seniority protects a worker who has been employed longer from being laid off while workers who have worked fewer years continue to work.

3.   A union contract provides a grievance procedure for an orderly way of settling disputes or grievances. The grievance procedure protects employees against unfair action on the part of the company. A company must prove just cause against an employee before he or she can be disciplined or fired.

4.   A union contract provides a written guarantee of working hours and overtime. Vacations and paid holidays are provided. Many contracts also include paid sick leave and cost-of-living adjustments to protect your wages against inflation.

These are only some of the clauses contained in a union contract. The contract is a legal document to which your employer must adhere. A union contract provides a better life and a more secure future.

****

Midwestern Production Workers Union, Local 000

Perceived degree of control in the job. Employees who perceive that they have little control over their work environments may look at union membership as a means to gain some of that control.

While each of these factors is important and should receive consideration some evidence suggests that dissatisfaction with job security and wages are the two most powerful motivators of employees in their votes for union representation.[5] Dissatisfaction based on these elements, when coupled with the perception of a lack of power to change things, causes interest in union activity to grow even more. The result is that one, or perhaps a few, employees will contact a union to come in and organize the workers.

The union organizing process can take quite a long time. Even so, organizations may not be aware of the process until it is nearly over and the authorization cards are being signed. Supervisors will be dealing, on a day-to-day basis, with the employees involved in the organizing. They need to be fully aware of what happens during the organizing process, mostly because there are certain things that supervisors, as representatives of the organization, are prevented by law from doing during this time period.

The union organizing process involves six steps: initial contact, building interest, signing authorization cards, the NLRB hearing, the pre-election campaign, and the NLRB election.

The Union Organizing Process

Initial Contact

The organizing process typically begins when a dissatisfied employee contacts a union. In some instances, however, a union may make the initial contact. Sometimes very large employers, are attractive to a union and so the union representative will make the first move. A union representative then visits the organization to determine whether enough employees are sufficiently interested in union representation to justify further effort on the part of the union.

Building Interest

It is common for the union representatives to identify those employees who seem to be most interested in the union and to create an organizing committee of these individuals. The members of the organizing committee will assume responsibility for contacting other employees in the effort to generate organizational support for the union.

Signing Authorization Cards

If the organizing committee is successful in generating interest in the union, they will begin asking employees to sign **authorization cards.** The union must gain the signatures of at least 30 percent of the employees before the NLRB can be petitioned for an election. When an employee signs an authorization card it means that the employee is interested in the union becoming his or her representative in collective bargaining with the employer. It does not mean that the employee is committed to voting for the union in a certification election. If the union gets the authorization card signatures of one more than 50 percent of the employees of an organization, it can ask the employer to recognize the union as the employee's bargaining agent without an NLRB election. While this has happened, it is much more common for the employer to refuse the request and insist upon an NLRB election.

To the Employees of JBS Manufacturing Corporation

****

Do your wages keep up with the cost of living? Are you treated well by your supervisor? Does your company listen to your legitimate complaints about your job? These are questions that, increasingly, are being asked by the workers in your company.

The Midwestern Production Workers Union believes that every employee has the right to a job that provides a decent standard of living, equal treatment, and comfortable working conditions. If you are interested in better working conditions and benefits, then you should know about the Midwestern Production Workers Union. We are the largest and strongest union in the Midwest, representing over 435,000 workers. If you want to improve things on your job, sign the card authorizing the Midwestern Production Workers Union to become your collective bargaining representative.

DON'T DELAY—SIGN TODAY

****

Midwestern Production Workers Union, Local 000

NLRB Hearing

After the union has petitioned the NLRB for an election, the NLRB will conduct a hearing to determine whether there is sufficient employee interest to hold an election. Again, sufficient interest is determined by the 30 percent authorization card signatures. If interest is indicated, the NLRB will usually set a date for the election sometime within thirty to sixty days.

An Open Letter to the Employees of JBS Manufacturing Corporation

****

A group of your fellow workers has asked Midwestern Production Workers Union, Local 000 to represent them and help them to make a collective bargaining agreement with the company. This agreement will recognize your rights as workers and protect you against unfair or inequitable treatment.

Midwestern Production Workers Union, Local 000 has been helping workers since 1942. Local 000 has helped to establish contracts with over 60 employers covering 37,000 workers. We firmly believe that we can help you improve your standard of living and gain increased respect from the management at JBS.

Joining a union where you will be represented by those who are experts in negotiations and contract administration will give you a voice that will be heard. The company is more likely to pay attention to a united group of employees than to any one of you alone. Join the Midwestern Production Workers Union for a better future. Sign a MWP authorization card today!

****

Midwestern Production Workers Union, Local 000

Pre-election Campaign

It is during the pre-election campaign that both the union and employer try to win more support for their positions. The union will emphasize such benefits of membership as higher wages and better working conditions. The employer will stress the disadvantages of unionism, such as union dues and strikes. The NLRB carefully watches the behavior of both labor and management during this time period so it is important that supervisors be very conscious of their words and actions during the pre-election campaign.

NLRB Election

The NLRB then holds an election and verifies the results. If a majority of the employees vote for union representation, the NLRB will authorize the union. This is called **certification.** Once a union is certified, the employer must bargain with it. If a majority do not vote for the union, another election may not be held for at least twelve months.

Supervisory Behavior During the Organizing Process

Supervisory behavior during the organizing process must be in accordance with the amended National Labor Relations Act. Significant violations of this act by supervisors or any representative of the organization can result in the election being set aside. This means that the union could be certified even though it lost the election. Carney has identified several examples of improper supervisory conduct.[6]

1. *Threats.* Supervisors must not threaten employees for their union activities. Threats of termination or discipline, changes in work assignments, loss of pay, and plant shutdown are all improper.
2. *Interrogation.* Supervisors must not question employees about their union activities or even what they think about unions.
3. *Promises.* Supervisors must not promise higher wages or other rewards in return for voting against the union.
4. *Surveillance.* Supervisors must not watch employees participating in union activities, nor can they attend union organizing meetings. This type of vigilance is called **surveillance.**
5. *Coercion.* Supervisors should not call employees into their offices or management conference rooms to talk about union activities. These settings are likely to be considered intimidating to employees. Any discussions with employees about unions should take place in a neutral site such as the cafeteria.
6. *Discrimination.* Supervisors should not treat pro-union and anti-union employees differently. Any favorable treatment of anti-union employees or unfavorable treatment of pro-union employees is prohibited.

While these provisions may seem restrictive, supervisors can exercise certain freedoms to act during an organizing campaign. Supervisors may remind employees that the organization prefers to remain nonunion, and of any benefits or working conditions that the organization has provided. It is also permissible to remind employees of the disadvantages of joining a union, and that even though they may have signed an authorization card they are free to vote to reject the union in the certification election. Supervisors may also correct any false statements made by the union.

NEWSLETTER
Midwestern Production Workers Local 000

****

Dear Employee of JBS Corporation:

A National Labor Relations Board Election will be held in the near future since a majority of your fellow employees at JBS have signed authorization cards indicating their interest in being represented by a union. This election will be conducted by the NLRB by secret ballot and will be completely anonymous. YOUR EMPLOYER WILL NOT KNOW HOW YOU VOTED.

Between now and the election you can expect JBS representatives to try to discredit the union. You may receive letters at home reminding you of what the company has done for you. You may also receive information listing the disadvantages of union membership. If you vote NO, against union representation, you are saying in effect that you are satisfied with the way JBS has treated you. However, many of you are dissatisfied. Dissatisfaction is what has led you to contact Midwestern Production Workers. If you vote YES, in favor of union representation, you are voting for improvements in your wages, hours, working conditions, and benefits.

Midwestern Production Workers, Local 000 is an established local union. We have represented workers in a variety of industries in the Midwest since 1942. Strikes can occur only when two-thirds of the members vote to go on strike. However, most collective bargaining agreements in the United States are reached without the use of a strike.

Let us help you reach an agreement with your employer that will protect your current benefits as well as gain the improvements in these benefits that you feel are necessary.

Sincerely,

Bob

Bob Sinclair, President
Midwestern Production
Workers, Local 000

****

Table 13.1	Excerpt From a Labor Agreement

Article 4
Hours of Work

Section 1. Eight (8) hours shall constitute a day's work, and shall be between 8:00 A.M. and 4:30 P.M. with one-half (½) hour for lunch from 12:00 noon until 12:30 P.M. A work week shall be five (5) days from Monday to Friday, inclusive.

Section 2. Employees shall not report at shop or on job before 7:45 A.M. or after 4:30 P.M. and must not leave the shop before 8:00 A.M. and must remain on job until quitting time.

Section 3. No employee shall work by the hour only, one-half day's pay being the minimum rate of wages journeymen shall receive for less than one-half day's work, except for overtime, which shall be at the rate of double time. This rule does not apply when journeymen quit work, or during a strike or unfavorable weather conditions.

Union Behavior During the Organizing Process

Union organizers have certain rights protected by the National Labor Relations Act. As a supervisor, you must know what these rights are so that you do not infringe upon them. Such infringement could cause the union to file an unfair labor practices charge against the organization. The right to organize is part of employees' right to engage in collective activity. This means that time outside normal work time may be used for organizing, even if it is on the organization's property. Time outside normal work time includes lunch, breaks, and the time both before and after work begins. The courts make a distinction between organizing by employees and nonemployees. Nonemployee union organizers may be prevented from soliciting union membership on the organization's property if solicitations by other nonemployee groups are also prohibited. If other nonemployee groups have been allowed to solicit on company property, then prohibiting nonemployee union organizers would likely be considered an unfair labor practice. The same is true of access to bulletin boards and meeting rooms. If employees have been allowed access to bulletin boards or meeting rooms in the past, the organization cannot deny them access for use in union organization activities.

Supervising under a Labor Agreement

Once a successful union organizing attempt has been made labor and management must come to terms under the guidance of this union representation. First, a labor agreement will be negotiated; typically, the supervisor is not heavily involved in this negotiation. Second, the labor agreement must be administered; this will involve the supervisor very directly. Knowledge of the negotiating process will, however, help supervisors in determining the true intent of the contract language and so will help them to administer the contract more effectively.

Union members picketing their employer during a strike

Photo: Wide World Photos, Inc.

Negotiating a Labor Agreement

If the union wins the NLRB election and is recognized as the employees' bargaining agent, negotiations with management representatives begin. The process by which a labor agreement is negotiated and administered is known as **collective bargaining.** Although no two labor agreements are exactly alike, most make provisions in a number of standard areas of concern. These include wages, benefits, working conditions, vacations and holidays, hours of work, overtime, seniority, layoffs and rehiring, grievance procedures, arbitration, and management's rights. Once all of the provisions of the labor contract have been made agreeable to both labor and management, the contract is signed, binding both parties to its terms for the specified length of the agreement. The labor agreement is a legal document and can be upheld by a court of law; however, most disagreements over contract provisions are handled through the grievance process as discussed in chapter 10.

If the two parties cannot come to agreement during collective bargaining, the process is said to have developed an **impasse.** At this point the union may call for a strike. A **strike** is a collective action taken by employees in which they do not report for work, and the purpose of which is to pressure the employer to agree to more favorable terms. Striking employees often **picket** in front of their place of employment in an effort to make the public aware of their disagreement with management and to try to win the support of that public. Management's version of a strike is called a **lockout** and takes place when management closes the company, thus preventing employees from working. Most labor agreements are negotiated without the occurrence of strikes and lockouts, despite the frequency with which strikes seem to be in the news.

There are two other alternatives available for dealing with an impasse. First, a request may be sent to the Federal Mediation and Conciliation Service for an outside mediator. A **mediator** is a trained negotiator whose function is to try to bring the two parties to an agreement, but who has no formal power or authority to force that agreement. The second alternative is for the two parties to call in an arbitrator. An **arbitrator** will hear both sides, review the facts, and make a decision that both parties must accept. It is understood before the arbitrator is called in that both parties will abide by the arbitrator's decision.

Administering a Labor Agreement

Supervisors have primary responsibility for interpreting and administering the **labor agreement** or contract; therefore, they must maintain a thorough knowledge of the provisions of that agreement. No labor agreement can spell out in advance all aspects of labor/management relations. Supervisors will be called upon, from time to time, to interpret unclear provisions of the contract. They may also be asked to make decisions in situations not specifically covered in the labor agreement. Supervisors also need to be aware of the constraints placed upon them by the labor agreement. For example, most labor agreements would not infringe upon the supervisor's right to discipline problem employees. The agreement may, however, determine what types of actions may be disciplined and what form that discipline may take.

Understand that your actions as a supervisor may affect the terms of the labor contract. For example, if the labor agreement provides for thirty minutes for lunch and you typically allow your employees to take forty-five minutes, your allowance of extra time could be interpreted by an arbitrator as consent to change the labor agreement.

The Union Steward

Supervisors must work closely with the union steward. A **union steward** is an employee elected to that position by the other union members in the department. Stewards represent the other employees in the department to the supervisor. For example, if one of the employees in the department wants to file a grievance, that person will first go to the union steward. The steward will hear the employee's complaint and then discuss it with the supervisor in an attempt to resolve the grievance. In addition, if an employee is called in by a supervisor for a disciplinary interview, the employee generally has the right to have the union steward present.

Supervisors and union stewards often find themselves in an adversary relationship. It is to your advantage as a supervisor, however, to try to develop a good working relationship with the steward. You will be working with the steward on grievances from time to time and it will benefit you greatly to have the cooperation of this individual. It is also likely that the steward could be of help to you in initiating any departmental changes that become necessary. A steward can help to facilitate a change or retard it. The time invested in developing a good relationship with the union steward may later pay dividends in those times when you find you need to institute major departmental changes. If the steward believes that you are fair and consistent in your dealings with employees, that individual is more likely to believe you when you suggest that a change is in the best interest of the employees as well as of the organization.

The Decertification Process

Neither employers nor their representatives are permitted to file a petition for a decertification election with the NLRB; nevertheless, there are some things that these individuals may do to assist the employees interested in doing so. Only an employee, group of employees, or their representative are eligible to file a petition for decertification. Just as is the case with a representation election, the petition must be accompanied by evidence that at least thirty percent of the bargaining-unit employees are in favor of such an election. It is quite legitimate for an employer to file a petition questioning whether the union continues to represent a majority of employees.[7] Employees typically become interested in decertification when they have ceased to believe that the union represents the interests of the employees; and decertification is most likely to occur when relations between employees and management are relatively good.

Supervisors must be very careful in their behavior during the decertification process. The NLRB will look closely at any assistance provided employees by the organization at this time. Holley and Jennings have identified a number of activities of employer representatives that would be considered by the board to be lawful, and others that would be considered unlawful if demonstrated during the decertification process.[8] It would be considered lawful:

1. to refer employees to the NLRB if they ask you questions concerning how to decertify the union.
2. to answer specific questions from employees about the decertification process; you should not, however, provide any information which has not been requested by an employee.
3. to provide employees with a current list of employee names and addresses.

It may be considered unlawful:

1. to obtain the necessary forms from the NLRB for employees interested in decertification.
2. to provide any type of clerical service (e.g., typing) or supplies (e.g., paper, typewriters) to employees interested in decertification.
3. to initiate discussions with employees concerning how to decertify the union.
4. to promote or encourage the decertification process.

As a general rule, you should refrain from any behavior that could be interpreted as an initiation of the decertification process, and any that could be perceived as encouraging employees to decertify their union.

Remaining Union-Free

Many organizations prefer to operate in a union-free environment. Sometimes this decision is made because the organization believes it can provide a better work environment without a union; other times it is because management believes that a union would interfere with its ability to effectively manage the organization. Regardless of the reason for management's desire to remain nonunion, it is likely that the supervisors will be called upon to assist the organization in its attempt to remain union-free.

When considering what can be done to keep an organization nonunion, some thought must be given to the reasons why employees choose to join unions. As discussed, employees decide to join unions most often because of dissatisfaction with pay, fringe benefits, working conditions, treatment by supervisors, job security, the work itself, or perceived lack of power. Some of these factors are beyond the control of the supervisor. Pay, fringe benefits, job security and, to a certain extent, working conditions, much more often fall into the domain of middle or upper management. Even if upper management sets pay levels or rates, supervisors may determine the amounts of pay raises or merit increases given to individuals. These raises and increases must be perceived as fair and equitable by employees.

The two factors over which supervisors have the greatest degree of control are treatment by supervisors and the perceived lack of power. The importance of fair and equitable treatment by supervisors cannot be overstated. Employees must perceive that your decisions are fair, impartial, and based upon job performance. Further, there is much that you can do to minimize the chances that your employees will begin to feel that they lack power or control over their work environment. You must be willing to listen to employee complaints and suggestions. If employees do not believe that the organization is even willing to listen to what they have to say, they may decide that the only way to be heard is to organize. Research suggests that dissatisfaction with pay or any other single feature of employment is not enough to make employees want to join a union.[9] It is when this dissatisfaction is coupled with a perceived lack of power that interest in collective action becomes much stronger. Supervisors may not be able to exert much influence upon levels of pay or fringe benefits, but they can serve as a pressure release valve for employees if they listen to what those individuals have to say about their work environment. It can sometimes be even more important to listen to a complaint than to do something about it.

Summary

While unions seem to be on the decline in this country, these groups still represent approximately 20 million employees. Even though unions represent fewer workers than in times past, union organizing attempts are just as frequent. This is why it is important for supervisors to have a clear understanding of the unionizing process.

This chapter presented three major labor laws. These are the National Labor Relations Act of 1935 (or Wagner Act); the Labor-Management Relations Act of 1947 (or Taft-Hartley Act); and the Labor-Management Reporting and Disclosure Act of 1959 (or Landrum-Griffin Act). Each of these pieces of legislation identifies illegal acts of labor or management, and are aimed at protecting employees' rights to organize and be represented by a union.

Employees typically decide to join a union because they are dissatisfied with some aspect of their employment. Once a dissatisfied employee contacts a union, the organizing process follows six steps: initial contact, building interest, signing authorization cards, the NLRB hearing, the pre-election campaign, and the NLRB election. If the union wins the NLRB election, it is certified as the employees' bargaining agent and management must bargain with it in good faith. If the union loses the election, it may not ask for another NLRB election for a twelve-month period.

During the organizing process, the NLRB carefully watches the behavior of labor and management. Supervisors must be sure to do nothing that could cause the election to be set aside and the union to be certified as the bargaining agent. Examples of illegal supervisory behaviors include threats, interrogation, promises in return for voting against the union, surveillance, coercion, and discrimination.

Supervisors must be familiar with the labor agreement, since it is their daily responsibility to administer it. An activity with which supervisors are frequently involved is the handling of grievances. Supervisors are wise to develop a good relationship with the union steward in order to more effectively handle these grievances and to facilitate change in the department, should the need for change arise.

Supervisors must know what they can and cannot do during the decertification process. They should also be aware of ways to be of assistance to the organization in keeping it union-free. While many activities are prohibited by law, supervisors are authorized to answer employee questions concerning the decertification process. The actions of supervisors can have a strong effect upon employee desires to unionize; therefore, it is critical to make decisions perceived as equitable, impartial, and job related. Supervisors must be willing to spend great amounts of time listening to the complaints and suggestions of employees with respect to their work environment. Failure to listen may contribute to their perception that they lack power in their work situations.

Key Terms

agency shop (p. 278)
arbitrator (p. 288)
authorization cards (p. 281)
certification (p. 284)
Civil Service Reform Act of 1978 (p. 278)
closed shop (p. 277)
collective bargaining (p. 287)
decertification (p. 276)
impasse (p. 287)
labor agreement (p. 288)
Labor-Management Relations Act of 1947 (p. 278)

Labor-Management Reporting and Disclosure Act of 1959 (p. 278)
lockout (p. 288)
mediator (p. 288)
National Labor Relations Act of 1935 (p. 277)
National Labor Relations Board (p. 277)
picket (p. 287)
"right-to-work" laws (p. 278)
strike (p. 287)
surveillance (p. 284)
union shop (p. 278)
union steward (p. 288)

Questions for Discussion

1. Why is it important for supervisors to be aware of labor law, and union organizing practices?
2. Identify the three major labor laws and describe the provisions of each. Which are pro-union? Which are pro-management?
3. What are "right-to-work" laws? Which states have them?
4. What are the primary reasons that employees join unions? Which of these reasons do you consider to be the most important? Why?
5. What can supervisors do to discourage employee interest in joining a union?
6. From your perspective as a supervisor or future supervisor, do unions always signify something negative? Is it at all advantageous to supervisors if their employees belong to a union?
7. Briefly describe the organizing process.
8. List and discuss several examples of illegal supervisory behavior during an organizing attempt.
9. What should supervisors do during a union organizing attempt?
10. Describe the relationship between supervisors and union stewards.
11. What action can a supervisor take when employees express an interest in decertification? What actions are prohibited?

References

1. W. J. Usery and D. Henne, "The American Labor Movement in the 1980s," *Employee Relations Law Journal* 7 (1981): 252.
2. Ibid.
3. W. E. Fulmer and T. A. Gilman, "Why Do Workers Vote for Union Decertification?" *Personnel* 58 (March–April 1981): 28–35.
4. C. F. Carney, "What Supervisors Can Do about Union Organizing," *Supervisory Management* 26 (January 1981): 10–15.
5. J. M. Brett, "Why Employees Want Unions," *Organizational Dynamics* 8 (Spring 1980): 47–59.
6. Carney, "What Supervisors Can Do," 10–15.
7. F. T. Coleman, "Once a Union, Not Always a Union," *Personnel Journal* 64 (1985): 42–45.

8. W. H. Holley and K. M. Jennings, *The Labor Relations Process.* 2d ed. (Chicago: Dryden Press, 1984).

9. Brett, "Why Employees Want Unions," 47–59.

Contact either a supervisor or union steward in a local organization and arrange a short interview. Find out how this person views his or her relationship with their counterpart. Ask for examples of recent dealings with the other party. Ask these individuals for advice or tips on dealing with their counterparts. When you return to class, compare the comments of supervisors and union stewards that were gathered during these interviews.

Exercise
The Supervisor / Steward Interview

Your instructor will assign you to either a management or a union negotiating team. Read the following description of the corporation and the accompanying set of bargaining issues. Then meet with your team to develop objectives, a negotiating strategy and a final agreement on each of these issues.

Exercise
Contract Negotiations

JBS Corporation

JBS Corporation is a large manufacturing firm located in a medium-sized city in the Midwest. The firm employs 2,300 production workers and 950 clerical workers. The production workers are represented by the Midwestern Production Workers, Local 1201; the clerical employees are represented by the Clerical Workers of the Midwest, Local 303. The firm is just beginning to recover from the recession and has experienced its first profitable year since 1980. While relations between the company and the unions have been good in recent years, the union was forced to make concessions during the last contract negotiations three years ago in order to keep the company in business. Now rumor is widespread that employees expect the company to make up for these lean years. The current labor agreement covering the clerical employees is due to expire at the end of the month. The results of the upcoming contract negotiation with the clerical employees are likely to affect negotiations with the production workers, whose contract expires in six months. The objective of the management team is to negotiate the lowest cost agreement possible. The objective of the union team is to achieve as many of their demands as possible.

Bargaining Issues

1. **Wages:** The current contract sets the wage rate for clerical employees as follows:
   Clerk-Typist, Level I: $3.75 per hour
   Clerk-Typist, Level II: $4.25 per hour
   Clerk-Typist, Level III: $4.90 per hour
   Administrative Assistant, Level I: $5.50 per hour
   Administrative Assistant, Level II: $6.30 per hour

The union wants an across-the-board wage rate increase of $.65 per hour. In addition, the union wants management to change clerical employees from an hourly payment method to a salary system. (Instead of a Clerk-Typist, Level I being paid $150 for forty hours of work per week, the union wants these employees to be paid $300 twice monthly.) The only significance of this change is that clerical employees would not have to clock in and out, and could take care of personal business without having to make up the time.

2. **Fringe Benefits:** The current contract calls for the following fringe benefits.
   Holidays. Ten paid holidays. The union wants this increased to fourteen paid days. This would cost JBS an additional $150,176 per year.
   Health insurance. Currently JBS pays 55 percent of an employee's health insurance. The union wants this increased to 75 percent and wants coverage to include dental care, as well. This would cost JBS an additional $190,000 per year.
   Vacation days. The current agreement provides for two weeks paid vacation after one year, three weeks after five years, and four weeks after twelve years. The union wants this changed to three weeks after three years, four weeks after seven years and five weeks after ten years.

3. **Job Posting:** Currently, JBS has no formal provision for job posting; nor does it have a promote-from-within policy. The union wants both to be written into the new contract. Specifically, the union wants to institute the requirement that every job be posted on a bulletin board outside the personnel department for five working days before it is advertised externally. This would provide current employees with the first opportunity to apply for any job opening.

4. **Flextime:** The current labor agreement calls for clerical employees to work a forty-hour week, eight hours per day. The union wants the organization to begin a flextime program for clerical employees whereby they can set their own hours of work. The union suggests that all clerical employees could be required to be at work during the core hours, between 10:00 A.M. and noon, and between 1:00 P.M. and 3:00 P.M. Outside these times, however, employees would be free to set their own hours. In the extreme, some employees could work ten hours per day for only four days per week.

Exercise

Debate: Are Unions Still Needed?

Your instructor will assign you to one of two debate teams. One team will prepare the argument that unions are no longer needed. The other team should take the position that unions are still needed. Be prepared to justify your positions.

Al, Mike, and Jerry walked quietly out of the personnel office after their meeting with George Klopic, the director of that department. Al spoke first. "George wasn't much help at all. JBS has never faced union organizing attempts before and no one has any experience in this area. I'm afraid we're on our own on this one."

"I basically agree with you, Al," Mike responded. "But I do think George gave us some useful information. He couldn't tell us exactly what we can and can't do, but he found out about the organizing attempt and took the time to collect some information that will be of use to us.

"We know now that the interest in unionization is centered within our division," Mike continued. "It apparently hasn't generated much support in other areas of the company. Our employees are the ones who seem most interested in pursuing this thing. We also know that we caught it early. They really haven't had the time to generate interest in these other areas. It seems to me we've got to find out exactly who is involved and what caused them to be so interested in joining a union in the first place. I also think we had better be very careful about what we say in front of our employees. Until this thing is over, let's plan on meeting in my office every afternoon after work."

Jerry spoke next. "I think meeting every afternoon is a good idea, but I'm not sure about your suggestion of finding out who is involved. It seems that I remember from a class I took a long time ago that things like surveillance and interrogation during a union organizing attempt are considered illegal. I think we should approach this problem on a broader level. Let's not worry about finding out what individuals are involved. Instead, let's deal with the employees as a group. Then we can't be accused of singling out particular employees and intimidating or coercing them."

Al agreed. "You're right Jerry. We've got to be very careful how we proceed. I wish I knew what caused our people to seek out a union. I always thought they were pretty well treated here. Granted, the pay isn't the highest in the area, but it's close. Working conditions are good. After we installed those new microcomputers last year, everyone's job got easier."

"That's exactly right," said Mike. "These employees have good jobs and don't appreciate them. You know, even after all the improvements we've implemented in the last few years, I've still gotten the feeling lately that some of my employees aren't satisfied. For several months after I took over this job, they came to me trying to tell me what needed to be done next. It seemed like they would never be satisfied. I got tired of this pretty quickly and told them to be happy with what they had. Furthermore, I told them I would run the department and didn't need to hear their opinions about how to do it."

"I know what you mean, Mike," Al responded, and Jerry nodded his agreement.

Questions

1. Why do you think these JBS employees are interested in joining a union? Be specific.
2. Assume that you are an outside consultant hired by JBS to help management deal with this organizing attempt. What would you advise these three supervisors to do? What would you advise them not to do?

Chapter 14

Managing Change and Training Employees

Learning Objectives

After reading this chapter, you should:

1. understand why change is important.
2. recognize the need for change.
3. be aware of different types of change.
4. understand why many people resist change.
5. be able to describe Lewin's change model.
6. know how to overcome resistance to change.
7. be able to explain how to make change permanent.
8. know how to identify training needs.
9. understand the advantages of the various training methods.
10. be able to write behavioral training objectives.
11. be aware of the legal aspects of employee training.

Introductory
Incident

Sam was confused. He was beginning to think that he didn't really know his employees as well as he thought he did. The company had spent several million dollars installing a new computer system that was supposed to make everyone's job easier. Now it looked as though nearly all of Sam's employees were against it.

JBS had recently purchased a new mainframe computer system with a network of small terminals. This has placed a terminal on the desks of every employee in the finance division. It has also produced quite a change in Sam's order processing department. Until the computers were brought in all orders and invoices had been processed by hand. Customers would call the department on toll-free lines, placing orders with his employees over the phone. The employees would write up these orders by hand and then deliver them to the keypunch room. At that point the orders were entered into the computerized billing system. Under the new system Sam's employees would be able to enter all orders into the computer as they were received over the phone. The system promised not only to save time and reduce errors, but was very likely to make the job of order processing much easier all the way around. Writing up orders by hand was a long and tedious job. It was not uncommon, either, for the keypunch department to punch in a wrong item number or quantity ordered. It was Sam's employees who would receive the calls from customers who received the wrong product, or twice as many or not enough of the items ordered. The new computer system was likely to reduce these errors because it would reduce the number of people who handled each order.

As soon as the equipment arrived, JBS announced to its employees that a new computer system had been purchased and that it was about to be installed. At that time it was also announced that formal training in the use of the new equipment was scheduled to begin in two weeks. Sam was surprised when his employees began making negative comments about the new system. He had tried to explain that their jobs would become easier and more enjoyable, but this seemed to produce little positive effect. He wondered how these employees could be so resistant to something that would benefit them.

Given the context in which organizations must function today, there is no real question about whether or not change will take place. In the face of the present rate of economic alteration, technological advance, government regulation, and foreign competition, continued change is one of the few things of which organizations can be sure.

The important question for organizations, and for supervisors, is one that asks how change can most effectively be managed. The ability to come up with a workable answer to this question requires an understanding of (a) why there is a need for change; (b) what types of change can occur in organizations; (c) why many people resist change, and; (d) how to overcome resistance to change.

The Need for Change

The need for change within an organization arises primarily from the alterations and evolutions that take place in the broader environment within which the organization is located. Figure 14.1 shows the variety of forces in the environment that are capable of creating a need for change within an organization. For instance, an organization operating in an environment where the demand for its product is highly variable would need to develop a means of adapting to these fluctuations. The organization could, for example, try to develop an additional line of products with more stable demand levels. From an organizational perspective, the key to dealing with change is adaptability. The organization must be able to adjust to changes in its environment.

Figure 14.1
Organizational
environment

Organizational adaptability is a quality that must be developed; in order to do so, it is necessary, from time to time, to introduce change at the individual or small group level. While supervisors are not the ones primarily responsible for developing this change, they tend to be heavily involved in the process. Most generally, supervisors are called upon to provide input with respect to the type of change that would be most appropriate for the situation, and the ways in which that change might best be implemented. Supervisors are many times made responsible for implementing change at the individual or small group level.

Change of sufficient magnitude sometimes creates the need for employee training programs. In the Introductory Incident, JBS has made a decision to change the way certain jobs are to be performed. The need for such a change may have stemmed from an environmental fluctuation like increased competition. JBS is responding to the environmental change of increased competition by attempting to provide quicker, more accurate service to its customers. The introduction of the new computers, however, is requiring that the employees be given extensive training in their use because most of these employees have had little or no exposure to computers.

Four types of change can be identified: (1) change in knowledge, (2) change in attitude, (3) change in individual behavior, and (4) change in group behavior.[1] Figure 14.2 indicates the relative difficulty of effecting each type of change. **Knowledge change** tends to be the easiest type of change to bring about; it only requires the presentation of new knowledge. Many of the organizational training programs aimed at improving employee job performance are based upon change in knowledge. Attitudes are learned ways of responding to a person, object, or idea and, because they are usually based upon emotion, tend to be more difficult to change than knowledge. When you like or dislike something you display an attitude. For example, many students unfortunately respond negatively to courses

Types of Change

Figure 14.2
Types and characteristics
of change

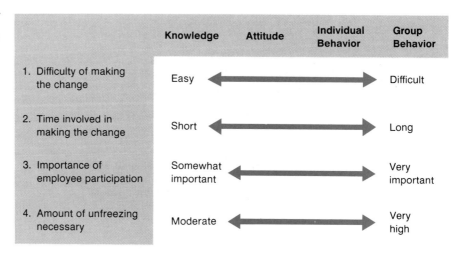

	Knowledge	Attitude	Individual Behavior	Group Behavior
1. Difficulty of making the change	Easy	←	→	Difficult
2. Time involved in making the change	Short	←	→	Long
3. Importance of employee participation	Somewhat important	←	→	Very important
4. Amount of unfreezing necessary	Moderate	←	→	Very high

that are quantitative or mathematical. When these students are faced with taking a quantitative course, they probably express this negative attitude. The more emotionally charged the attitude, the more difficult it is to change. If you are highly sensitive about some issue, you are unlikely to be willing to listen to, much less accept, any new information that stands in conflict with your attitude. Training programs designed to improve interpersonal relationships or increase cooperation often involve **attitude change.**

While attitudes are difficult to change, it is even more difficult to bring about **individual behavior change.** Many people have some habit they would like to change; they know they smoke too much, drink too much coffee, or eat too much and would like to stop. They may have successfully completed knowledge and attitude change, but find behavioral change to be another matter entirely. The individual may know, for example, that smoking increases the risk of heart attack, and may have developed a negative attitude toward the activity of smoking, yet still find the behavior difficult to change. Remember the old saying, "It's easy to quit smoking. I've done it hundreds of times!"

Group behavior change is the most difficult type of change to produce. Chapter 11 explained that groups many times have goals and standards of behavior quite apart from those of the individuals who make up that group. Groups reinforce members for striving to achieve group goals and for adhering to group standards. This is why any organizational change that requires modification of these goals and standards will be difficult to bring about. Changing group behavior entails a great deal more than producing independent change in the behavior of a number of individuals. The individual might believe in the need for a particular change, but will very often set that belief aside to conform to the group if the group is against the change.

All four types of organizational change are important to organizational function. In fact, most situations calling for modification within the work environment, and which involve supervisors, will call for some degree of change at all four of these levels. The alteration process starts by providing employees with

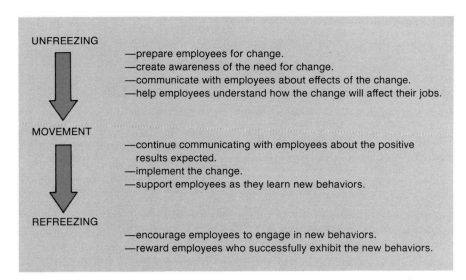

Figure 14.3
Lewin's model of the
change process

knowledge about the change. If knowledge change has been effective, attitudes should begin to change. Since attitudes affect how we respond to particular objects, ideas, or persons, attitude change will give rise to behavioral change. If the proposed organizational modification is to involve a group, then the attitudes, goals, and behaviors of the group must be changed at the same time as individual behavior is changed.

Kurt Lewin developed a classic model of change that incorporates these four types of change into a three-step process (see fig. 14.3).[2]

Lewin's Change Model

Unfreezing

The first step in Lewin's process is **unfreezing,** or convincing others of the need for change. Old behaviors and attitudes must be shown to be less effective than the proposed new ones; that is, people must be shown that there are more effective behaviors or ways of doing things. The need to discard the old behaviors and begin considering new ones must be made apparent. This may involve documenting performance problems so that employees cannot deny that they exist.

Movement

In the second stage of the process, change starts to be implemented and people are allowed to begin experimenting with the new behaviors. Lewin's model refers to this as **movement.** According to Schein, movement is facilitated if both identification and internalization occur.[3] **Identification** has taken place when an individual learns new behaviors from models, a concept bearing a close similarity to that underlying social learning theory. **Internalization** has occurred when new behaviors replace the old in the individual's normal patterns of behavior.

Refreezing

The last step in Lewin's change model is known as refreezing. **Refreezing** is action taken to make the change as permanent as possible. When refreezing has occurred, individuals have not only experienced knowledge change, but have undergone attitude and behavioral change, as well. They not only exhibit the new behaviors, but display favorable attitudes toward the change.

Lewin's change model focuses primarily upon preparing people for change and reducing their resistance to it. It is helpful to know some of the reasons why so many people are resistant toward change.

Why Many People Resist Change

People may resist change for a variety of reasons most of which can be overcome by the supervisor during the change process. The following are common reasons that individuals oppose change.

Fear of the unknown   When the organization has not done a good job in communicating to employees about the need for change and how it is likely to affect their jobs, it creates a resistance to change in employees that is based upon a fear of the unknown. In these situations individuals oppose change simply because they know what change will mean to them, personally. This resistance, quite obviously, may be avoided entirely through adequate communication in advance of the implementation of any change.

Fear of failure   Fear of failure arises because of a lack of information, as well. While employees who resist change for this reason may be more informed about the nature of the change than those who fear the unknown, these individuals lack more specific information about what will be required of them when the change is made. They may be aware, for example, of the need for the change, and of the general type of change that is to take place. They are not sure, however, of the implications this may have where their specific jobs are concerned; hence, the uncertainty about whether they will be able to handle their changed jobs leads them to oppose the change altogether.

Satisfaction with the status quo   Some employees may be quite satisfied with the existing organizational situation. There is nothing necessarily wrong with such an outlook; but if making the modification will benefit the organization, then the attitudes of these employees must be "unfreezed." These individuals must be convinced that, even though things are not bad right now, they will be even better after the proposed change has been implemented.

Fear of change in social relationships   Sometimes employees fear that a change in their jobs or in the organizational structure will upset other long-standing social relationships. Remember from chapter 11 what a strong influence informal groups can exert upon their members. If employees have found that important social needs have been satisfied through interaction with the people around them on the job, it is not surprising that they would be concerned that a proposed change might in some way affect those relationships. For

example, the employees in the Introductory Incident may have shown opposition to the installation of computers because they were afraid that the
new technology would remove some of the opportunity to talk with one another that they had enjoyed in the past. If this form of interaction satisfied
important needs, then no matter how much easier the change could make
their jobs, the employees would be likely to resist it. Any plans for organizational or work-related change should, from the outset, include a consideration of its likely effect upon social relationships.

Lack of trust   Any existing lack of trust between supervisors and employees
makes it very difficult to initiate change. Employees sometimes have a hard
time believing that management would consider their best interests in making
any organizational decisions. Or, workers may decide to resist the change
simply to make things more difficult for management. Trust is something
that must be developed over a long period of time. If you are the supervisor,
it is likely to be too late to try to develop the trust of your employees if you
wait until the time when you want to initiate change.

Fortunately, in no case where these reasons for resisting change are found
should the situation be considered irremediable. Supervisors have several courses
of action they may take to overcome employee resistance to change.

Overcoming Resistance to Change

The key to overcoming resistance to change is to prepare employees for the change.
Proper preparation can replace employees' potential resistance to change with
outright commitment to it.[4]

The basic steps to overcoming resistance to change are listed in table 14.1.
The first of these, planning, should start long before any final decision has been
made to implement a change. As a supervisor, you should begin at this time to
consider what, when and how to communicate with employees about the possibility of change. You may also want to consider asking employees for their inputs
at this point. If you ask employees to participate before the decision is actually
made, they may react more positively than if you make the decision and then ask
for their inputs. Too often, managers and supervisors get so caught up in the
decision of *whether* to implement a change that they neglect to give enough
thought to *how* it should be implemented.

Communication to employees about the change should start very early in the
process. Employees need specific information about the change being considered.
They will need to know when the decision is to be made, when the change is likely
to be implemented, and most importantly, how the change will affect the specific
jobs of individuals. The latter will be the responsibility of the supervisors. Failing
to provide this information increases the risk that resistance to the change will
develop.

Allowing employees to participate in both the making of the decision and in
the planning of the implementation of the change often reduces resistance.[5] Asking
employees for their input on the matter will give them more of a sense of involvement in the process. There is a big difference between a statement that says,

Table 14.1	Overcoming Resistance to Change

1. Plan the change
2. Communicate with employees
3. Allow employee participation
4. Provide support
5. Offer rewards
6. Be prepared to use force

"We are considering implementing the following changes. Do you see any problems this might cause in your work area?" and one that says "We have decided to make the following changes. Do you foresee any problems?" The former suggests to the employees that their opinion is important enough to consider before important decisions are made. The latter may be perceived as an attempt to make it look like management is allowing employees to participate in decisions, when in fact the decision has already been made.

Once all preliminary plans and preparations have been made and the process of implementation is under way, the role of the supervisor becomes one in which support and encouragement is given to employees. Employees may be agreed that the change is for the best, but still feel apprehensive about it during the implementation process. Supervisors must provide two types of support to employees: facilitative support and emotional support.[6] As a source of **facilitative support,** the supervisor makes sure that employees have the necessary tools, equipment, supplies, and training to make the change work and to carry out the new assignments that result from the change. In supplying **emotional support,** the supervisor gives counseling to employees, attempts to reduce their anxieties, answers their questions, deals with their problems, coaches them, and encourages them to perform to the best of their abilities. Both types of support are important in making any change successful.

Rewards, properly chosen and administered, can be used to encourage employees to accept the change. Rewarding employees for complying with the change and helping to make it work will make these employees more disposed to continue this behavior. Rewarding those who cooperate may also induce others, who have previously resisted the change, to join the effort to make the change work. Reward does not have to be higher pay, necessarily, although money is a strong incentive for most people. An organization's willingness to reward employees financially for helping implement change is an indication of the degree of importance management is placing upon that change. Other rewards such as praise or recognition can work very effectively.

Finally, as a strategy of last resort, you may rely on your power to force the change. In a situation where the change must be implemented quickly, force may be the most appropriate alternative. The other strategies, while clearly more effective over the long run, require considerable amount of time to put into practice. If time is scarce and employees seem to be resistant to the change, you may have no other choice but to rely upon your formal power and your ability to administer punishment. While you are not likely to get employees to become highly involved and committed to the change through the use of force, you are likely to get immediate compliance with your requests.

In sum, the effective management of change requires that time be spent planning the implementation of the change as well as the details of the change, itself. It can be just as important to weigh the potential effects the change upon individual employees and social relationships within the organization as it is to consider the implications of the more technical aspects of the change. The prospect of any organizational change takes into serious account both the technical and the behavioral components of that change if it is to be successfully put into practice.

The training of employees is one area of change in which supervisors have frequent and substantial involvement. It will often be necessary to give new employees some training in the technical aspects of their jobs before they can be productive. Furthermore, it is part of a more general response to environmental change that it has become increasingly common to give additional training to older, more experienced employees in order to help them meet the changing demands of their jobs.[7] As a supervisor, you must be capable of determining what specific types of training are needed in particular situations and which training method is most appropriate.

Training Employees

Determining Training Needs

The first step in any training process is to determine training needs. Determining the training needs of newly-hired employees can be a relatively easy task. The specific responsibilities involved in the new employee's job can be presented and taught to the individual as separate activities. Determining the training needs of current employees is often more difficult. Typically, supervisors become aware of the need for additional training only after performance or quality problems arise. If, however, these problems are not the result of inadequate training, the introduction of a training program would be a mistake. If the problem happens, instead, to be that of low motivation produced by low pay or old equipment, then training is not likely to be the solution. On the other hand, if new technology has created a change in the way the work is performed, then additional training may be appropriate. Supervisors can determine specific training needs in a number of ways.

1. *Observing.* One simple observation of employees as they perform their jobs may suggest training needs. Many employees, despite the fact that they were trained in their jobs when they were first hired, begin to alter their work patterns after some time on the job. Think back to the days when you were learning to drive a car. Most of us took great care to buckle our seat belts, check the mirrors and lock the door. Compare this with what you do now

when you prepare to drive. The point is that as we become familiar with some activity, we tend to alter how we execute it. Often, this alteration means a reduction in the amount of the activity performed or the degree of effort put into that performance. Decreases of either kind are rarely desirable in a work setting and, if the activity is important, can create the need for refresher training.

2. *Soliciting employee suggestions.* Since employees are performing these jobs on a day-to-day basis, who should know better than they if they need training that would make them better able to perform? Asking employees about the problems they face on the job may uncover other training needs.

3. *Analyzing productivity problems.* As mentioned, problems in output, quality, rejection rates, and waste are not absolute signs that additional training is required. In any case, however, the cause of the productivity problem should be analyzed to determine if additional training could be the solution. Sometimes customer complaints, or complaints from other departments within the organization, will alert you to the particular problem areas.

4. *Evaluating performance.* A performance evaluation properly conducted, should alert a supervisor to training needs if they exist. If you find that most of your employees have received low ratings in the same area, the need for additional training in that area could be indicated. The problem area might lie outside of any of the technical concerns of the job. For example, if the work of your department requires a high degree of interdependence with that of other departments, yet there seems to be a high level of interpersonal conflict among your employees, it might suggest that training involving team-building activities is called for.

5. *Learning from rates of accidents, absenteeism, grievance, and turnover.* Increased occurrences within any of the problem areas of accidents, absenteeism, grievance, and turnover may signal the need for new or additional training. For example, employees may have high absentee rates just because they are unsure of their own abilities to perform. Frustration over inability to perform may, in turn, lead some employees to file more grievances. Training in those areas about which employees feel insecure should then help to reduce the incidence of absenteeism and the number of grievances filed.

One other factor should be considered when determining training needs. As has been pointed out, your first decision is whether or not training is the solution to the problem. Second, you must try to determine the specific training required by the situation. Such decisions must be made on an employee-by-employee basis. Not everyone will require the same types of training; yet, too often, organizations require all employees to attend the training sessions that are developed. Requiring employees to take training that they do not need may result in morale or motivation problems. Employees are not likely to be motivated to learn what they already know. They are also likely to wonder why they are being forced to attend this training session, perhaps thinking that the organization does not care enough about its employees to keep track of the training and education that each has completed.

Training Methods

A variety of methods may be used to train employees. Some of these are more appropriate than others for specific types of training. In order to be able to choose the most effective training method, you must be aware of the strengths and weaknesses of each method.

On-the-Job Training

On-the-job training (OJT) is one of the most widely-used forms of training. It simply places an employee in the job situation and that individual is then shown how to perform the responsibilities of the job by the supervisor or an experienced coworker. The advantages of this approach are its low cost and the simplicity with which it can be put into practice. The potential problems associated with this technique can be very serious, however. The supervisor or employee who conducts the OJT not only has to be a skilled instructor, but must also be willing to teach the trainee how to perform the job as it should be performed.

Imagine a large organization in which OJT is the training method used and that a new supervisor has just been hired. In this particular case, the training procedures require that the supervisor spend an entire day with each of several of the employees in the department in order to learn the technical aspects of the job. These employees could very easily resent having to train a supervisor. They could feel that there is something inappropriate, somehow, about training the very person who will be their boss. At the extreme, the employees could take the attitude that if this person is so smart, why does he need to be shown what to do by his future employees? In such a case employees are not only unmotivated to train new supervisors, but are not trained to train them. Many people can tell you what they do, but not why or how it affects other work areas. Individuals who conduct the OJT programs must also be trained in instructional methods. In addition, they must be given some reason, typically, that of reward, for doing a good job of training.

Programmed Learning

Programmed learning usually involves three steps: (1) providing information to the trainee; (2) asking questions about the information and allowing the trainee to respond; and (3) providing feedback on the accuracy of the trainee's answers.

Differences among programmed learning methods rest primarily in the mode in which the information is presented to the trainee (e.g., books, mechanical devices). Recent and rapid advances in microcomputer technology have developed software on a variety of topics and made it available in a programmed learning format. For example, several software manufacturers also market computerized programmed learning software explaining how to use the company's word processing, data base, and spread sheet software. The major advantages to training of the programmed learning approach is that it typically trains people in less time, provides immediate feedback, and allows trainees to proceed at their own pace.[8]

Vestibule Training or Simulation

Vestibule training or simulation takes place away from the work site. The environment in which training occurs, however, is structured to be as similar to the actual work environment as possible. To the extent that this is accomplished, the vestibule training method enjoys many of the advantages of OJT. This approach is typically used where trainer mistakes could be costly or dangerous. Trainees can learn in a realistic but unhazardous setting where mistakes can be used as learning experiences. An example of vestibule training is the flight simulator used in pilot training.

Lecture

The major advantage of training through the **lecture** method or formal class is that a great deal of information can be transmitted in a relatively short period of time. There are several variations to the lecture method. These include (1) the straight formal lecture with little trainee participation, (2) the lecture with questions or discussion, (3) the lecture followed by case analysis and discussion, (4) the lecture followed by an experiential game, exercise, or role playing, and (5) the group discussion in which the formal lecture is minimized. In general, some form of active participation by trainees is preferred to the straight formal lecture.

Job Rotation

In **job rotation** employees move from job to job within the department in order to create a situation in which individuals can learn to perform the tasks required of several positions. The job rotation training method gives the supervisor increased flexibility in making job assignments.

Audiovisual Techniques

Some organizations make use of **audiovisual techniques** in training programs, preparing films, videotapes, or video cassette recordings for play over closed circuit television. The advantage of these techniques is that a large number of people can be reached at one time and the film or videotape can be replayed at a later date for a new group of trainees. A disadvantage is the lack of opportunity in such large groups for participation. Trainees must remain relatively passive during the presentation of the material.

Choosing a Training Method

Any discussion of choosing an appropriate training method must include a consideration of how people learn. Knowles has suggested that adult employees learn in ways different from students.[9] Many classroom settings use some variation of the lecture method. Students are relatively passive, simply receiving the information transmitted by the lecturer. Knowles argues that adult employees are more independent and action-oriented than students. Knowles also contends that

Relative Effectiveness of Training Methods

Table 14.2

| Training Method | Training Objective | | | |
	Knowledge Acquisition	Problem Solving	Participant Acceptance	Knowledge Retention
1. Lecture	4	4	4	4
2. Discussion	3	2	1	3
3. Case Study	2	1	2	2
4. Programmed Learning	1	3	3	1

Source: Based on Carroll, S. J., Paine, F. T., and J. J. Ivancevich, "The Relative Effectiveness of Training Methods—Expert Opinion and Research," *Personnel Psychology,* 1972, 25, 495–509.

employees are more likely to show greater interest in the ways that a concept can be used or applied than in the concept, itself. Training methods should, therefore, include trainee participation and a discussion of the potential job application of these concepts.

Table 14.2 encapsulates the results of a study that asked 200 training directors from Fortune 500 companies to compare the effectiveness of various training methods. These results indicate that the most appropriate method depends upon the specific training objective.[10] For example, programmed learning was ranked highest in those situations that the training objective is knowledge acquisition or knowledge retention. If the training objective is to develop problem-solving skills, the case study was considered to be the best training method to use. It was concluded that the group discussion method was most effective in achieving participant acceptance. The straight lecture method was not judged to be the most effective for any of the training objectives considered.

In deciding upon the best training method, the focus should be upon what, specifically, needs to be accomplished in the training program. A good way to establish and maintain this focus is to develop behavioral training objectives. Cherrington has suggested that a good behavioral training objective (1) can be described in specific, behavioral terms using action verbs (to make, to use, to correct); (2) specifies the expected level of performance (in number, in degree, in accuracy); and (3) specifies time limitations for performing the behavior.[11]

Behavioral training objectives not only keep the attention concentrated upon the specific results expected as a result of the training program, they also provide a standard against which the effectiveness of the program may be measured. Expressed in specific and quantitative terms, these figures can be used to determine whether the desired results have been achieved.

Setting Behavioral Training Objectives

Legal Aspects of Training

Employee training is subject to the same equal employment opportunity legislation discussed in chapter 2. Discrimination in employee training decisions is prohibited by Title VII of the amended Civil Rights Act of 1964; the Equal Pay Act of 1973; and the Age Discrimination in Employment Act of 1967. Furthermore, the Vocational Rehabilitation Act of 1973 requires that employers who perform more than $2,500 worth of work for the federal government take affirmative action to hire qualified handicapped employees. Under legislative provisions employers can be required to redesign equipment, to build wheelchair ramps making certain equipment accessible to handicapped employees, and to develop specialized training programs to accommodate handicapped employees.

The same legislation stipulates that the requirements for entry into training programs, and all decisions upon which employees are chosen to enter training programs, be job related. All employees must, therefore, be given the same training opportunities. It is a good idea to maintain detailed records of all decisions associated with the selection of employees for training programs, as well as of the evaluations of their progress in these programs.

Summary

Change is inevitable in the modern organization. Supervisors must be prepared to manage change rather than simply react to it. Four types of change were identified: (1) knowledge change, (2) attitude change, (3) individual behavior change, and (4) group behavior change.

Lewin's change model includes three steps: unfreezing, movement, and refreezing. This model follows a basic chronological sequence of activities beginning with preparing people to accept change, followed by introducing the change, and concluding with taking the necessary steps toward making the change permanent.

There are a variety of reasons why people resist change. Most can be overcome or at least minimized through the careful planning of the change. Fear of the unknown, fear of failure, satisfaction with the status quo, fear of change in social relationships, and lack of trust between employees and management are all reasons why people may tend to resist change. Methods for overcoming resistance to change include establishing high levels of communication, encouraging employee participation, and promoting the effective use of rewards.

The decision to institute organizational change often creates a need for the training and development of the employees whose job lives will be altered because of it. Determining the training needs of current employees can be difficult; but several methods may be used by supervisors to make that determination. Methods include observing employees at work, asking for employee suggestions, reading the signs related to productivity problems, and assessing performance evaluations.

When a particular training need has been identified, an appropriate training method must be chosen. Available methods of training include on-the-job training (OJT), programmed learning, vestibule training or simulation, and the lecture.

Each of these training methods has advantages and disadvantages of which the supervisor should be aware. All employees must be given equal opportunity to enter training programs.

attitude change (p. 300)
audiovisual techniques (p. 308)
emotional support (p. 304)
facilitative support (p. 304)
group behavior change (p. 300)
identification (p. 301)
individual behavior change (p. 300)
internalization (p. 301)
job rotation (p. 308)

knowledge change (p. 299)
lecture (p. 308)
movement (p. 301)
on-the-job training (p. 307)
programmed learning (p. 307)
refreezing (p. 302)
unfreezing (p. 301)
vestibule training or simulation (p. 308)

1. What makes change such an important element of organizational operation today?
2. What is the relationship between change and an organization's environment?
3. Select an organization with which you are familiar. What are the parts of its environment that are exerting pressures for change right now? Would you expect these forces to change in the near future? Why or why not?
4. Explain the four types of change presented in the chapter. Include a discussion of the relative difficulty with which they are produced, the need for employee participation, the time it takes to make each type of change, and the amount of unfreezing required.
5. Explain Lewin's change model. What action should supervisors be taking at each step of this model?
6. Why do many people resist change? Which of these reasons do you think it would be most difficult to deal with as a supervisor?
7. How can supervisors overcome resistance to change?
8. What specific types of communication should supervisors use during the change process.
9. Explain the differences between facilitative and emotional support. Which is more important?
10. By what methods can supervisors determine the training needs of their current employees? Which of these methods do you think is most effective? Why?
11. Compare the various training methods. Which of these methods do you think would be most effective in training (a) an assembly line worker who solders wires in electronic equipment; (b) a skilled mechanic who is not familiar with the particular type of machinery he will be responsible for repairing; and (c) a quality control inspector at a meat packing plant.
12. What are the factors to consider when choosing a training method?

References

1. P. Hersey and K. H. Blanchard, "The Management of Change," *Training and Development Journal* 34 (June 1980): 80–98.
2. K. Lewin, "Group Decision and Social Change," in *Readings in Social Psychology,* ed. E. E. Maccoby, T. M. Newcomb, and E. L. Hartly (New York: Holt, Rinehart & Winston, 1958), 197–211.
3. E. H. Schein, "Management Development as a Process of Influence," *Industrial Management Review* 2 (1961): 59–77.
4. W. Berry, "Overcoming Resistance to Change," *Supervisory Management* 28 (February 1983): 26–31.
5. J. P. Kotter and L. A. Schlesinger, "Choosing Strategies for Change," *Harvard Business Review* 57 (1979): 106–113.
6. R. B. Dunham, *Organizational Behavior: People and Processes in Management* (Homewood, Ill.: Richard D. Irwin, 1984), 477.
7. B. Rosen and T. H. Jerdee, "A Model Program for Combating Employee Obsolescence," *Personnel Administrator* 30 (1985): 86–92.
8. A. W. Nash, J. P. Muczyk, and F. L. Vettori, "The Relative Practical Effectiveness of Programmed Instruction," *Personnel Psychology* 24 (1971): 397–418.
9. M. Knowles, *The Adult Learner: A Neglected Species* (Houston: Gulf Publishing Co., 1978).
10. S. J. Carroll, F. T. Paine, and J. M. Ivancevich, "The Relative Effectiveness of Training Methods—Expert Opinion and Research," *Personnel Psychology* 25 (1972): 495–509.
11. D. J. Cherrington, *Personnel Management: The Management of Human Resources* (Dubuque, Iowa: Wm. C. Brown Publishers, 1983).

Exercise

Choosing the Appropriate Training Method

For each of the subjects listed below, select the training method you believe would be most appropriate. Be prepared to justify your answer.

1. budgeting
2. letter and report writing
3. handling dangerous chemicals
4. oral communication skills
5. setting objectives
6. sales techniques
7. speaking in front of a group
8. working as a team
9. repair and maintenance of a drill press
10. safety in the use of a drill press
11. a computer language

Exercise

Writing Behavioral Training Objectives

Think of one or two activities with which you are very familiar (e.g., changing the oil in a car, writing a very simple BASIC program, building a birdhouse). Write specific behavioral training objectives for each of these activities.

Val Perkins was not sure how she was going to like being transferred to JBS Manufacturing's regional facility in Arenzville, Illinois. The facility there consists of a regional warehouse and shipping dock for the midwest region as well as a large retail outlet for JBS products. Arenzville, itself, is a relatively small city, but the retail outlet serves a number of small towns, villages, and farms in the surrounding area. Market research shows that the population of the seven-county area is 527,934. With this size population, the sales of the regional facility's retail outlet should be much higher than it has been. The nearest similar facility, operated by a competitor, is more than sixty miles away. This means that a large number of people are driving long distances to purchase from the competitor.

Val was assigned to the regional facility specifically to improve operations of this retail outlet called JBS Sales. She decided that the best way to get a clear idea of the existing problem was to work alongside the other employees as a retail sales clerk. The facility employs twenty-five full-time and thirty-two part-time sales clerks. Because it serves a primarily agricultural community, the store has been operating until 9:00 each night, Monday through Saturday, and from 1:00 P.M. to 6:00 P.M. on Sunday afternoons. During the spring, a few extra part-time employees are hired and everyone else puts in a great deal of overtime.

Val spent a two-week period working on the floor with the retail sales clerks, the first day of which she noticed two major problems. One was customer relations. These sales clerks just don't know how to deal with customers, Val thought to herself. It wasn't that the clerks were rude to customers; it was more that they were not as helpful as they should be. When customers entered the store, the clerks would walk up and ask if any assistance could be given. If the reply they received from the customer was, "I'm just browsing," the clerk would walk away and forget about that customer. If the individual eventually found something to purchase or had a question, there was no clerk to be found. Unless they were helping a customer, the clerks tended to cluster in the back of the store and talk to one another. Val decided that this could be corrected with a little training.

The second problem was more serious. JBS Sales carried a large variety of agricultural supplies such as nuts, bolts, nails, tools, garden equipment, fertilizer, agricultural chemicals, pesticides, seeds, paint, and a small supply of lumber. Recently, the front of the store had been remodeled and stocked with such kitchen and household supplies as pots and pans, dishes, and small appliances. The problem was that the clerks did not seem to know the locations of these items in the store. When a customer came in and asked for something specific, like a particular type and size of bolt, the clerk had to run around and ask all the other clerks until someone was found who knew where the item was kept. In the meantime, other clerks would look throughout the store for the item, keeping one another posted on their progress by shouting across the aisles. It seemed to be a game they enjoyed. The clerk who found the item first won the game. Most customers seemed embarrassed or upset by this display. Val knew she had to put a stop to it, but she also knew that the clerks enjoyed the game that they had been allowed to play for several years.

A related part of the problem was that few of the clerks had much knowledge of the tools carried by the store. When customers asked for a recommendation on a drill bit or sanding disk, most of the clerks could not produce an informative answer.

Case

The Regional Facility

Case continues . . .

Case (cont.)

Val's final analysis was that the clerks needed training in two areas: dealing with customers and staying informed about the items carried by the store, where they are kept and how they are to be used.

Questions

1. Write specific behavioral training objectives for Val's training program.
2. What would you consider to be the proper training method for each of these training needs?

Chapter 15
Supervising Special Types of Employees

Learning Ojectives

After reading this chapter, you should:

1. be aware of the recent changes in the labor force.
2. understand what the general changes in the labor force predict about the more specific qualities and characteristics of the employees that you are likely to supervise.
3. be aware of several ways in which women have been stereotyped.
4. be able to refute several existing myths about older employees.
5. understand the problems faced by an employee in a nontraditional occupation.
6. recognize the problems faced by handicapped employees.
7. understand the nature of part-time and temporary employment.
8. know how to supervise creative and professional employees.

Introductory
Incident

After graduating from JBS Corporation's six-month supervisory training course, Joan and Roger were assigned as supervisors within the same department at JBS. They had just finished their first six months on the job and received their first regularly-scheduled performance evaluations. The two compared notes as they walked to their cars after work.

Roger: It sounds as if we were told about the same thing.

Joan: Yeah. Our performances are basically quite good, except we might be a little too soft on our employees.

Roger: You know, management appears to be aware of the low motivation of the employees in this division and seems to be looking for ways to improve things. But I think they're looking in the wrong direction. Encouraging supervisors to get tougher with these people isn't going to help. Look at the situation. We have a large department of clerical employees. Most of these employees are women without college degrees or specialized training. Most of them have families, but the income is more to them than just extra money. Nevertheless, it has historically been the case that JBS has treated these people as if their jobs weren't important. It's as if management has assumed that these employees weren't interested in a career when they took their jobs, but only wanted to pick up a few extra dollars. The way I see it, these jobs are as important to these people as your job is to you. I think we're making a big mistake treating them like second-class employees.

Joan: I agree. I had a talk with Mary not long ago. She's a senior employee and I knew she could fill me in on the history of the company and of the department. At one point I asked her if any JBS clerical employee had ever been promoted into a supervisory position. From her reaction, you'd have thought I had told the best joke she had ever heard. Unfortunately, neither you nor I are likely to be able to change the attitudes of an entire corporation. Management wants us to get tougher. So, if we want to keep these new jobs of ours, we'd better *get* tougher— even though I think toughness is the opposite of what is really needed.

Roger: I'm afraid you're right. See you tomorrow for lunch in the cafeteria.

Earlier chapters dealt with the legal protection of particular groups of employees such as women, the handicapped and older workers. This chapter is concerned, not with the legalities of their employment, but with the factors that motivate special types of employees to work at their potential in the effort to accomplish organizational goals. The purpose of this chapter is to look beyond what the law requires or prohibits with respect to the treatment of, and provisions made for, these individuals in their places of work. It makes a closer examination of the particular problems faced by these special groups and relates these concerns to the practice of supervisors.

Changes in the Labor Force

The U.S. labor force and population is undergoing significant change. One product of this change has been a marked growth in the number of several distinct groups within the work force. The increased participation of women, the aging of the population, and changing work values have all contributed to the basic alteration of the characteristics of the labor force.

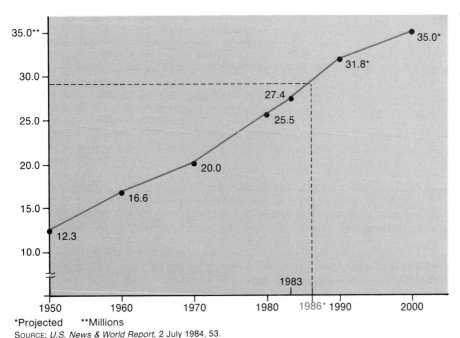

Figure 15.1
Number of Americans
aged sixty-five and over

Source: Based on U.S. News
& World Report, *July 2, 1984,
53.*

*Projected   **Millions
SOURCE: *U.S. News & World Report*, 2 July 1984, 53.

Increased Participation of Women

Often observed as one of the most significant social or demographic variations
of recent times is the increased participation rate of women in the labor force.
From 1947 to 1980 the number of women in the work force increased 151 percent
while the number of males increased only 37 percent over the same period. In
1984, more than half (53.6 percent) of all adult women worked outside the home.
Projections are that 60 percent of all adult women will belong to the work force
by 1990, and that these women will compose approximately 47 percent of the
U.S. work force. This is not to suggest that women have been successful in their
quest for equality in employment. While fair employment legislation has no doubt
reduced the incidence of discrimination, it has not eliminated such practices. For
example, women make up only a small percentage of many traditionally male
occupations (e.g., managerial and administrative positions), and are typically paid
lower salaries than men in similar positions.[1]

An Aging Population

Today, the "baby boom" babies (those born just after World War II) are in their
mid- to late thirties and are having children of their own. These children will
become part of the labor force in the 1990s. Life expectancies are still on the
increase; in 1980 men could expect to live seventy years and women, eighty years.
Examining the pattern established by these figures in conjunction with the recent

Table 15.1   Civilian Noninstitutional Population, 1975–1995

Age Group	1975	1985	1995
16–24	34,479*	33,376**	28,543
25–34	30,025	38,894	37,193
35–44	22,388	30,885	39,620
45–54	23,530	22,246	30,533
55–64	19,562	21,510	20,375
Over 65	21,285	25,939	29,770

*In thousands. **Figures for 1985 and 1995 are projected.

Source: Based on Fullerton, H. N., "The 1995 Labor Force: A First Look," *Monthly Labor Review,* December 1980, 14.

trend toward postponing retirement, it becomes understandable why the average age of the work force is increasing. The aging of the work force has produced several trends in supervisory practices.

According to table 15.1, the number of people aged thirty-five to forty-four years is expected to have increased from 22.4 million in 1975 to 39.6 million people by 1995. Such an increase is likely to reduce promotional opportunities for employees in this age group. In turn, supervisors will be faced with employees who are qualified for and interested in promotion, but who are locked into their jobs because no job openings above them exist. To the extent that advancement and increased challenge and responsibility are regarded as important, these individuals may grow dissatisfied, lose motivation, or exhibit an even more unfavorable reaction to the situation. Supervisors may have to develop different ways of providing employees with challenge and responsibility in the jobs currently held. Techniques such as task design, job enrichment, participation, and quality circles may be used to offset the lack of promotional opportunities.

While the balance of the labor force is upset, on one hand, by an oversupply of workers ranging in age from thirty-five to fifty-four, there is a projected undersupply of workers in the group aged sixteen to twenty-four years. Such a projection predicts a future shortage of people available for low- or semi-skilled entry level positions.

Changing Work Values

The argument has been put forward that the work ethic has disappeared in this country.[2] That argument suggests that people are no longer willing to work hard in order to get ahead. Two studies by Yankelovich conducted more than ten years apart support this contention.[3] In the 1960s, 50 percent of the American workers Yankelovich surveyed viewed work as a source of personal fulfillment. In 1979, only 25 percent were found to agree with that sentiment.

Others argue that the work ethic survives, but that today's employees must receive certain types of satisfaction from the job in order for them to expend a great amount of effort. These types of satisfaction are not the product of good wages and adequate working conditions, alone. Such satisfaction stems from meaningful, challenging and interesting work about which employees are given some degree of freedom to offer opinions regarding how, when, and by whom the work is to be done.

A rising level of education seems to be closely associated with, and quite possibly is one of the causes underlying, the ascending level of employee expectations. In 1950 the median number of years of education in the U.S. was 9.3 years; that figure had risen to 12.6 years by 1983. The percentage of the population twenty-five years and older with at least four years of high school increased from 52.3 percent in 1970 to 72.1 percent in 1983. It is quite probable, therefore, that rising educational levels have stimulated a corresponding rise in the expectations that employees hold with regard to the things that work should provide. Workers are no longer content to passively accept what the organization chooses to provide. Individuals want more active participation in, and control over, their jobs. Many employees are unwilling to unquestioningly submit to the authority of a supervisor or manager. Instead, they may ask for or demand some justification for the course of action chosen or the rationale underlying a supervisory request before agreeing to follow it. Rosow reports that in 1969 nearly 70 percent of younger people accepted authority without question. In 1979, however, 70 percent said that they did not feel they had to take orders from a supervisor at work if they disagreed with the orders.[4] Supervisors, today, who wish to be successful cannot afford to rely solely or even primarily on their formal authority. The changing work values among employees have made it more important than ever that supervisors develop informal authority.

Further evidence that workers today expect more from their jobs appears in the form of increased involvement in **Quality of Work Life (QWL)** programs in recent years. A variety of types of these programs are in operation; most support, in some manner, the increased control of employees over their work environment. A report by the U.S. Department of Human Services has listed the features of the work environment for which QWL programs strive.[5]

1. Equitable compensation and fringe benefits.
2. Job security.
3. A safe and healthful work environment.
4. Recognition for achievement through promotion, pay, and other rewards.
5. Due process in resolving grievances, terminations, and other work-related problems.
6. Employee participation in decision making.
7. Some employee control over the daily work process.
8. Adaptability in work time arrangements through such measures as flextime or a compressed work week.
9. Emphasis on the education, training, and career development of employees.
10. Use of nonbureaucratic forms of organization.
11. Consideration of the social aspects of the job environment.

12. Open communication and adequate feedback to employees.
13. Organizational recognition of the competing demands of work, family, community, and leisure activities.
14. Redesign of work through job enrichment, or task design.

Regardless of which combination of these factors is included in an organization's QWL program, it is clear that these programs are an attempt to provide more meaningful and challenging jobs for the more demanding workers of today.

Changes in Jobs

Closely related to changing attitudes toward work, another recent development has been the change that has taken place in the structure of jobs. Several new alternatives to the traditional eight-hour day, five-day work week have been developed in response to alterations in life-styles and to the changing attitudes that have accompanied life-style change.

Flextime allows employees to set their own work hours, at least to some degree. Many companies, for example, determine a **core time** when all employees must be on the job, say from 10:00 A.M. to 3:00 P.M., excluding lunch. Outside of core time, employees are free to set their own hours, as long as they work the required number of hours each week (e.g., a forty-hour work week).

For certain types of jobs, flextime is inappropriate. These are jobs which involve some type of customer contact or contact with other organizations who conduct a normal 8:00 A.M. to 5:00 P.M. business day. Flextime may also cause problems in terms of supervision. Some employees may work from 7:00 A.M. until 4:00 P.M. while others work from 10:00 A.M. until 6:00 P.M. Such an arrangement would require that (a) the supervisor work longer hours each day, (b) the department operate without supervision part of the day, or (c) that the organization hire additional supervisors.

In the practice of **job sharing** two people share one full-time job. To illustrate, several years ago a manufacturing company was finding it difficult to fill jobs on the midnight to 8:00 A.M. shift. The company contacted a local college and hired a number of college students to share several full-time positions. Alone, these students could not both hold a full-time job and stay awake in class, but through job sharing could work four hours a night and remain full-time students.

Women in the Work Force

Women are guaranteed equal opportunity in employment by Title VII of the Civil Rights Act of 1964, as amended in 1972, and by the Sex Discrimination Act of 1965. As has already been noted, however, there is evidence that employment discrimination continues to exist. The character of this discrimination may be more subtle than in previous years, but its effect is to deny women opportunities for advancement. Women face certain specifiable problems as members of the work force, in general. They often face additional problems when they enter a traditionally male-dominated occupation.

Common Stereotypes of Women

Several stereotypes of women employees are commonly held. To the extent that they are accepted by supervisors, these stereotypes may work to limit opportunities for the female employee. No evidence has been found to support any of the following stereotypes.[6]

1. Women are too emotional to make rational decisions.
2. Women don't work for the same reasons men do. Women work only for extra money.
3. Women are not interested in careers or long-term employment. They quit work when they get married or have children.
4. Women have a low commitment to work.
5. Women are more content than men with dull, repetitive jobs.
6. Women do not have the necessary education or experience to perform in challenging, responsible jobs.

Such stereotypes, if believed, are likely to cause managers and supervisors to assume that women are inappropriate for certain types of jobs. Women, therefore, may never be considered for these jobs regardless of their objective job qualifications.

Equal employment legislation against discrimination on the basis of sex cannot prevent subtle forms of discrimination against women. Women must be given the opportunity to grow and develop as employees. Where supervisors largely ignore women employees or are unwilling to delegate activities to them, women are denied the opportunity to develop within the organization. There is some evidence to suggest that this situation is found less frequently than in the past. In a 1982 study, male supervisors assigned equal numbers of tasks to male and female employees.[7] While studies done years earlier suggested that male managers tended to discriminate in delegation by assigning dull, routine tasks to women and more challenging or important tasks to males, this more recent study paints a more positive picture.[8] Hopefully, this implies that traditional stereotypes regarding women are breaking down, and that women throughout the work force will receive similar increases in their job opportunities.

Problems Women Face

Because of these stereotypes and the conflicting demands of work and marriage, women face potential problems that male employees do not. In a study of 150,000 working women, Koontz found pervasive feelings of loneliness and isolation.[9] This finding suggests that women are not fully accepted by their male counterparts in the work situation. Where the work group is predominantly male, women may be accepted into the formal structure of the organization, but not be recognized as part of the informal structure. Discrimination, the conflicting demands of marriage and work, and social isolation are sources of stress in the work-place that women usually experience to a greater degree than do their male co-workers.[10] Supervisors may be able to substantially reduce the amount of stress experienced by female employees by serving as a mentor or advisor.[11] A **mentor** is the type of boss who takes employees under their wing, who coaches them, and who helps them to advance within the organization. Displaying confidence in the female employee's ability to perform, delegating important tasks to the female employee, and making sure that the female employee is included in lunches and other social activities are the first steps to be taken toward overcoming social isolation.

Nontra-ditional Occupations

Employees who choose to enter **nontraditional occupations** face some of the same problems as do women in many work settings. Women are increasingly entering jobs that were once considered "male jobs," such as those of the police officer, firefighter, construction worker, and supervisor. More recently, men have begun entering occupations traditionally thought to be "female jobs," such as those of the registered nurse, secretary, child care worker, and retail salesperson. Movement into nontraditional work roles is likely to escalate as traditional sex roles continue to erode. The problems associated with entering a nontraditional occupation are essentially the same for both men and women.

A major problem for the employee in a nontraditional occupation is the social isolation they undergo if members of the majority sex exclude them from activities or refuse to accept them into the group. Coworkers are likely, at least initially, to view the worker in a nontraditional job with some suspicion, creating sentiment that is apt to prevent the employee from being readily accepted into the social structure of the work environment. For example, many people seem reluctant to accept the idea that men may be happy in clerical or secretarial positions. When men first began staying at home and opting to be "house-husbands" while their wives worked outside the home, many people wondered what could be wrong with them. Society seems to expect that men will be aggressive, career-oriented, and motivated to get ahead. Women, on the other hand, are expected to be passive, home-oriented, and uninterested in careers. Certain jobs reinforce each stereotype. When men or women crossover into opposite-sex stereotyped activities or jobs, some people have difficulty accepting their decisions.

Older Workers

The Age Discrimination in Employment Act of 1967 protects employees between the ages of forty and seventy from discrimination in decisions affecting their employment. Just as with women, however, legislation cannot eliminate all forms of discrimination. Older employees may still be denied opportunities for promotions or for assignments to challenging and important tasks. A supervisor may feel that important tasks are more suitably assigned to younger employees with

Common Stereotypes of Older Employees	Table 15.2

1. High absenteeism
2. High turnover
3. Low productivity
4. Inflexible and resistant to change
5. Tire or fatigue easily
6. Not as creative as younger employees
7. Declining strength, vision, hearing, and reaction speed
8. Accident-prone
9. Uninterested in additional responsibility or challenging tasks
10. Costs employers more than younger workers

many years ahead of them to devote to the company, than to older employees nearer retirement.[12] The reasoning of these supervisors seems to be that tasks which can help employees develop and improve should not be given to older employees who are about to retire and leave the organization. A number of stereotypes about older employees may lead supervisors to deny promotional or developmental opportunities to these employees, also. These stereotypes are listed in table 15.2.

It would be hard to support the argument that age does not slow people down at all. Nevertheless, the literature suggests that the strength, vision, and hearing of older workers does not decline as rapidly with age as was previously thought.[13] Neither is there any evidence to indicate that older workers are less productive than younger workers. Little support has been found for the contentions that older workers are more accident-prone, have higher absenteeism, or higher turnover rates. In fact, a review of the research related to these questions found just the opposite to be true.[14] Older workers were discovered to be less likely than younger employees to be absent, to shift jobs, or to have accidents. Furthermore, older employees were found to have higher levels of job satisfaction, job involvement, motivation, and organizational commitment.

Such findings suggest that organizations can benefit by hiring and retaining older workers, and by seeing to it that these older workers are given adequate opportunity to grow and develop within the jobs they currently hold. Older employees can constitute a satisfied, motivated, involved, and committed part of the work force. A study undertaken in 1979 by the Work in America Institute and titled "The Future of Older Workers in America" suggested that many stereotypes of older workers are incorrect. The report asserts that each person ages differently—at a different pace and in different ways.[15] The value of older workers, therefore, should be judged not on the basis of age, but on the basis of accomplishment, just as any other worker is judged.

Table 15.3	Productive Older Employees
	President of the United States Ronald Reagan, 74.
	Supreme Court Justice William Brennan, Jr., 78.
	Nobel scientist Barbara McClintock, 82.
	Heart transplant surgeon Michael DeBakey, 75.
	Boston Marathon runner Johnny Kelley, 76.
	Director of the Chicago Symphony Sir Georg Solti, 71.
	Author and trust officer for RepublicBank in Houston, Texas, Jackie Greer, 75.
	Restaurateur Bruce Randolph, Sr., 84.
	Petersburg, Indiana attorney-at-law, Carl Gray, 88.
	Nun, disk jockey, and organizer of Meals on Wheels in Astoria, Oregon, Sister Patricia McCann, 73.

Source: Based on *U.S. News & World Report,* July 2, 1984, 48–50.

Handicapped Workers

In 1980 there were approximately 15 million disabled people in the United States; only about half, however, were members of the labor force.[16] While the rights of the handicapped to equal opportunity in employment are protected by law, some organizations have been found to adhere rather loosely to the provisions of this legislation. In 1980 the Department of Labor surveyed 300 companies and found 90 percent of them to be in violation of laws protecting the employment rights of handicapped persons.[17] Individuals are considered to be handicapped if they suffer from (a) sensory impairment (e.g., sight or hearing); (b) mobility problems (e.g., confinement to a wheelchair); (c) missing, malformed, damaged, or paralyzed limbs; (d) cerebral palsy, spinal cord or brain damage, stroke, diabetes, epilepsy, blood disorders, heart disease, kidney disease, or disease of other organs; (e) learning disabilities (e.g., dyslexia); (f) mental retardation; or, (g) unusually short stature.[18]

As is the case with women and older employees, the way in which handicapped people have been stereotyped may prevent them from being considered for positions or, if hired, may prevent them from being considered for advancement. Table 15.4 lists some of these stereotypes. In a Du Pont study of 1,452 employees, all of whom had some form of disability, Nathanson found no evidence to support any of these stereotypes.[19] For example, 96 percent of the disabled employees were given average or better than average ratings on their safety records. Compared to the total company work force, 79 percent of the disabled workers had average or better attendance. Du Pont supervisors also rated 91 percent of their disabled workers average or better on job performance. The Du Pont study found little difference between handicapped and nonhandicapped workers in terms of ability to get along with coworkers. Like any other person, the study reported, a disabled worker may be likable, friendly, and pleasant—or he may not.[20] Neither is it likely that a handicapped worker will require any expensive accommodations in order to perform the job. Few such accommodations cost more than $100.[21]

Common Stereotypes of Handicapped People	Table 15.4

1. Handicapped employees make other workers uncomfortable.

2. Handicapped workers are not as productive as other workers.

3. Handicapped workers are frequently absent from work.

4. Handicapped workers are accident-prone.

5. Hiring handicapped workers will increase the company's insurance costs.

6. Hiring handicapped workers will require a substantial investment in special work arrangements and accommodations.

7. Handicapped workers have high turnover rates.

Typically, any alterations of the work environment for handicapped workers involve nothing more complex than raising a desk so a wheelchair will fit underneath, modifying a telephone for a hearing-impaired worker, or marking equipment in braille for a blind person. The most important consideration, for the handicapped and for any worker, is to match the worker with the job. The properly placed handicapped worker is likely to perform just as well as the properly placed nonhandicapped worker. Improperly placed workers, handicapped or not, are likely to have performance problems.

Part-time employees are those people who work fewer than forty hours per week; the number of these employees has increased dramatically in the past few years. In fact, the part-time work force has grown at twice the rate of the full-time work force since 1954.[22] It has been estimated that one of every five employees works on a part-time basis.[23] While some of these employees prefer to work full-time, research indicates that 80 percent favor their part-time status.[24]

Part-time and Temporary Employees

The number of part-time workers is likely to continue to increase as many more employers begin to realize the benefits of hiring part-time employees. The part-time employee typically gets paid less than the full-time employee in a similar position; they receive few, if any, fringe benefits; and, part-time workers can be used as buffers in organizations that experience a seasonal or varying demand for their products or services.[25] Organizations may maintain a core of permanent, full-time employees, but hire part-time employees on a temporary basis during periods of heavy demand. These part-time jobs can then be eliminated in periods of low demand, thus, allowing the organization to circumvent the problem of having to lay off permanent, full-time employees.

Temporary workers are another important segment of the labor force. **Temporary employees** are those who work fewer than twelve months per year, no matter whether that work is done on a full-time or part-time basis. In 1976, part-time and temporary workers, (known, collectively as **peripheral employees**) represented approximately 46 percent of the entire work force of 48 million.

Peripheral workers sometimes suffer the same problems as the other special categories of workers discussed. Supervisors have been known to stereotype peripheral workers in a fashion similar to women. Peripheral workers are viewed as uninterested in a career, capable of handling only routine and repetitive tasks, unlikely to be good performers, and prone to be absent and to quit without notice. On the basis of these beliefs, many peripheral workers receive different treatment on the job than their full-time, permanent counterparts.[26]

It *is* true that peripheral employees (a) receive lower pay than full-time employees; (b) receive few, if any, fringe benefits; (c) receive few opportunities for promotion or advancement; (d) are seldom included in decision making, even when those decisions will affect their jobs, and; (e) are typically assigned to undesirable jobs. Where peripheral workers have proven to be unreliable or their performances unsatisfactory, it is as likely to be the fault of the supervisor or organization as that of the workers. Werther points out that "since their tasks and pay offer few attractions . . . and since their jobs are essentially dead ends, unreliable behavior can only be penalized by the loss of a meaningless job. Obviously, there is little incentive to be dependable and hard-working.[27] To the extent that peripheral workers are unsatisfactory, it may be attributable to the treatment given them by their supervisors and by the organization for which they work. What would happen if these peripheral workers were given the same treatment and offered the same opportunities as permanent full-time employees? Logically, their performances and the reliability they demonstrate should be no different than that of the full-time, permanent employees. To apply the comment made with respect to handicapped workers, some peripheral workers are likely to be hard-working and reliable—and some are not. Workers should not be prejudged because they are part-time or temporary; rather, they should be evaluated in terms of their job performances and the contributions made to the organization.

A number of organizations recognize and utilize the advantage of employing peripheral workers. Hospitals, for example, typically employ a substantial number of nurses on a peripheral basis. The hospital enjoys the benefits of lower labor costs, lower turnover, lower absenteeism, and increased scheduling flexibility. The nurses who choose to work on a part-time or temporary basis have jobs that more closely coincide with their other responsibilities or interests. Essential to the effective use of peripheral employees is that the treatment they are given by supervisors be the same as that given all other employees. Peripheral employees must be allowed to participate in the making of decisions affecting their work, they must be assigned meaningful and challenging work, and they must be given opportunity for growth and advancement.

Creative and Professional Employees

Certain types of employees, because they are likely to be somewhat unconventional in their approach to the job, may need supervision according to methods that are somewhat unconventional, also. Creative employees and professional employees are two such types. **Creative employees** are known for their nonconformity, lack of respect for authority, unorthodox dress, low commitment to the employing organization, and at times, rather strange behavior. Professionals are included in this discussion because they, very often, are called upon to be creative in their work. Supervisors must be prepared to accept and encourage unconventional behavior when the job calls for creativity and original thoughts. This will mean that the supervisor will need to encourage high levels of decentralization, participation, and communication while minimizing the formality and rigidity of organizational demands. Steiner identifies the creative organization in terms of the following practices:[28]

1. Provides open channels of communication
2. Places little emphasis on status or position
3. Maintains high levels of decentralization
4. Allows high levels of autonomy
5. Engages in supervisory practices that encourage risk taking
6. Encourages participative decision making
7. Practices supervisory methods that encourage new ideas over conventional practice
8. Encourages employees to develop contacts outside the organization

Conversely, consider the activities that are likely to stifle creativity. Shapero identifies the organization that would seek to eliminate creativity in terms of the following practices:[29]

1. Discourages and penalizes risk taking
2. Discourages and ridicules new ideas
3. Rejects and discourages any use of unusual methods
4. Makes sure all communications follow formal channels
5. Discourages communications with people outside the immediate organization
6. Discourages nonconformity of any kind
7. Discourages joking and humor
8. Provides no recognition
9. Provides no resources

Professionals and creative employees are likely to be motivated more by the intrinsic aspects of the work than with money or working conditions. While the lack of loyalty to the employing organization may trouble some supervisors, this should not necessarily be viewed as negative. It means only that these individuals identify more strongly with their profession than with the organization. A professor in the management department at State University may, for example, think of himself or herself as a professor of management rather than a professor at State University. Such a perspective is no indication that the person will be a poor performer or problem employee; instead, it is more likely that the individual will be highly involved in the work. It does mean, however, that they are unlikely to respond favorably to attempts to control their behavior, or to the imposition of inflexible rules and procedures. As much as possible, supervisors should keep a loose rein on creative employees. Objectives and deadlines can still be set, but it then becomes the duty of the supervisor to make sure that the creative process is not stifled.

Summary

Current trends in the labor force and in the general population are bringing about corresponding changes in the role of the supervisor. A variety of new groups of employees are joining the work force in ever greater numbers and management practices must accommodate those differences. The labor force is getting older along with the population. One potential result of this demographic change is that the work force of future years may experience a shortage of younger people to fill entry level positions. At the same time, there may be an oversupply of people for middle- and upper-level positions. More and more women and handicapped people are entering the labor force. Unfortunately, these women, older people, and the handicapped must battle a variety of stereotypes which continue to limit their opportunities for employment and advancement. Research has shown that these stereotypes are beliefs not supported by factual evidence. Increasing numbers of men and women are entering fields of work that have been traditionally viewed as occupations belonging to the opposite sex. This movement into nontraditional occupations is representative of other, more broadly-based, changes in attitudes toward work that are now taking place. While some who have studied this attitude change believe that the work ethic is dead, others have concluded that workers today have developed higher expectations regarding their jobs, and that these expectations are largely the product of higher levels of education. Workers today are not as likely as those of the past to be satisfied with good pay and working conditions. They want their work to be challenging and meaningful, and, increasingly, require some degree of control over the work environment. These individuals are less likely, also, to accept supervisory authority without question. Efforts to accommodate the more demanding worker of today have been made through the implementation of such programs as Quality of Work Life (QWL) flextime, and job sharing.

Finally, creative employees and professionals typically require relatively high levels of autonomy and greater degrees of participation in decision making with respect to their jobs. The behavior of such individuals is sometimes unconventional and these employees may tend to identify more strongly with their work or profession than with their organization. In work environments characterized by decentralization, participation, open communication, and limited rules and regulations, however, the performances of creative and professional employees may be exceptional.

Key Terms

core time (p. 320)
creative employees (p. 326)
flextime (p. 320)
job sharing (p. 320)
mentor (p. 322)

nontraditional occupations (p. 322)
part-time employees (p. 325)
peripheral employees (p. 325)
Quality of Work Life (QWL) (p. 319)
temporary employees (p. 325)

1. What are some of the developmental trends occurring in the labor force and in the general population that are affecting the job of the supervisor? Have you observed any trends that were not discussed in the chapter?
2. What solution could you propose in anticipation of the problem of a shortage of younger people for entry-level jobs and an oversupply of middle-aged and older people for higher level positions?
3. What would you do as a supervisor of several older employees with strong desires for greater responsibility and challenge, but for whom there are no promotional opportunities available?
4. What specific problems do working women face?
5. How do the problems that men face as they enter traditionally female occupations differ from those of females entering traditionally male occupations?
6. Suppose you are a supervisor who has just hired a handicapped individual who will be working closely with several other employees. The reaction of these employees is negative and they ignore the handicapped employee on the job. What would you do to remedy such a situation?

Questions for Discussion

References

1. M. D. Keyserling, "The Economic Status of Women in the United States," *American Economic Review* 7 (May 1976): 205–212; D. K. Rubin, "Fifth Annual Salary Survey: Who Makes What, Where?" *Working Woman* 9 (1984): 59–63; L. Larwood and G. N. Powell, "Isn't It Time We Were Moving On?: Necessary Future Research on Women in Management," *Group and Organization Studies* 6 (1981): 63–72.
2. D. Cherrington, "The Values of Younger Workers," *Business Horizons,* November 1977, 18–30.
3. D. Yankelovich, "Changing Values," *Industry Week* 20 (6 August 1979), 60.
4. J. M. Rosow, "Changing Attitudes to Work and Life Styles," *Journal of Contemporary Business* 8 (1979): 5–18.
5. P. Bernstein, "Career Education and the Quality of Working Life," *Monographs on Career Education* (Washington, D.C.: U.S. Department of Health, Education and Welfare, 1980), 13–16.
6. J. E. Crowley, T. E. Levitin and R. P. Quinn, "Seven Deadly Half-truths about Women," *Psychology Today,* March 1973, 94–95; G. E. Biles and H. A. Prytel, "Myths, Management, and Women," *Personnel Journal* 57 (October 1978): 572–577.
7. C. F. Cohen, O. W. Baskin and D. N. Harlow, "The Effects of Manager's Sex and Attitudes toward Women," in *Proceedings of the Forty-Second Annual Meeting of the Academy of Management,* edited by K. H. Chung, New York: Academy of Management, August 1982, 395–398.
8. J. R. Terborg and D. R. Ilgen, "A Theoretical Approach to Sex Discrimination in Traditionally Masculine Occupations," *Organizational Behavior and Human Performance* 13 (1975): 352–376.
9. E. D. Koontz, *A Step toward Equality: A Progress Report* (Washington, D.C.: National Manpower Institute, 1979).
10. D. L. Nelson and J. C. Quick, "Professional Women: Are Distress and Disease Inevitable?" *Academy of Management Review* 10 (1985): 206–218.

11. E. G. C. Collins and P. Scott, "Everyone Who Makes It Has a Mentor," *Harvard Business Review* 36 (1978): 4–5.
12. B. Rosen and T. H. Jerdee, "Too Old or Not Too Old," *Harvard Business Review* 55 (November–December 1977): 97–106.
13. A. C. Laufer and W. M. Fowler, "Work Potential of the Aging," *Personnel Administrator* 16 (March–April 1971): 20–25.
14. S. R. Rhodes, "Age-related Differences in Work Attitudes and Behavior: A Review and Conceptual Analysis," *Psychological Bulletin* 93 (1983): 328–367.
15. J. M. Rosow and R. Zagar, "Work in America Institute's Recommendations Grapple with the Future of the Older Worker," *Personnel Administrator* 26 (October 1981): 47–54, 80.
16. U.S. Department of Labor, *Affirmative Action for the Handicapped* (Washington, D.C.: Government Printing Office, April 1980), 104.
17. Ibid., 102.
18. J. S. Macleod, "Integrating Handicapped People into the Work Force," *Employment Relations Today,* Autumn 1984, 261–265.
19. R. B. Nathanson, "The Disabled Employee: Separating Myth from Fact," *Harvard Business Review* 55 (1977): 6–8.
20. Ibid.
21. F. Bowe, "Intercompany Action to Adapt Jobs for the Handicapped," *Harvard Business Review* 63 (January–February 1985): 166–168.
22. R. Graham, "In Permanent Part-time Work, You Can't Beat the Hours," *Nation's Business* 67 (1979): 65–66.
23. S. L. Terry, "Work Experience of the Population in 1979," *Monthly Labor Review* 104 (1981): 48–52.
24. J. D. Owen, "Why Part-time Workers Tend to be in Low-wage Jobs," *Monthly Labor Review* 101 (1978): 11–14.
25. G. L. Mangum, D. Mayall and K. Nelson, "One Person's Job Security is Another's Insecurity—But 'Help' Is on the Way," *Personnel Administrator* 30 (March 1985): 93–101.
26. P. W. Hom, "Effects of Job Peripherality and Personal Characteristics on the Job Satisfaction of Part-time Workers," *Academy of Management Journal* 22 (1979): 551–565.
27. W. B. Werther, "Part-timers: Overlooked and Undervalued," *Business Horizons* 18 (February 1975): 13–20.
28. G. A. Steiner, *The Creative Organization* (Chicago: University of Chicago Press, 1965).
29. A. Shapero, "Managing Creative Professionals," *Research Management* 28 (March–April 1985): 23–28.

Exercise

Interviewing Special Types of Employees

Perhaps you know someone who has entered a nontraditional occupation, or who belongs to one of the special categories of employees discussed in this chapter. Interview that person and prepare a report for the class. Your questions should focus on the special problems that person has faced, the things they have done to cope with stereotypes or discriminatory treatment, and their outlook upon their own future as well as that of the handicapped, in general. Report your findings at the next class meeting.

Terry and Joan met in the JBS cafeteria for coffee as they did every afternoon. Joan sensed immediately that something was bothering Terry. "Care to talk about it?", Joan asked. "It shows, huh?" Terry responded. "I knew when I took this supervisory position that there would be people problems. I know that comes with the territory—that's what appeals to me about being a supervisor. It's a real challenge to try to accomplish objectives by directing the work of others. But when your own boss becomes an obstacle, the challenge disappears and the frustration begins."

"Wow. It sounds like you're really upset about something," Joan said. "What happened?"

"Do you know Grady Filson?" Terry began.

Joan thought she did. "Isn't he that handicapped Vietnam veteran that Susan hired a couple of years ago to work in her accounts payable department?"

"That's right," Terry said. "He has been an excellent employee. I understand the 'power' here at JBS was somewhat reluctant to hire someone confined to a wheelchair. They were afraid that they would have to spend all kinds of money so that this person could get around. As it turned out, they only had to raise his desk about six inches. Ramps had already been cut into the curbs in the parking lot, so access to the building was no problem. The whole thing couldn't have cost fifty dollars.

"Anyway, I've got this opening in my department," Terry continued. "I just got formal approval for the new position. The job involves arranging transportation for our shipments from various raw material suppliers. Most of this person's time would be spent on the phone. It's an important job because these shipments usually represent a lot of money. This person would have to select and arrange the most economical and timely mode of transportation, whether that be commercial truck lines, railroads, or the JBS trucking system."

This is where Terry had run into his opposition. "I talked to my boss about offering the job to Grady, and I couldn't believe his reaction," he said. "He said he didn't think Grady was ready for such an important position within JBS. It was obvious to me that he just didn't want to promote a handicapped person into such a responsible position. I talked with Susan, and she has nothing but positive things to say about Grady. His performance has been good and he has never had any attendance problems. I think Grady not only deserves the promotion, but he's the best qualified person for the job. His handicap shouldn't be a factor in this decision. Unfortunately, my boss doesn't seem to agree. How would you handle this situation, Joan? Should I let it drop and start interviewing other employees, or should I go back and try to convince him that Grady is the right person for the job?"

Joan thought for a couple of minutes before she spoke. "You've got a sticky situation here. If Grady really is the best person for the job, then it's hard to argue against hiring him. On the other hand, if your boss stereotypes handicapped people as being incapable of certain things, you've got an uphill battle ahead of you if you really want Grady for the job. If you don't get to hire the person you want, you may never be completely satisfied with anyone else, no matter how well they perform. I wish I could be more help, but I think you're the only one who can make this decision."

Questions

1. Put yourself in Terry's shoes. How would you handle this situation? Assuming that Terry decided to try to talk his boss into giving Grady the promotion, what sort of argument would you use to support your case?
2. Assuming you were successful and hired Grady, what steps would you take to ensure that he was accepted by the other employees in the department?

Index